Brave New West

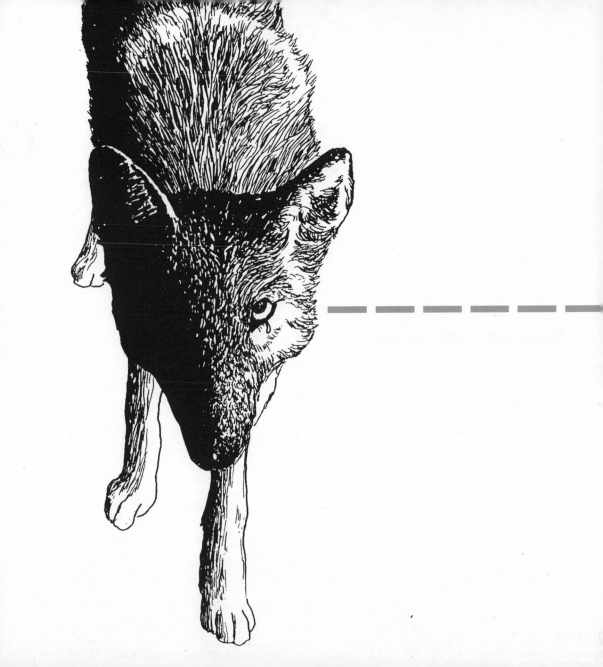

Brave NEW West

Morphing Moab at the Speed of Greed

JIM STILES

THE UNIVERSITY OF ARIZONA PRESS | TUCSON

The University of Arizona Press
©2007 by Jim Stiles

Library of Congress Cataloging-in-Publication Data
Stiles, Jim.
Brave new West : morphing Moab at the speed
of greed / Jim Stiles.
    p. cm.
ISBN-13: 978-0-8165-2474-7 (pbk. : alk. paper)
1. Moab (Utah)—Economic conditions.
2. Tourism—Economic aspects—Utah—Moab.
3. Rural development—Environmental aspects—
Utah—Moab. 4. Rural development—Social
aspects—Utah—Moab. 5. Social change—West
(U.S.)—Case studies. I. Title.
HC108.M777S75   2007
338.9792'58—dc22   2006026089

Manufactured in Canada on acid-free, archival-
quality paper containing 100% post-consumer
waste and processed chlorine free.

12   11   10   09   08   07

6   5   4   3   2   1

For Bill Benge, 1946–2006

"It was good to be alive."

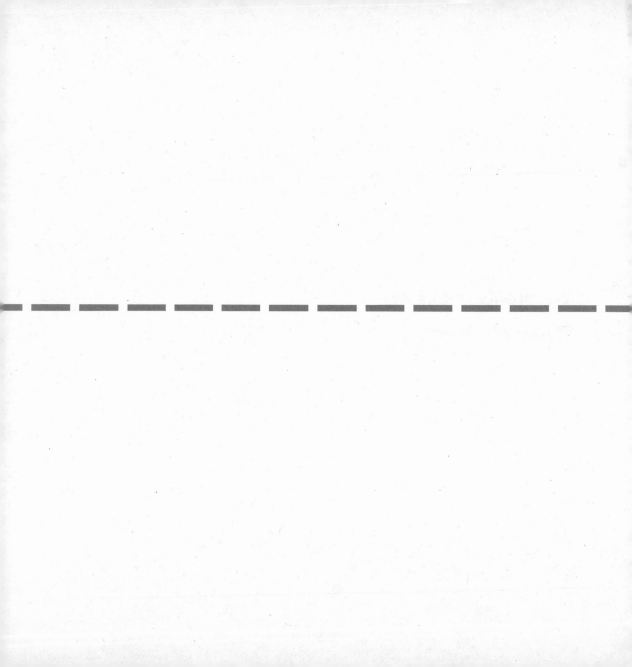

You touch the great lonely land,
only to plant upon it some ugliness
about which, never dreaming of the grace
of apology or contrition,
you then proceed to brag with
a cynicism of your own.
. . . and I should owe you my grudge
for every disfigurement and every violence,
for every wound with which you have
caused the face of the land to bleed.

Is the germ of anything finely human . . .
supposably planted in such conditions of
endless stretching and such boundless spreading
as shall appear finally to minister
but to the triumph of the superficial
and the apotheosis of the raw?

Oh for a split or a chasm . . .
Oh for an unbridgeable abyss
or an insuperable mountain.

— HENRY JAMES

Contents

Introduction

Almost thirty years ago, I wandered into a remote town in the Four Corners area of the American Southwest called Moab, Utah. My first glimpse was fleeting and cold, but its imprint on me was dramatic and permanent, and I returned the next summer. A year later, I moved in. Even before I became a resident, I knew I'd found home. It was a pre-cognitive experience—I was convinced I'd dreamed of this extraordinary place as a child, years before I'd heard of slickrock or canyon country.

As I came to know the town, I realized that the community and the landscape comple-mented each other in a very peculiar but almost addictive way. I couldn't bear to be away. I longed for it like a man yearns for a woman, and returning always caused my heart to race. I thought I would feel this way forever.

But one day, I crawled out of bed and rubbed my eyes, and the Moab I had known and loved for a quarter century was gone. In my heart of hearts I had seen its departure com-

ing for a long time, and only my self-delusional skills allowed me to ignore the inevitable. Finally, there was no way to avoid reality any more. Moab, for me, was gone—physically, metaphysically gone. Where did Moab go?

Well, in order to discover where Moab went, it's important to know where it was, *what* it was, why it became the thing that it is, and where it's headed now that it's left. Perhaps most critically, we have to ask why it should matter. What difference does it make? Who gives a damn? The vast majority of you don't live in Moab. So Moab's vanishing should not matter a whit to anyone with the good sense to stay out of an ultimately useless and hopeless debate about an age-old subject: eternal change.

But it does matter, and that is what this book is about. Moab is a town with a rich and varied past, an uncertain and unsettling present, and the potential at least for a dull, shallow, and homogenized future. My town is doing everything it can to look exactly like every other community in the West, or in America, for that matter. Where does this dim-witted passion for bland unoriginality come from? The West, the Nouveau West, the Brave New West, if you will, has a thing for banality during these strange days of the twenty-first century, although I've never understood the attraction. From contrived quaintness to outright ugliness, Moab is another *faux adobe* clone, another Brave New West microcosm. Chances are, this extended diatribe will sound all too familiar. If you grew up in the rural West or arrived here more than a decade ago, you will wade through the pages that follow, shake your head violently at times, and mutter to yourself, "Yeah, the same goddamn thing happened here in [choose one: Jackson, Telluride, Park City, Aspen, Santa Fe, Taos, Sedona, Flagstaff, Durango]." Over and over, infinity, God help us all.

If you arrived in the West recently—or to inject the generation gap into this polemic early on, if you are under thirty-five—you probably won't have any idea what I'm talking about. You might even suggest that my words sound more like a whine than a lament. I won't completely disagree with you. One might argue, and some do, that the transformation of these little towns across the rural West from lonely, quiet backwaters with a marked absence of cultural, social, and educational opportunities is not only inevitable and unavoidable but perhaps even preferable. Many environmentalists believe that bringing an amenities economy to the rural West will reinvigorate it, that it will replace the old extractive industries that the rural West survived on for a century with something cleaner and more lucrative.

Other environmentalists try to block the sight of these New West towns from their fields of view altogether. They insist that they've drawn a line around the new boomtowns and vow to fight that final battle to save the dwindling wildlands that lie beyond them. But it won't work. Towns like Moab aren't last lines of defense. They're embarkation points, and we've made them that.

With a current U.S. population of 300 million and its expected rise to over 400 million by midcentury, the transformation of the rural West by fleeing urbanites is probably inevitable. While I'd love to believe that there is still time to inspire a dramatic reversal of the course that much of the West has attached its star to, I'm not brimming with hope, although angry outraged optimists like me don't give up easily.

We may call Moab a New West town, but there's really nothing new about it. The rural West has always been influenced, even driven, by the extractive industries of cattle, timber, and mining. People came west to get rich. Few ever did, but some of them stayed on because they'd discovered a different kind of wealth—the riches that come from open land, solitude, and the freedom to live an uncluttered life.

Today many people come here because they already are rich. They come here to extract the very beauty of the land that they claim to love. What's happening today is extractive, too, and in the long run much more efficient and much more destructive. The old miners peeled off the West's skin; today we're removing her soul.

The West's dwindling wildlands are being done a disservice by a great deal of dishonesty. Many of the extractors try to pass themselves off as environmentalists, but it's a lie. There are still many brave and courageous environmentalists out here who fight for the land because it is simply the right thing to do, because wilderness, of and by itself, has value. They are not here because they stand to make a profit. But their efforts are being thwarted by environmental consumers or, even worse, enviropreneurs, those peddlers of beauty who eye unlimited high-end tourism and gated communities with the same greedy lust as that of a Forty-niner. Commodifiers of nature threaten its very existence.

Moab is just one town among many across the rural West that faces an uncertain future. Or maybe it's not so uncertain at all. Perhaps the rural West's future as a commercialized nature theme park, with controlled access and plenty of rules, is already cast. Can we put the resource under glass at the cost of freedom, solitude, silence, the very intangible aspects of wilderness that so many of us revere and long for, but that so many more apparently disdain and even fear? To me the tangible and intangible are inseparable.

This is not a book that will dwell on or attempt to describe the beauty of the canyon country of southeastern Utah. I will not regale you with tales of my inspiring hikes to seldom-visited secret places, though I've had more than my fair share. Go find your own goddamn secret places, and when you do, don't tell anyone what you've found. My need for secrecy is not driven by selfishness—far from it. But nothing worth having is free. Earn the right to be overwhelmed. Create your own special corners of the world. It's so much more satisfying.

In 1968, when Edward Abbey wrote *Desert Solitaire*, nobody knew where Moab was. Few had even seen pictures, and if they had, they thought they were looking at the Grand Canyon. Today anyone who's seen a Toyota X-Terra commercial or a Mountain Dew ad or has been bombarded with adventure-tour Web sites and brochures knows how beautiful it is around here. We have $150 running shoes named after our town for godsake. Moab has been discovered.

So there's no need for me to describe in a new way the power and majesty of a red-rock sunset. If you don't know about a canyon-country sunset already, I doubt if my words can inspire you. I am not here to bring tears to your eyes or describe this land in such alluring and seductive prose that you feel moved to grab your titanium bike and Lycra outfit and zip over here for the weekend in your Lexus suv.

I'm not going to do that. I can't. I'll leave that chore to others. Abbey once said, "The idea of wilderness needs no defense. It needs more defenders." If you read the public opinion polls, wilderness support is up these days. But if every wilderness supporter tries to experience wilderness simultaneously, we've got a problem. It's an old cliché by now, but too many of us, waxing poetic over nature's beauty and simultaneously trampling her to shreds, will surely destroy the object of our affections.

My friend, Terry Tempest Williams, once said, "There is a healing and a joy that comes from the land itself. The land literally brings us back to a reverential state of mind, where the health of the land is the health of the people. It is about spirit."

I respect Terry, but I'm not sure I totally agree. The land is indeed healing to those who genuinely seek her recuperative powers, but to others it never will be anything but a commodity to be marketed and sold. Today, as lines become blurred and values twisted, I sometimes can't differentiate the exploiters of the land from its defenders. Many years ago, Scott Groene, then an attorney for the Southern Utah Wilderness Alliance and a *Zephyr* contributor, said to me, "You think things are bad *now* fighting our adversaries. Wait until we start battling our friends." He was even more prophetic than he knew. Wilderness as a spiritual and moral issue has been replaced by economic and political considerations, from both ends of the ideological spectrum. Passion is what we need right now. We need the acetylene torch that Abbey lit beneath us thirty-five years ago, not the scented candles and reams of lawsuits and injunctions that have replaced the fire and Ed.

I'll tell you at the outset that I am a shameless disciple of Ed Abbey, as I have been since *Desert Solitaire* was dropped in my lap decades ago, and I will never hesitate to quote him or invoke his memory. He changed my life early on. He was my friend and my mentor, and I wish he were still here among us. I don't think any of us who loved him have ever quite recovered from Ed's sudden departure. We're adrift, still trying to find our way in the Brave New West.

In the twenty-some years I've lived in southeastern Utah, I've seen it evolve (or devolve) through the unique perspective of three different lenses. First, I came here as a tourist. I spent several years longing for the red-rock canyons from the green and humid forests of Kentucky, plotting the next trip to Moab and dreaming of the day when I'd stay. Even back East, I kept my watch set to Mountain Time. Then I made the great leap westward and spent a decade as a seasonal ranger at Arches National Park, in the heart of the canyon country. It's where I decided to build my life, and Moab became home.

For the fifteen years since I started a small alternative publication called the *Canyon Country Zephyr*, I've been reporting the ups and downs of my little town and the red desert that surrounds it. The *Zephyr* began in my mind with uncharacteristically great enthusiasm and hope. I thought Moab was inspired. I'd like to be able to say that those days were really as blissful as I remember them, and sometimes they were. But I never dreamed it might end up like this. But there's the rub: this isn't "the end" either. Decades from now, my young friends, now in their twenties, will look back on *these* times and say, "Those were the good old days." And they just might be right.

Return to Moab, 2040 A.D.

I don't know what made me do it. Some kind of grim, masochistic satisfaction, I suppose. To prove to myself, at least, that Moab really had become as bad, weird, and ugly as I'd feared it would, that I hadn't been a lifelong cynic for no damn reason at all. Now I knew that everything we'd feared was here.

In 2009 I moved away from the United States and relocated to a small island chain in the South Pacific called Funafuti. I was a fool to go there, because I had been warned. Global warming and rising sea levels jeopardized the island atoll as far back as 1999. By the year I arrived much of the island system began to disappear, and by 2016 Funafuti was gone. Its inhabitants were allowed to immigrate to New Zealand and Australia. I was lucky enough to find a sponsor in Western Australia and moved to a small town called Gnowangerup, which was northeast of Tambelup, a bit east of Kojunup, and thirty kilometers north of Broome Hill. I bought a small farm, married a woman of Aboriginal and

Welsh descent, and raised sheep until I was almost eighty years old. For a man who once loathed hoofed creatures, the irony was striking. But recently I'd begun to wonder about the place I'd called home for more than thirty years.

I wasn't sure I'd be allowed to return to Moab. Transportation schedules had become much more rigid in the last decade, and international flights were exorbitantly expensive and difficult to book. The background and security checks alone required a two-year wait and a $10,000 fee. In the United States just getting around was frustrating; the country's highway infrastructure had deteriorated badly. The government simply could not keep up with the demand that 400 million citizens placed upon it.

By the mid-2020s, oil and its $200-per-barrel price tag had put a virtual end to leisure driving as we knew it back in the "good old days" of the late twentieth century. I longed for my old GMC pickup, even if it did suck gasoline like a terminal alcoholic.

In 2030 President Jenna Bush proposed and implemented a massive government-financed program to develop alternative energy sources. Earlier efforts to rekindle the nuclear power industry had collapsed after the Paso Nobles disaster in 2018 (by 2040, 7000 square miles around the doomed plant were still too radioactive for human entry). But fifteen years later, an economically viable process to convert coal to a burnable and affordable fluid for internal combustion engines was made commercially available, and suddenly America's highways were running beyond capacity again.

The downside to coal-fired cars was their inability to meet pollution standards, so President Bush and Congress relaxed clean-air requirements. The result was a degraded view and increasing health problems. President Bush drew criticism when an off-camera comment made headlines. Referring to the bad air, Ms. Bush had said, "So a few more die from the stinking air. We could *use* a few more deaths in this country." With the U.S. population passing the 400 million mark, some Americans understood the president's comments better than others. Protests from the international community about the clean-air revisions were modest. Most countries had long ago abandoned the Kyoto accords when their own desires for economic growth outweighed any health effects. By 2040 everyone in the world wanted to be just like us. We set the trends; Asia produced the stuff.

But the impact on the nation's highway system was staggering. Although coal-powered cars had made travel inexpensive again, the cost of highway maintenance became exorbitant. The U.S. government was faced with some options: it could raise taxes to levels sure to trigger a major downturn in this booming economy, or it could restrict use and hope to extend the lifetime of the rapidly crumbling interstate system. More restrictions could also be justified under the newly revised Patriot Act. So, of course, the government chose the latter.

I spent a small fortune on my jet ticket, applied for a U.S. domestic travel visa, and hoped for the best, but without expecting it to happen. Even if I was given a visa, I was in no condition to drive. I had to give it up years ago, not because I'd lost my driving edge, but because I could never grasp the new technology. I liked using a steering wheel and pointing the vehicle where I wanted it to go. These auto-lane sensors were an annoyance to me, and I kept trying to override the system. I may be pushing ninety, but I didn't need some damn computer system to tell me where to go. My travel prospects looked bleak. Then, as in much of my life, coincidence and good luck changed my fortunes.

A few weeks ago, out of the ether came a faintly familiar sound. The caller had put an electronic block on the video transmission, but the voice and the words shook long-forgotten memories from remote corners of my brain.

"Jim Stiles! It's your good friend Rich Ingebretsen!"

I stared at the static on the monitor. My hands began to tremble. "Jesus Christ," I muttered. Rich flipped a switch at the other end, and his remarkably well-preserved face appeared before me.

"No, I'm still a Latter Day Saint, and I haven't ascended to that level. At least not yet."

"I can't believe it. How are you Rich?"

"Still waiting to see them drain the lake."

"I heard you'd come close."

"I'll tell you all about it. I hear you need a sponsor for a visit to our fair land. It's already arranged."

Dr. Ingebretsen had done well for himself in the years since I'd left Moab. A physician by trade and a tireless proponent of the movement to drain the Powell Reservoir in the early twenty-first century, Ingebretsen had done much to legitimize the issue. His reasonable approach to many environmental causes thrust him into politics. In 2018 he was elected lieutenant governor of Utah and was reelected twice. Now in retirement, Rich was as hospitable as ever.

So, we arranged for him and his wife Nadine to pick me up at the jetport in Los Angeles. Then we'd travel by I-10 to Phoenix, then north on I-17 all the way to Moab, Utah.

"There's an interstate in Moab?" I asked.

"Been there since 2025."

With lane sensors, the drive was effortless, although the traffic was insane. Even with driving restrictions, cars and trucks were bumper to bumper and moving at 140 kilometers per hour. (The U.S. finally converted to the metric system in 2026.) We bypassed Phoenix and Flagstaff during the long night drive, but I wondered about a side trip to the South Rim.

"Can't do it," Rich advised. "Not unless you made a reservation five or six years ago."

"Five or six years? That's impossible."

Rich chuckled, "You're in for a shock, my friend. It's going to get worse."

He explained that all national parks in the U.S. system required advanced booking. Every morning at dawn, hundreds of travelers seeking permits to see the Grand Canyon gathered at a huge reserve parking lot near Cameron, Arizona, and waited for the 7:00 a.m. lottery numbers to be called. An extra fifty permits were provided each day for a handful of lucky and persistent Grand Canyon aficionados.

"I've never won anything in my life. I guess stopping would be a waste of time."

"I guarantee it," Rich said. "Keep going driver."

We hurtled north through Monument Valley at sunrise and into Utah. The nearby scenery looked the same—or what I could see of it—but the long vistas were gone.

"What is this haze? Is there a forest fire?" I asked.

"Stiles, you've been away too long. This is 'Blade Runner' come to life. Remember the old movie with that actor? What was his name?"

"Harrison Ford?"

"Yeah, the guy who became governor of Wyoming. *This* is the way it is. The crap blowing in is from California, Phoenix, Las Vegas, St. George, Salt Lake. It's brown sky by day and orange sky by night. But most of this is from Kaiparowits. Remember all that coal?"

"Yeah, back in the nineties they said there was enough coal to supply the country's energy needs for four hundred years. You mean they've dug up the coal from Kaiparowits?"

"That's it, and they built six coal-fired plants around it. Most of the plateau is gone. Makes Kennecott look like a little sand box. In fact, they reversed the national monument designation, just so they could mine the coal. Said it was a national emergency."

Old Highway 191 was gone, swallowed by the interstate. At Devils Canyon, near Monticello, Utah, I glanced over my shoulder, then turned away. I didn't want to know. Hole 'n the Rock was now a freeway off-ramp, but what shocked me more was the exit sign: "South Moab." According to the Fodor's Guide in Rich's dashboard monitor, Moab's population had recently passed 40,000, far more than what build-out studies in the 1990s calculated the valley could handle. Sure enough, the growth had spilled over Blue Hill and even beyond the now-defunct tourist attraction. Nadine told me that a Chinese firm bought Christensen's sandstone home-in-the-rock in 2027, now using it as a private vacation resort for many of its high-level executives.

Finally, we descended Blue Hill and into Moab, thirteen miles south of the old city limit. In 2037 Grand County finally annexed thirty-five square miles of neighboring San

Juan County. A year later, after almost a century of debate, the county and city governments consolidated. The vote was close, and many of the old Moabites were furious. In the early days of the twenty-first century, after the passage of an anti-junk ordinance, many of Moab's residents had moved across the county line, where building codes and land ordinances were less strict. With consolidation, the city moved to condemn and remove many of the residents and their modular homes, trailers, and vehicles.

They had all sought refuge in San Juan County, and now they faced an uncertain future. Carl Rappe, a longtime Moabite, tried to organize a protest, but nobody was particularly interested. Some of the old owners could derive some comfort from the price their land brought—a five-acre ranchette lot with water and power sold for about $1 million—but for many the money meant nothing. There was no place else to go.

Many of the old homes in Moab were gone, torn down to make room for more high-density housing developments. I tried to find my old house on Locust Lane, but couldn't even find the street, much less the structure. Incredibly, Dave's Corner Market was still standing at Fourth East and Mill Creek Drive. But the store was now called Maynard's & Maynard's, and it featured optional nude shopping in its adult section.

Downtown was unrecognizable. Most of the old buildings had vanished. Of course, there weren't all that many old buildings left in 2009, because Moabites never could leave things alone. Much of the valley was covered with ten- to twenty-story condo developments. Something had been needed to handle the swelling throngs of emigrants from the big cities.

I was determined to find some of my old camping spots and spend the night under the few remaining stars that could pierce the haze.

I asked Rich to go north toward Arches National Park, when he reminded me, "I told you before. No reservation, no entry to the parks!"

"I know Rich. I'm not headed for Arches. I want to take that old jeep road by Dalton Wells. I've got to get away from all this."

"Stiles, you just don't get it. You can't, can *not* get off this road. This vehicle is programmed to go where we're allowed to go. All that public land out there is closed, just like the parks, the wilderness zones, all of it. There's a waiting list three years long just to do an overnight at the Dalton Wells camping area. Of course, there's a Marriott at Dalton, four hundred dollars for double occupancy."

I stared blankly out the window. "Somehow I never dreamed it would be *this* bad. What's it like in Thompson?"

"Don't ask."

I was feeling hopeless. Rich programmed the vehicle for a return trajectory and back to Moab. As we returned to town via the bypass, I could see Charlie Steen's cliff-side home high above the valley on what used to be Moab's northern end. The 1950s mansion of the Uranium King was clearly visible in the late-afternoon sky.

"Hey," I wondered, "does the Steen family still own Mi Vida?"

"It's in litigation," Rich said. "The youngest son, Mark, finally gained custody of the home. For a while, he apparently tried to restore some of the ambience and excitement of the boom days, but . . ."

"What?"

"Well, one night he tried to recreate one of Charlie's great parties. Invited about five hundred guests to the hilltop mansion. Everyone had to dress fifties-style, and the folks were all having a wonderful time. But then Mark, who was feeling particularly . . . exuberant, fell off the railing and cracked his head. He was seventy-three. Now the kids are fighting over the estate. Litigation seems to run in the family. But I guess the party was a nice gesture."

As we passed the northern Moab Portal, a massive entryway built of fake adobe and pine logs, I thought about Ed Abbey and Ken Sleight. Just north of what used to be Moab's city limit, we passed the Moab Springs Condos. It was once a restaurant called the Grand Old Ranch House; before that, when my old buddy Doug Treadway lived there in the off-season, it was just "the ranch house." I'd met Ed Abbey in the front room of that old building. Just beyond the new Chi Chi's chain Mexican restaurant, Ken Sleight had owned a little bookstore. I remembered the day we celebrated Ed's new novel *The Monkey Wrench Gang.*

"How's the environmental movement going these days, Rich?" I asked. "As if it mattered."

"As if," Rich echoed. "Well, they finally got what they wanted. The big drought did most of the ranchers in, and big-city speculators snatched up most of the land. Remember Escalante? It's got a population of 15,000 now. They have their own classical music festival, and I hear they've got the highest median income in Utah except for Park City and Panguitch."

"What about a wilderness bill?"

"The Congress passed the Red Rocks Wilderness Bill in 2020. The Sierra Club, the Southern Utah Wilderness Alliance, all of them were happy, but . . ."

"But?"

"They got their nine million acres or whatever it was. But with so many people moving here and with the increased travel, the easily accessible wilderness areas got slammed—unbelievable damage from millions of well-meaning morons. Finally, the government allowed the construction of designated trails inside the wilderness areas and restricted private use to those routes. Armed compliance rangers work the trails all the time. The fines for leaving wilderness trails are severe."

"Some wilderness."

"Yeah, but it gets worse. The environmental groups and the recreational industry got together and proposed that most wilderness travel be restricted to commercial use. The industry sold the enviros on the idea that they could control impacts and limit abuse much better than letting these yahoos wander about on their own. There are a lot of yahoos these days."

"Better a yahoo than a lemming."

"So, today, if you want to take a hike up Courthouse Wash, you can wait an eternity for a permit, or we can sign you up right now for one of the senior tours. These companies have covered every angle. They've got a package for every demographic. If you've got the money, they've got the tour."

"I feel sick."

"Hey, not to despair. They're all 'proud members of the Utah Wildlands Alliance.' All the groups consolidated in 2025, in conjunction with the Outdoor Products Environmental Enterprises. Remember, they were your pals."

"If you recall, I moved to the South Pacific."

I could feel my metabolism rising again, the old ticker pounding. I reached into my shirt pocket and popped a couple of little blue pills. "So tell me, is there resistance to any of this? Is there any youth uprising opposing all these restrictions and controls, this total sellout?"

Rich shrugged, "Look, none of these kids even *remembers* what it was like to have freedom. Even forty years ago, you could see that, what with the War on Terror and all."

"The War on Terror," I sighed. "When will it end?"

"Hey, there is one good bit of news," said Rich. "We *almost* drained the reservoir."

I laughed bitterly. "What was it we used to say? *Almost* only counts in horseshoes and hand grenades."

"Well, the water needs of the Southwest became so acute that by 2030 the value of a gallon of water far exceeded the electrical energy that the dam produced, especially after they started burning coal. They needed the Colorado's water downstream in California and Arizona, not in the middle of Utah. But all the growing little towns on the Colorado Plateau wanted some of it as well. It was weird. Here was the Utah chapter of the Sierra Club arguing in *favor* of a pipeline from Lake Powell to Escalante, Panguitch, and Kanab, when they'd opposed the St. George deal back in 1999. Finally, they reached a compromise. The dam would stay but the Bureau of Land Management (BLM) would draw down the level of the reservoir by a hundred meters. It opened up a lot of the upper parts of Glen Canyon. We got Cathedral back. But Music Temple is still under seventy-five meters of water. And, of course, like everything else, the waiting list to float down the re-exposed parts of the river is several years long. The best way to see it is to volunteer for the restoration project. It's quite an undertaking."

We drove to the southern end of what used to be Spanish Valley, mostly in silence. But we were using up our allotment of urban miles and needed to find a place to sleep.

"Damn it, Rich. I refuse to go to a hotel. I want to camp out. Just let me out and I'll take my chances. Pick me up right here tomorrow morning at seven o'clock."

"You're crazy. For one thing, you're over eighty years old. You look like hell. I doubt if you'd get a hundred meters. And, second, it's illegal. They have sensors along this road. A security patrol would be here in ten minutes."

"I don't care. Stop the car."

Rich's driver slowed and pulled to the shoulder of the highway. I pushed open the door and stared into the late afternoon sun. In an hour the light would fade behind the great ramparts of the West Wall. I had often thought of exploring all those cracks, crevices, and broken canyons. Decades ago, each time I drove south I'd stare longingly at those mysteriously beautiful, harsh, yet inviting towers. Somehow, I'd never stopped.

"Are you sure?"

"See you in the morning, Rich."

I stepped over the Russian thistle that still grew prolifically along the interstate and slid down the embankment. With great difficulty I climbed the three-strand barbed-wire fence and tore my old jeans in the process. Damn, I'd had those Wranglers for forty-five years.

The roar of traffic behind me was inescapable, but I ignored it, put it away in some other part of my brain. *This* is why I came. I saw an old juniper tree, its weathered silver trunk caught in the late-afternoon sun, each swirl of bark and wood delineated and accentuated by the light. I saw a bird. I looked closer and recognized a Say's phoebe as she landed on one of the skeletal branches just above my head. I listened. Her song was as melancholy and sad as the first time I'd heard it, sixty years earlier. I began to weep.

Biting midges swirled about my head, crawled in to my scalp, and bit me mercilessly. I could only smile. I took off my boots, my beloved Redwings, and dug my wrinkled and withered old feet into the hot red sand. I leaned against the juniper's trunk and looked up. Above the burnt green berries, the foliage, the phoebe, and the streaked canyon walls, I could still see what was left of a desert sky. I could almost see stars.

In the distance, from the north, the sound of sirens grew louder and louder.

You Can't Get Here from There Anymore

Moab, Utah, is one of the hottest places in North America, and the first time I saw it, I was in the process of freezing to death. Moab's daytime summer temperatures often exceed 100 degrees and can stay there for days, weeks, or even months at a time. But I chose to make my first Moab pilgrimage in the bitter cold of winter, on a brutal day in January over thirty years ago, driving a Volkswagen Squareback without a heater. I had been sleeping on Barry Schreiber's couch at the Alto Nido Apartments in a vile and evil place several hundred miles away called Hollywood, California. Schreiber and I were exiles from our home in Kentucky. Barry was enrolled in film school with dreams of a Spielbergian future. I was broke and tired of drifting up and down the Big Sur coast in search of enlightenment. As always, Barry's generosity knew no limits, and he invited me to kick back at the Alto Nido while he pursued movie immortality.

I was miserable there. I stayed a month, but just couldn't fit into the L.A. scene. After a series of humiliating experiences, I left Hollywood and swore I would never return, even after I was cleared of those armed robbery allegations. I'd been minding my own business at the corner of Hollywood and Ivar when two undercover cops leapt from an unmarked car and slammed me against a wall. I hadn't even been close to the Bank of America on the day in question, and why those legalized thugs thought I had anything to do with it still irritates me.

Then my Squareback was smashed one afternoon while parked along Ivar Street in front of the Alto Nido, which naturally left me upset. A local tow truck operator had inflicted the damage, but he begged me not to mention it to his boss. He explained that towing was a sideline—he was really a screenwriter. He promised to include me and my crushed car in his treatment of a story about tow trucks, which he was sure he could pitch as a series to the networks, if only I would keep this incident between the two of us. Somehow this was supposed to appease me.

But I think what put me over the edge was the run-in at the Whisky a Go Go with a renowned drummer named Buddy and the unkind and unethical way he treated Schreiber over a proposed purchase of massive quantities of marijuana at discount prices. I never did get over that. Besides, the music at the Whisky a Go Go was just too damn loud.

The Squareback still ran, barely, but it seemed like a good time to make a run for it. The tow-truck driver's boss had repaired my car, reluctantly, but as sort of a mischievous send-off, he adjusted the brakes so tightly that the wheels would barely turn. I didn't notice the adjustment until San Bernardino, when smoke began to pour from all four wheels and my powder blue Volkswagen looked like an Atlas rocket entering the upper ionosphere. I'd burned up half the brake pads in seventy-five miles, but I didn't care. I could see the clean crisp desert ahead of me, the foul inhuman stench of Los Angeles fading in my rear-view mirror, and no reason to ever turn around and go back. I never did.

All I had was fifty dollars and my father's Gulf Oil credit card, but I felt wealthier than a fat Republican. Of course, my father *was* a Republican and proud of it, and I had stolen his card. But I had not yet come to terms with hypocrisy or guilt and all their ramifications. I was much too young for those kinds of complications. After readjusting the brakes, the Squareback ran reasonably well for a vehicle that was on the verge of falling apart. So I decided to detour from my intended route back to Kentucky and go north from Flagstaff into the remote canyonlands of southeastern Utah.

I made it as far as the Grand Canyon that first day, and I slept in my car in the parking lot of the El Tovar Lodge at the South Rim. During the night, the weather shifted a bit and temperatures plummeted to near zero. I'd been wise enough to park the car on a hill, though, and when the battery wouldn't even give the starter a groan, I released the brake, turned on the ignition, popped the clutch, and lurched forward into the frigid crystal morning, bound for a place called Moab, hoping for better weather.

I arrived in Moab on one of the coldest afternoons in recorded history. As long as the sun was up and beaming though my windows, the day had been tolerable. But now, with sunset rapidly approaching, I came down Blue Hill into the Moab Valley and saw an odd sight just ahead of me. It was my first encounter with a real American West valley inversion, that strange meteorological event that occurs when cold air at the bottom of a valley becomes trapped by warm air above it. I drove into a dense fog that instantly engulfed me and the Squareback. The inside of my windshield appeared to fog up, until I realized it wasn't fog at all—it was ice. I was driving along US 160, steering with one hand and scraping the inside of my windshield with the other. I could no longer feel my feet at all.

Moab was buried under a heavy blanket of snow. Plows had pushed it into huge piles in the center of Main Street, and even seeing what was on the other side of the road was nearly impossible. I stopped at Jack West's Chevron for gas and a chance to warm up.

"Is it always this cold?" I asked Jack through chattering teeth.

"This son-of-a-bitchin' snow is a goddamn son of a bitch!" replied Jack. "I hate the god-damn stuff. Son-of-a-bitchin' white shit. Hate it!"

I nodded, and I wondered how Jack might reply to a question about the heat in July to a total stranger.

Then I crossed the street to Walker's drug store and bought two cans of Sterno—canned heat, it was called. Before Primus stoves there was paraffin in a can, but I had no intention of cooking anything except maybe my ass. I pried open the lid of both cans with a screwdriver, placed them on the floorboard between my legs, and lit them. The flames leapt beneath my knees, and I accidentally ignited my first copy of Moab's venerable weekly newspaper, the *Times-Independent*. But I didn't care if I burned to death at that point. It seemed like a reasonable, even desirable, alternative.

Driving north toward us 6, I had just stomped out the last of the *Times-Independent* embers when I noticed the entrance to Arches National Park, five miles north of town. It didn't look like much from the highway, buried under three feet of snow at the bottom of a gloomy canyon on that bitter January day. I was unaware what lay just over the hill. For that matter, I was unaware of almost anything but my frostbitten limbs and the frozen mucus in my nose. I was oblivious to an entirely new world that loomed in the growing shadows, just beyond the reach of my headlights.

What lay within those shadows would change me forever. But at the moment, I couldn't have cared less, because my feet were blue and about to fall off. They felt brittle, and I feared stomping them to increase circulation might cause them to shatter. I pushed my Squareback to the limit as the flames from the Sterno cast a soft and golden glow on my face. It was 110 miles to Grand Junction, Colorado, and a Holiday Inn that honored my dad's Gulf Oil card. With gritty determination I pushed onward. Two hours later, I was snug in my rented bed and had cranked the heat to eighty degrees. Alfred Hitchcock's "Vertigo" played on the television. Huddled beneath extra blankets, the feeling in my feet slowly returned. As I drifted toward sleep, I thought of all I'd seen that day, and

I thought about Moab. I wondered what it looks like when it's not snowing. I wondered when I'd be back. I wondered if my car would start in the morning.

I returned to Moab the following summer and then again and again, making the long drive from my home in Kentucky to the red-rock canyons. It was like a pilgrimage of sorts, at least in the beginning. "I'm going to Moab" meant something marvelous to me. I felt like I was on a mission, like I'd received some admonition from on high to protect this sacred place. It seems silly now, but there was dedication and commitment in the words, as if going there was an honored assignment. Within a couple of years, I gave up Kentucky, moved to Utah, and changed my license plate. At last, I was home in Moab.

What I noticed about Moab, almost from the get-go, was that I had come to live in a mutant landscape in a land of mutants. I came to love and appreciate the fact that many of Moab's residents were as strange, twisted, colorful, and weird as the rocks that surrounded them. The slickrock and the citizens peculiarly complemented each other, though it might be a stretch to say they lived symbiotically. Men are always trying to extract something from the land here, as we do almost everywhere. For over a century, it's been that way around Moab, though the kind of treasure we've sought keeps changing.

▬▬▬ ▬▬▬ ▬▬▬ For millennia, the canyons of southeastern Utah were left to their own devices. As recently as 15,000 years ago, humans had failed to make an appearance. Places we know so easily now, icons like Delicate Arch, the windswept summit of Mount Tukunikivats in the La Sal Mountains, the dizzying precipice of Dead Horse Point, all looked much as they do today. Of course, before we arrived they had no names for there was no one then to name them—nor to photograph or videotape them. Not a soul existed to rappel from Balanced Rock or to BASE jump from Grand View Point. No one proposed to use Castle Rock as a backdrop for a Chevy ad or otherwise exploit its commercial value.

No one waxed poetic about the scenery and wrote love sonnets to their girlfriends while being properly inspired by the light and color of a canyon-country sunset. Inspiration, if there is such a thing, was left to the croaking ravens, the laughing coyotes, and the chattering chipmunks. Did such scenery move them in any measurable way? Probably not, yet they managed to be excellent stewards of the land for more centuries than we can begin to grasp. Just a good clean place to live is all they needed, and the land gave them that and a bit more. It gave them a room with a view.

Thousands of years ago, the Anasazi Indians wandered south into the canyon country of southeastern Utah and western Colorado and made their homes there. They were the first inhabitants, though that fact may not have occurred to them. Wherever most of the early Americans traveled in those times, they were breaking new ground.

I recently found buried beneath my driveway the intact remains of three crude earthen pots, made some 1500 years ago. My driveway had been a Basketmaker III cook site, according to renowned amateur archaeologist and southern Utah's most beloved misanthrope, Orville Serafin. The cook site had been a hut of modest efficiency, built of sticks and branches, but offering enough protection from the elements to provide a comfortable kitchen. Orville and I looked a bit harder and found remnants of the pit house, just a few feet further up the slope.

A family had lived here, just a hundred yards from the site of my own home. They'd lived, worked, laughed, loved, fought, and cried under the same skyline I enjoy every evening. And, like me, they were neglectful cooks—from all appearances, one of their cook fires got away from them and burned down the hut. Eventually they moved on.

But did this family and others like them really love the majestic scenery that embraced them? Or was the monumental landscape just another obstacle to be dealt with in their daily struggle to survive in a harsh and hostile environment? One of my favorite petroglyphs is at what is now Arches National Park. High on the wall along the rim of Salt Valley, the two figures chiseled in Entrada sandstone are holding hands and one of them has the unmistakable hint of a smile. They're facing west, gazing at the same vista that makes all of us smile, especially at sunset. So, yes, I think they got it.

The Anasazi vanished as quickly as they'd come, and mystery shrouds their disappearance. Centuries passed, the kivas and granaries filtered the howling winds and provided homes for the packrats whose middens marked the passage of time. Ute Indians arrived in the seventeenth century, on horses that they'd taken from the Spaniards a century earlier. They left their images on rock walls near Salt Valley Wash in Arches. In 1776 the Spanish came to the Moab Valley and followed the base of the West Wall south to the Abajos Mountains and then southeast toward New Mexico. Their route became the Santa Fe Trail, and remnants of the trail remain today.

Still, the Moab Valley mostly slumbered. In 1844 a French fur trapper named Denis Julien from St. Louis, one of America's first rugged individualists, passed through Arches, probably on his way to Robidoux's Trading Post near present-day Duchesne, Utah. On May 12 of that year, Julien paused along the Devils Garden ridge to camp for the night. He took the time to carve his name in the sandstone fin adjacent to his camp. In fact, he chiseled his signature over the top of an Anasazi petroglyph, making Julien the first white man (but not the last) to deface an archaeological site in Arches. He escaped without receiving a federal citation. In fact, his signature would go unnoticed for 135 years, until I happened to stumble on it one day while trying to hide from tourists.

Three hundred miles north, Brigham Young's Latter Day Saints finally thought they'd found a place remote enough to be free from persecution and prosecution. In 1847 the vanguard of the emigrants made their way through the canyons of the Wasatch Mountains to the barren flats above the Great Salt Lake. Within a few years Salt Lake City was booming, and Brigham sent his Saints to settle other parts of the territory. Alfred Billings got the call to travel southeast and establish a settlement near the river known then as the Grand. Billings and forty-three others left Manti in the spring of 1855 and traveled south, crossed the river near today's highway bridge, and immediately set about the task of establishing the Elk Mountain Mission, near what is today Moab. They built structures and created an irrigation ditch to divert water and grow crops. The Ute Indians were not happy with their new neighbors, and hostilities increased between the Mormons and the Utes. When a Mormon was killed by a Ute arrow, Billings ordered the evacuation of the settlement and they returned to the Salt Lake Valley.

But in their haste, the Mormons forgot to turn off their irrigation canal. The diverted water flowed for another thirty-five years. The ditch was a familiar landmark in Moab until the 1950s, when bulldozers filled the last remnants of it. Until a few years ago, it was claimed that rocks from the mission lined the garden of a home at the corner of Fifth West and the main highway. The rocks, like much of Moab's history, have recently been discarded.

The Moab Valley returned to normal for another three decades until ranchers from Colorado and Texas, searching for new grasslands for their cattle, discovered the La Sal Mountains and the high green meadows. A motley collection of cowboys and prospectors, scoundrels and Christians, entrepreneurs and drifters made their way to the valley. One of the earliest to earn a lasting reputation was William Granstaff, known to his friends and enemies alike as "Nigger Bill." He ran cattle that may or may not have been stolen with his partner, identified only and forever as "Frenchie." Bill may have even sold land he didn't own to Mormons, who finally returned to the valley in the early 1880s. Granstaff and the others set a tone for the valley that would set Moab apart from other Utah towns and cities to this very day. The town grew up wild.

Early on it was also given a name. The early accounts, such as Fawn McConkie Tanner's *History of Moab*, suggest that the town's first postmaster, William Pierce, chose the name "Moab" from the Bible for its alleged references to the "far country" in the Old Testament's books of Ruth and Jeremiah. But in his excellent slim volume *Coyote's History of Moab*, longtime Moabite José Knighton took issue with the official version. Knighton pointed out that "Moab" first appears as a person, not a place. Genesis 19:36–37 says, "Both the daughters of Lot were with child by their father. The first-born bore a son, and called his name Moab; he is the father of the Moabites to this day." Knighton noted that, "Lot, famous as the righteous refugee from Sodom, obviously succumbed to further temptations. The name Moab literally means 'of my father,' and is a direct reference to the original Moab's incestuous origin. The land of Moab which he settled became infamous as a haven for genealogical embarrassments like himself. . . . In definition and allusion, the Biblical meaning of Moab is a far cry from anything as neutrally romantic as the 'far country.'"

So where does the name come from? Knighton offered a far more compelling explanation, one that had everything to do with itching and scratching. Until very recently, Moab was inhabited by a very small human population and about 50 trillion mosquitoes, especially during the late spring and summer months. The low-lying areas near the Colorado River, known for decades as The Sloughs, were perfect breeding grounds for the little blood-sucking bastards. Old-timers, even today, recall with bitterness the "good old days" when sitting on the front porch in Moab was a test of wills with their buzzing, biting adversaries.

According to Knighton, "the Paiute word *moapa* (mo-ah-pah) means 'mosquito water.' Ute and Paiute are sibling languages. . . . Perhaps William Pierce recognized the similarity of the native name to the target of a prophet's jeremiads, and chose it for its poetic echo of Paiute. The name of Moab may be more a reminiscence of the place of mosquitoes than of any infamous Biblical landscape."

Besides the mosquitoes, cattle dominated the landscape of southeastern Utah until the early twentieth century. Huge cattle companies used every square mile of rangeland they could find for their burgeoning herds. From the high meadows of the La Sal Mountains to the scrawny blackbrush and sage land on the plains and valleys below, cattle were everywhere. Cattle rustling was a natural offspring of the industry, and stories of Butch Cassidy and the Wild Bunch and the Robbers Roost Gang and their exploits are legendary. Butch's friend Harvey Logan killed the Grand County sheriff over the death of a friend. The Robbers Roost Gang frequently used Salt Wash in Arches as an alternative route north to avoid the authorities. The town had more saloons than churches, and Moab built a reputation as a lawless and wide-open community.

But by the early 1900s, the ranchers and a fair number of sheep barons had over-played their hand. They had laid waste to the vast acreage they used and abused to feed their herds. The British-owned Carlyle Cattle Company pulled its holdings from the dec-imated and burned out country and moved to greener pastures in Montana. The rustlers found themselves out of work as a consequence, and the town cleaned itself up, even if it didn't want to. Moab had no choice but to go straight. For decades Moab would slumber yet again. For many, slumbering was an excellent way to pass the time.

As a little girl in the 1920s, Toots McDougald lived an idyllic life in Moab, a place that seemed to have been forgotten by the rest of the world. Her stepfather, Marv Turnbow, ran a few cattle in a remote part of the county. Sometimes he occupied a rough-hewn cabin near Salt Wash that had been built twenty years earlier by a refugee from Ohio named John Wesley Wolfe. Wolfe came to the canyon country for his health, grew weary of the solitude and the desolate surroundings after a decade, and abandoned the prem-ises. Turnbow and others made infrequent use of the ruins thereafter.

Toots spent summers at what came to be known as Turnbow Cabin, helping Marv with the chores and often wandering into the strange twisted red rocks that virtually sur-rounded her summer home. Just a mile and a half up the slickrock was a natural stone arch that some locals called the School Marm's Bloomers. Turnbow found the fantastic red-rock jungle a nuisance more than a wonder. "Hell of a place to lose a cow" is the way many early residents described the Colorado Plateau.

But a few did take notice of the scenery. Alex Ringhoffer, a Hungarian-born prospec-tor with an eye for odd beauty, wandered into a labyrinth of canyons north of Moab and was overwhelmed by what he saw. He may have been Moab's first New West entrepre-neur, because the unworldly scenery he discovered touched him in a very capitalistic way. In July 1923, Ringhoffer contacted Frank Wadleigh of the Denver & Rio Grande Western Railroad. Wadleigh was in charge of passenger operations, and Ringhoffer felt sure he had just discovered America's newest scenic wonder. A few months later, Ring-hoffer took a delegation from the railroad to a place he called the Devils Garden, about fifteen miles south of the rail line at Thompson Springs, Utah.

Wadleigh shared Ringhoffer's awe and contacted his friend Steven Mather, then direc-tor of the National Park Service, to see if Ringhoffer's discovery might qualify for national monument status. Mather dispatched a crew but could not find Ringhoffer's Devils Gar-den; however, they did locate other magnificent stone arches and monoliths a few miles south and recommended this area for federal protection. The Coolidge administration initially balked at the idea of creating yet another monument. In fact, then Secretary of the Interior Hubert Work proposed returning some of the already-designated monu-ments to the states, an idea that would still warm the hearts of many rural Utahns in the twenty-first century. Finally, a small parcel of land, about 5000 acres, was proclaimed by President Hoover as Arches National Park in 1929. President Roosevelt expanded the boundaries to more than 33,000 acres in 1936. But it would not be until 1969 that another park expansion by President Johnson finally included Ringhoffer's original Dev-ils Garden, now called the Klondike Bluffs.

It was Ringhoffer's discovery that would someday trigger an enormous multimillion-dollar tourist and recreation economy. But when Roosevelt expanded Arches National Park in 1936, tourists were as rare as money in Depression-struck America. Still, the National Park Service seemed determined to establish a foothold of sorts in the Arches and Moab area and sent Henry D. "Hank" Schmidt to work as the monument's first full-time custodian. Schmidt's homespun monthly reports gave a colorful and accurate description of the Arches country during those years. Hank spent much of his time shov-eling sand and filling potholes on the old dirt two-tracks that led the occasional visitor inside the monument.

On June 21, 1940, Hank wrote, "This monument still has a road into the Windows sec-tion, across the very sandy Willow Flats, in spite of the combined efforts of high winds and blown sand to wipe it out. My long-handled shovel and I do our bit every day in order that our visitors may cross the dunes safely in their trip to the Arches. It is necessary to patrol the road regularly to assist those motorists who bog down in the sand or who stall their cars via the overheated fuel pump method." Yet, Schmidt cheerfully reported, "Travel to the monument has dropped considerably in comparison with the month of May, [but] it has shown a good increase over June 1939." Arches hosted 213 visitors in June 1940.

With the arrival of a Civilian Conservation Corps (ccc) crew in late 1940, Schmidt and others hoped that a new road into the monument might become a reality. Local boosters like J. W. "Doc" Williams and the Moab *Times-Independent* publisher Loren "Bish" Taylor were particularly pleased to see the work begin. They had long advocated a tourism-based economy for Moab, if only they could make it a bit easier for the tourist to get here. The ccc boys attacked the job with a vengeance, and local optimists like Taylor and Williams believed that the job might be completed in a few years, barring the unexpected.

But the unexpected was just eighteen months away: the attack on Pearl Harbor and the nation's entry into World War II would delay that road project by eighteen years. Moab, like the rest of the nation, threw itself behind the war effort, but it would not be evident for years just how intimate a role Moab would play in America's ultimate victory.

Every small town has its staunch promoters, and Moab was no different. For years, Bish Taylor and his *Times-Independent* dreamed of a Moab future driven by some extraordinary mineral and/or oil discovery. In the 1920s an oil well, Shafer No. 1 along the Kane Creek anticline south of town, caused Taylor to proclaim it "The Greatest Oil Strike in the State's History." But the well caught fire, which burned the rig to the ground, water seeped into the hole from other geological formations, and the story died. Rumors of copper-rich "glory holes" came later. A proposed magnesium processing plant to be built near Crescent Junction in the late 1930s inspired Bish Taylor to boast that the plant would provide the world's magnesium needs "for 3000 years."

But in the late 1930s, another often-overlooked mineral was modestly sought in the canyon country of southeastern Utah. Howard Balsley found a market for the mineral with a firm in Pittsburgh called the Vitro Manufacturing Company, which used pigments derived from the mineral in ceramics and pottery. In the years and decades ahead, however, that same mineral would transform Moab, the nation, and the world. That mineral was uranium.

Few besides Balsley even knew what uranium was, and no one knew of its potential. Vanadium, a related mineral, was sought and mined in the canyon country during World War II. The United States needed vanadium, a vital element used in the hardening of steel, and there was plenty of it in southeastern Utah. In 1943 the government banned the sale of uranium-producing ore for any kind of industrial purpose in the private sector, but few noticed. Quietly the government accumulated a stockpile of uranium from the vanadium tailings. On August 6, 1945, the United States used a portion of it to destroy Hiroshima. Moabites soon learned that the ingredients for the first atomic bombs had been mined practically from their own backyards.

As postwar America returned to some semblance of normalcy, Moab tried to pick up where it had left off. Tourism was front-page news again. Stories that the Bureau of Reclamation planned to build a series of high dams on the Colorado River convinced many that Moab might become a tourist mecca, despite the fact that an early plan of the bureau called for the flooding of the Moab Valley itself. Construction of a dam along a remote part of the river called Glen Canyon began in 1956, despite the protests of a small group of river runners, including a skinny, crew-cut, former tire salesman from Salt Lake City named Ken Sleight.

That same year a recent graduate of the University of New Mexico reported for duty at Arches National Park as a seasonal ranger. His name was Edward Abbey, and according to his supervisor, Lloyd Pierson, the only thing remarkable about him was his hat size.

"Ed had the biggest head I've ever seen," recalled Pierson decades later. "We couldn't find an official 'smokey hat' that fit. We finally gave him a pith helmet to wear. It was the best we could do."

But in the early 1950s, something else lurked just beyond the shadows that would transform Moab forever. The Cold War and the American dream were about to collide with each other in this sleepy little orchard town. In a matter of months Moab would become "The Uranium Capital of the World," and Charlie Steen would become its king.

Charlie Steen hardly looked the part of a man about to change the course of Moab's history. Short, skinny, and balding, with thick tortoise-rimmed glasses and dressed perpetually in khaki work shirt and trousers, Charlie was an out-of-work geologist from Texas who was convinced he could find uranium where the experts said it didn't exist. He looked in odd places, in great part because the obvious locations for uranium ore had already been staked.

Charlie searched for geological conditions that would cause uranium to collect and concentrate and in favorable locations that could be discovered with a drilling rig. He began to prospect in an area called the Cutler Formation. As his youngest son Mark recalled years later, "His theory was ridiculed and criticized by AEC [Atomic Energy Commission] geologists who were familiar with the country, and company geologists figured they knew more about uranium ore deposits than some newcomer from Texas."

Ultimately Charlie was right, the AEC geologists were wrong, and the bespectacled man from Texas became staggeringly wealthy in a matter of months. He made millions, built a mansion on a hill overlooking Moab, constructed a uranium-processing mill on the banks of the Colorado River (with the gratitude of the U.S. government and its citizens), and became an integral player in the nation's Cold War with the Russians. He fought with those of his friends who resented his success, yet he displayed incredible generosity with other friends and strangers alike. More than once, Charlie invited the entire town of Moab to fabulous picnics and barbeques. He spoiled his kids rotten, unwittingly creating a family nightmare that exists to this day. Mark Steen talks frequently of the tell-all book he will someday write, entitled "All the Misery that Money Can Buy."

Eventually Charlie lost it all, but in those glory days of the 1950s, everyone in America dreamed of becoming the next Charlie Steen. His life story was even played out on television, with Jackie Cooper as Charlie. Thousands of hopeful Americans, most with no skill or training in mining at all, descended on Moab. The town exploded, with its population tripling in a year. The schools were unable to keep up with the town's exponential growth. Waiting for their three minutes on Moab's only public pay phone, lines of would-be callers queued for hours. But still the prospectors came. Armed with nothing more than a jeep and a cheap Geiger counter, they fanned out over the canyon country in all directions, madly staking claims anywhere they could. Sometimes the same ground was staked three or four times, and eventually the lawyers were the ones who made all the money (as it has always been and always will be).

Unwittingly, the prospectors were building Moab's future, one arduous bumpy cross-country trip into the desolate red-rock country of southeastern Utah at a time. Their legacy would not be in the riches they found but in the trails they left behind. Before 1952 the canyon country was traversed by only a few roads and trails, created mainly by cattlemen and sheepherders searching for strays. But by 1960 a vast network of jeep tracks, trails, seismic lines, and even airstrips had been laid down over the pristine landscape. In the fragile desert, those tracks would not go away quickly. Decades later, they would be rediscovered and become the recreational avenues for thousands of motorized and non-motorized recreationists who would descend upon the same land in even greater numbers. They would become a source of acrimony and outrage between environmentalists, who wanted to shut down almost all the old roads, and die-hard recreationists, who not only wanted to leave them all open but create even more.

In the interim, however, life finally began to pause a bit in Moab. The uranium boom melted away, and Charlie Steen moved to Reno in the mid-1960s. Uranium mining continued but without the gleeful enthusiasm of a decade before. The uranium mill, now owned by the Atlas Corporation, began to leak heavy metals and toxins into the Colorado River, but few took notice.

Tourism grew with the creation of Canyonlands National Park in 1964, but many roads remained rough and unpaved, and southeastern Utah was still thought to be one of the most isolated parts of the contiguous United States. Moab found itself slumbering yet again. Many residents who had experienced the uranium-boom years schemed and dreamed of a way to put Moab back on track. Others liked the slower pace, and some were actually drawn to Moab for that very reason.

In the 1970s, Moab became a strange, oddly diverse community of miners and cowboys waiting for the next boom and a hodgepodge of young idealists, river runners, and seasonal park rangers seeking a simpler life. Though it was a troubled and sometimes hostile coexistence, it was also never dull. For many, the strange diversity was downright entertaining. It was about then that someone found a new way to describe Moab: it became known as "a funky little town."

And that's when I arrived.

Abbey's Decade

Webster's defines a *landmark* as "a conspicuous object . . . that distinguishes a locality." It takes time, prominence, and a reputation to earn the honor. Delicate Arch is *the* landmark of Arches National Park. It's composed of quartz sand tightly cemented by calcium carbonate to form Entrada sandstone. The particles were squeezed together millions of years ago, compressed by the weight of 1000 vertical feet of sediment and rock deposited above it. The arch waited, unformed, through millions of years as erosion worked tirelessly and perpetually to free it. Peeling back the rock, one grain at a time, the intricately sculpted work of art finally emerged from the rock massif thousands of years ago. But it wasn't until humans like Toots McDougald came along and gave the arch a name that it finally became the landmark we revere today.

Humans generally don't have the patience of nature when it comes to landmarks. We like to grow our own, even when that's not our intent. I doubt if anyone could have predicted the future or the landmark-to-be when a small cottonwood seedling was planted at the corner of First South and Third East in Moab during the spring of 1886. Documents from the Grand County Recorder's Office indicate that Leonidas L. Crapo filed on the land on November 14, 1885, as a homestead property, a few months before the seedling began to take root, but no one knows for sure who planted it.

I'd like to believe that it was someone who took a long view of life. Wendell Berry once wrote, "Invest in the Millennium . . . plant sequoias." No one who plants a tree, unless they're growing Chinese elms, can ever be called a seeker of instant gratification. Trees take time, care, and patience. Whoever it was, I'm certain he (or she) dug the hole with great love and affection, careful to make it wide enough and deep enough for the roots to grow freely. He might have transplanted the tree from a location along Mill Creek, just a few blocks away, carefully wrapping the roots in wet burlap as he hauled the seedling back to its new home. The planter surely found some good manure from the neighbor's cow to mix with the sandy soil until it reached a consistency best suited for a cottonwood.

The tree may have gone into shock from its sudden unearthing and relocation. Its leaves might have begun to show signs of stress and wither in the late spring heat. But with loving care and enough water, the cottonwood survived and began to grow, quite slowly at first. The planter might have wondered in those early years if the tree would ever provide decent shade on a scorching July day. But as the century drew to a close, the tree's roots had reached deep into the sandy soil of the Moab Valley and tapped into the underground aquifer. The cottonwood tree took off.

By the 1920s, Moab residents were already referring to it as the "Big Tree." No one had to ask, "Which big tree?" Among great trees, the First South cottonwood was the greatest. The Big Tree became a reference point for Moabites and especially for new arrivals.

Almost a century after it found a home on First South, I saw the Big Tree for the first time. I still recall its gigantic gnarled old trunk—each lump, bump, and scar looked as

if it had a story to tell. But more than anything I remember the cool shade it provided, even on a hot August afternoon. I stood beneath the Big Tree and gazed skyward at its soft green translucence as light filtered through branch after leafy branch.

I could have stood there all afternoon without attracting the slightest amount of attention, because there didn't seem to be anyone around. On a Sunday afternoon in the middle of late summer, Moab had every appearance of being deserted. I was visiting an old friend of mine on East Center, near the bottom of the cliffs, whom I'd met the year before in Jackson Hole. Nelle Holmes was a remarkable lady. At seventy-five she had recently endured breast cancer surgery, a double radical mastectomy. Now, just a couple months later, Nelle was digging holes in her garden. I tried to help, but she was determined to plant those rose bushes herself. She sent me on an errand, probably to get rid of me for a while.

As I headed for my car, she yelled, "Why not walk? It's just a mile or so and you'll get a better feel for the town."

I made my way down Center Street, diverted a block to get a closer look at the Big Tree, and saw a man toiling in his garden across the street. A couple years later, I'd learn his name was Dave Baker. He was the maintenance foreman at Arches National Park and the keeper of Moab's finest backyard garden.

I crossed Main Street near the same gas station I'd visited during the January freeze. I thought I could hear Jack West cursing the heat from a lube bay at his Chevron station, but I wasn't sure. It may have been the 100-degree temperature playing tricks on me. Main Street was almost empty—not a truck or motor home in sight. I could have laid down in the middle of the pavement and taken a little nap, but after loitering a few moments along the center line, I moved on.

I was looking for a man named Conrad Sorensen, owner of Lifestream Health Foods, and one of the reasons Moab was earning a reputation as a funky little town. Conrad was inside his shop, though the sign on the door said "Closed." I took the sign at its word and started to leave, but he waved at me to come in. If I recall, even then Conrad was drinking what he called his "green slime." It was some strange concoction of wheat grass, spinach leaves, and bananas. It was a frightening combination to be sure, and little green strings dripped from his beard. He offered to make me one, but I foolishly declined.

I picked up Nelle's jar of organically grown, all-natural peanut butter, and Conrad welcomed me to Moab, convinced even before I was that Moab was destined to become my home. Moab affected people in different ways, but the effect was rarely subtle. Either you *got* this place or you didn't. And when you did, Moab got *you* in spades.

That summer Moab was still trying to determine its identity and its future. The uranium boom was long gone, but the mining industry continued to provide decent incomes for many of Moab's residents. The Atlas Mill, constructed in the 1950s on the Colorado River flood plain north of town, was Grand County's largest employer. Tourism lingered as a second option for some, but Moab had never been able to sell itself as a true destination for the millions of tourists wandering the highways of the West. For many, it was just too bloody hot, with summer temperatures exceeding 100 degrees for as many as fifty days a year.

Still, annual visitation had increased at Arches National Park from the 10,000 or so who used to bounce their way up the old dirt-and-gravel entrance road when Ed Abbey worked there in the mid-1950s to more than 300,000 in the late 1970s. Grandiose plans to build new paved highways into Canyonlands National Park and into the heart of the Escalante Canyons west of Moab convinced tourist promoters that a new economy lay just ahead, an unsettling thought for the likes of someone like me.

Besides, I wasn't ready to put down roots of my own quite yet. At the time, I was on a far greater mission. Had I shared my secret plan with Conrad, he might have saved me a lot of trouble, but I kept my planned pilgrimage to myself. A few days later, I said goodbye to Nelle and Conrad and assured them I'd be back. But today I was off to find Wolf Hole and Edward Abbey.

It has always been a relief to me that I first stumbled into Moab *before* I read *Desert Solitaire* and not after. I'd like to think that some aspect of my formative years wasn't affected by Edward Abbey, though in truth, much of it was. Ed Abbey changed my life—he saved me from becoming a Republican, though decades later, I haven't much use for the Democrats either.

Only a few months after my frigid Sterno drive through Moab, a friend and coworker of my father's, a closet eco-rebel and Sears Roebuck display manager named Bill Parker, tossed a well-thumbed paperback of Abbey's masterpiece at me. He said, "Here. Read this now, before it's too late and you end up working for Sears, too."

I listened to Bill and read Ed. Almost immediately I abandoned my family's misguided dedication to Richard Nixon and the GOP and became one of those annoying young eco-Abbey freaks who drove Volkswagens covered with inflammatory bumper stickers. I always carried a copy of The Book in my hip pocket.

It's almost impossible to understand how integral Abbey's voice was in those heady and exciting days, when we were young, idealistic, and convinced that our collective voices might make a difference. When Bill gave me The Book, I was young, stupid, and impulsive and my head spun with unarticulated notions that I couldn't quite bring into focus. And then Abbey came along. No one saw with more crystalline clarity what we humans need to do to keep this battered planet of ours from sinking into a sea of sludge. Yet, he never claimed to be a vision of perfection himself. Abbey detested the various crowns and accolades we tried to thrust upon him.

"I'm not a goddamn guru," he'd grouse. "And I'm not an 'environmental leader.' I just like to throw words around."

No one hurled them better. He lit fires. Before Abbey, writers like Thoreau and Muir spoke eloquently but gently in defense of the Earth. Their message was clear but so slumberingly lyrical. Then Abbey came along with a clenched fist and a heart full of joyful passionate anger. I loved the way he challenged us to do something—*anything*. Apathy disgusted him. Complacency infuriated him. It's why Abbey enjoyed the company of men and women who vehemently disagreed with him. He admired their passion, even if he thought it was wrong-headed.

Ed Abbey also reveled in his own ironies. He was contradictory, but he was so damn proud of his contradictions. He was once expounding on population control, and the young feminist interviewer thought she had Ed by the short squigglies.

"But, Mr. Abbey," she asked with unbridled scorn, "don't you have five children of your own?"

Abbey's eyes brightened. "Yes I do," he answered. "But they're by five wives. That's only one per wife. I think every woman is entitled to one child. Don't you?" Pure Abbey.

▬▬▬ ▬▬▬ ▬▬▬ More than twenty-five years ago, I wanted to shake his hand. Just a few weeks after the release of *The Monkey Wrench Gang*, and invigorated even more by Abbey's latest fiery rhetoric, I was in search of my only hero. I wanted to say hello, and I came bearing gifts. Carefully rolled up in a cardboard tube was a drawing of mine, a cartoon extravaganza of Glen Canyon Dam blown to smithereens. The cartoon was of mediocre quality, for I've never really been a very good technical artist, but my intentions were noble. I wanted to give my pen-and-ink doodle to my favorite author and was determined to find him before winter fell. The jacket of *The Monkey Wrench Gang* said that Abbey lived in a remote little corner of the Southwest called Wolf Hole, Arizona. After long hours eyeballing road maps, I found the hole, a tiny speck of a place on the Arizona Strip, a remote stretch of land south of St. George, Utah, and north of the Grand Canyon. Of course, that's where Abbey would live, I sighed. I started for Wolf Hole the next afternoon.

One of the risks associated with traveling alone is the never-ending opportunity to think useless thoughts. For me, thinking too much has never led me anywhere but into the arms of a paranoid neurotic episode. As I left Moab and turned south toward Hanksville, I considered my imminent meeting with the great Abbey. Would he be happy to see me? Would he appreciate the effort I'd made to pay my respects? Was there any hope whatsoever I'd be able to hold up my end of a conversation? Would he think I was a blithering moron? These thoughts haunted me as I made camp in the San Rafael Desert. A full moon hung over the San Rafael Swell as I drifted toward a fitful sleep.

The next morning I stopped in Hanksville, at an eatery then called Jim 'n' Elle's Café. I continued to ponder the conversation that awaited me in Wolf Hole. I tried to think of interesting witty things I might say. Nothing came to me. My mind was a blank.

I was sipping coffee, when this guy walked in. He looked vaguely familiar. Although he was dressed in typical cowboy garb, there was something unusual about the man, something rough but regal. I can still recall his outfit, a beat up straw hat, red snap-front shirt, faded Levis, pointy-toed engraved cowboy boots. He asked the waitress a question, then turned and strutted out the door.

"It couldn't be," I thought. Then I saw the waitress swoon, clutch her heart, and slowly descend to the floor. I jumped up to catch her, but she had already settled onto the carpet. I looked down at her.

"Was that Robert Redford?" I asked.

She nodded as she continued fanning herself with a menu.

I stepped outside to find all kinds of activity going on. Several of Redford's associates were scurrying about. Redford was talking on a pay phone, just fifty feet or so beyond my Volkswagen. Muckluk, my independent-minded dog, was asleep beneath the rear wheel, unmoved by anything but the cool morning air and the bright desert light. I decided to check my oil.

I had barely pulled out the dipstick when I heard Redford say, "Okay, see you in a few days." For the love of God, he was coming my way.

He walked by on his way back to the diner. I knew this was it, perhaps my only chance in a lifetime to converse with Robert Redford. I thought of Abbey—if I could speak intelligently and articulately to Redford, surely that would restore my self-confidence and I could quit fretting about Wolf Hole. Beyond that, maybe Redford would be impressed by my knowledge of environmental issues threatening southeastern Utah. We could discuss the controversial proposed Kaiparowits Power Project, which he had publicly opposed. Maybe he'd invite me back to Sundance for the weekend. Perhaps he might see a certain quality that made me perfect for a supporting role in his next film. This is the kind of seminal moment that can change a young man's life!

"Excuse me!" I blurted. I saw him hesitate. "Aren't you Robert Redford?"

He stopped dead in his tracks, spun ever so gracefully in a 180 degree arc on his Justin boots, crouched slightly as he addressed me head-on, and said, "I sure am."

I felt my brain start to cloud over. He smiled at me slightly, but it felt menacing, as if Redford was calling a bluff in a gunfight. Okay, buddy, you got my attention. Now what are you going to do?

It felt like hours that I stood there flat-footed and deeply fearful, but it was probably only a matter of seconds. I shifted uneasily from foot to foot, racking my brain for the one line that might turn this improbable moment into my hour of destiny.

I cleared my throat, put my hands on my hips, and said with great authority and conviction, "Next to 'The Wizard of Oz,' 'Jeremiah Johnson' is my favorite movie."

There was an awful silence. I knew I was finished. I thought of trying to crawl through the dipstick hole on my Volkswagen, but it was too late to hide. I saw Redford's smile tighten and disappear. He stared at the ground, but maybe there was time for recovery.

"So, what brings you to Hanksville?" I asked.

"I like it here," he replied curtly. It seemed to me, he was becoming a bit taciturn.

Meanwhile, Muckluk had stirred from beneath the car. She crawled out of the shade and walked toward Redford. Muckluk was a magnificent looking animal—half husky, half German shepherd—with knowing eyes and a certain insouciance that usually belongs to cats. Redford seemed interested. Perhaps my dog would save the day. By then Muck was standing directly in front of Redford but facing me.

Redford said, "Nice looking dog you've got."

He bent over and reached out to stroke Muckluk's back. But before he could ever touch hand to fur, the dog simply walked away from him. That goddamn insouciance again. She left him stroking air, and that was enough for Robert Redford. He couldn't even bear to look at me again. He said, "See ya" to the sidewalk as he turned and disappeared inside the café.

I got Muckluk, jumped in my car, and drove away through Capitol Reef, bound for Wolf Hole, absolutely crushed. Muck assumed her position in the passenger seat, her head hanging from the window, her long tongue flapping in the hot wind. I scolded her for ruining my chances at stardom. She acted like she didn't hear me, but the truth is, the damn dog just didn't care.

Shattered, I faced my immediate future in a state of near terror. Doubt plagued me, but I kept going. I made the long difficult passage over dusty corrugated dirt roads to find Edward Abbey, legendary writer, the inspirer of my soul, and, it turned out, legendary liar.

He wasn't there. Nothing was there, not even a fence post. Wolf Hole. I couldn't even find a hole. I walked away from the car into the dry grass and looked for miles across the dusty expanse of meadow and pygmy forest, beyond the trees to Mount Trumbull. I considered hollering out his name, pleadingly, "Abbey, you bastard! Where are you?" But it would have seemed too melodramatic, too pointless. Besides, I was relieved in a way, grateful that I no longer faced the possibility of humiliating myself twice in less than a week.

Muckluk hopped down from the front seat, stretched briefly, rolled in the dust, and then pissed on my tires, guy style. She looked dubiously at me for a moment, then climbed back into the car. Muck was growing weary of my antics. I shrugged and gave up. But before I turned the Volkswagen around and headed out of Wolf Hole, I pulled my line drawing from its tube. At the bottom of the cartoon, I had written, "To Edward Abbey." Now I scrawled beneath it, "Wherever you are."

I abandoned my quest, stuffed the tube under the back seat, and spent the next month totally alone except for the dog, on a remote finger of land along the North Rim. At

Parissawampits Point, I considered my immediate future. It seemed as bleak as the winter that was casting a gray pall on autumn much sooner than I'd expected. For weeks we wandered the North Rim, watching the aspens turn gold and the days grow short. Finally, on the verge of going mad from too much solitude, I loaded up the Volkswagen and rattled my way back over forty miles of dirt road to the main highway, then north toward Moab. Conrad had been right. It already felt like home.

Then, without warning, everything went right. I must have looked cold and lonely the day I wandered into the visitor center, and some sympathetic park rangers at Natural Bridges National Monument suggested I apply for a volunteer job at Arches. They'd just heard there was an opening. Three bucks a day and an apartment sounded extravagant, and I leapt at the chance.

Then I discovered that Abbey had been in Moab all along. In fact, he lived in a ranch-style home on Spanish Valley Drive with his beautiful nineteen-year-old wife Renée, and he was friends with most of the seasonal rangers at Arches and Canyonlands. A mutual park service buddy, Jim Conklin, arranged for a meeting, but I wasn't sure if I was ready—or worthy. I kept thinking about Hanksville and Redford.

"Christ!" I said to Conklin, "What if I say something stupid like that to Abbey?"

Conklin weighed my concerns gravely. "Hmmm . . . you very well might," he nodded. "It would probably be better to say nothing at all. If he asks you a question, just answer it as simply as you can. Don't elaborate. The less you say, the better. Quiet people are more mysterious. Maybe he'll even think you're deep."

Abbey was playing poker that night at the ranch house, north of town. Today it's called Moab Springs Guest Ranch and Condos, a high-end development that charges $200 a night to sleep next to one of the busiest truck highways in America. But then it was just a ramshackle old brick home that once belonged to the family of Bobby Kennedy's wife—they'd stayed there on their honeymoon—and that was rented by seasonal ranger and ne'er-do-well Doug Treadway and his three big dogs.

Doug greeted Conklin and me at the back door and led us into the brightly lit but drafty old home. "Ed," Treadway shouted, "the guy with the drawing of Glen Canyon Dam is here."

The lights in the front bedroom were off, but it faced the highway. Reflected light from passing traffic revealed the silhouette of a man standing in the front window. The dark figure turned slowly and walked toward me. Out of the shadows and into the light stepped my hero, Edward Abbey. Conklin poked me gently and whispered, "Remember, don't say much."

But Abbey could not have been kinder or more gracious. He asked how long I'd been in Moab and was especially pleased to hear I was about to start work as a volunteer at Arches National Park.

"Good!" he said. "We need more radicals in the park service."

I finally unfurled my Glen Canyon Damn drawing. Ed threw back his head and laughed. "My God! Floyd Dominy Falls at last!" I pointed out some of the smaller and subtler aspects of the drawing, including the tiny inscription on a large chunk of smashed concrete in the foreground that read, "Ken Sleight was here for the ride."

"Have you met Ken yet?" Ed asked.

I had. Just a week earlier Abbey's old pal Ken Sleight, the inspiration for Seldom Seen Smith in *The Monkey Wrench Gang*, had wandered into the Arches Visitor Center. In the course of a few days, I had met both Abbey and Sleight and had managed to survive both encounters without seriously humiliating myself. I hoped it would be the start of some very long and genuine friendships.

In the weeks and months that followed, I saw Abbey from time to time, usually at the post office. In April I began my first full year as a seasonal ranger at Arches National Park. My duty station was the Devils Garden campground, eighteen miles from the park entrance, and my living quarters was a dilapidated old trailer that was positioned near the beginning of the campground road. It would be home to me and several hundred deer mice over the next decade. By the time the National Park Service finally hauled that old relic away in the 1990s, mouse turds must have doubled its weight. I should have been revered as a miracle of science since I never succumbed to the dreaded Hantavirus, the deadly disease carried in mouse droppings.

I tried to convince myself that I was following in Abbey's footsteps in some way. Among the hordes of tourists that now swarmed over the park were hundreds of Abbeyphiles, who, like me, came to Arches looking for Abbey or to capture the feeling of *Desert Solitaire* for themselves. A few wanted to take a piece of Abbey home with them. I realized how serious the Abbey phenomenon was when I found an erstwhile young camper trying to pry a shard of tin from my little trailer.

"I just wanted to take a bit of Abbey's home with me," he explained lamely.

I went inside, found a piece of paper and a marker, scribbled "This Was Not Edward Abbey's Trailer," and stuck it to the door.

Still they came, and for the next ten years I was there to greet them.

▬▬ ▬▬ ▬▬ It's a pity that we rarely appreciate the things we have when we have them. Twenty years after Abbey's tour of duty, Arches National Park bore little resemblance to the desert outpost he had described. I found myself waxing nostalgic for a time I had never experienced. The park's development plans were almost complete. Twenty-three miles of paved road took visitors to all the major features. "Yes, Ma'am," I'd say wearily, over and over and over again, "you can see *four* major arches without ever leaving your vehicle, if you just stay on this paved road." Only the Delicate Arch trailhead remained accessible by dirt road.

The old dirt road crossed two washes, which remained dry 360 days out of the year. But when the late summer storms came, flash floods filled the sandy bottoms with foam, debris, and torrents of raging water. Tourists caught on the trailhead side of Salt Valley Wash had to wait until the waters subsided, and it was often the highlight of their otherwise overplanned vacations. Several times, the waters stayed high all night and we noble rangers waded through the water with sandwiches, coffee, tents, and sleeping bags to keep our stranded guests as comfortable as possible. They could not have been happier.

Still, with 300,000 visitors a year and the numbers rising annually, it seemed to me from the beginning that something had been lost here with all the pavement, rules and regulations, and comfort stations. But I simply did not realize—could not even grasp—just how much worse things could get.

The future development of Arches National Park and other public lands in southeastern Utah was a source of endless argument, and Moab's residents never tired of it. Our passion for debate seemed limitless, and throughout the 1970s and 1980s Moabites argued about practically everything. From paving the roads in Canyonlands National Park, to building a high-level nuclear waste storage facility, to the always-contentious issue of wilderness designation, Moab's citizens never failed to turn out in droves to contribute their own views. The historic old Star Hall on Center Street served as the gathering place for dozens of meetings and hearings, and both sides always managed to produce a good crowd.

It was better than a movie, especially in Moab, which usually saw films reach the local theater about a year after their release. Our locally produced public fights were far more entertaining, and, best of all, we knew the actors. Some of them were stellar. When uranium miner Joe Stocks took the microphone, we could expect a brilliant performance, even if we didn't agree with a word he said. From the few but vocal enviros, we could always count on one of our drunk, stoned, disheveled, and just a little insane buddies to stagger to the podium. He'd ramble incoherently, far beyond his allotted five minutes, about our Mother Earth being screwed by the goddamn forces of evil until one of his less impaired friends finally led him gently back to his seat.

But on July 4, 1980, I realized just how conservative most Moabites still were. More than a thousand of my fellow citizens, led by County Commissioner Ray Tibbetts, marched down Main Street to protest recent road closures by the BLM. Wilderness study areas were being established by the bureau, and locals were furious to see their favorite jeep trails shut down overnight. The protesters gathered at Negro Bill Canyon, while Tibbetts fired up a D7 Caterpillar bulldozer, pushed the "Road Closed" sign aside, and reopened the trail, to the hoarse cheers of his followers.

Moab was still a mining town and was determined to stay that way. The new road closures were a direct threat to their very existence, something I didn't grasp at the time. I was impressed by the turnout but hardly sympathetic to their cause. To me, all of the extractive industries—mining, drilling, ranching, timber—constituted a threat to what remained of the pristine West. Somehow we environmentalists thought that if these kinds of threats were eliminated or reduced, *all* threats to the land would cease. It never occurred to any of us that if these industries failed, something else would take their place. But it was this event that would define the polarization between Old Westerners and New Westerners for the next twenty-five years and beyond.

Environmentalists responded in kind. In the early 1980s, Grant Johnson, Clive Kincaid, and Robert Weed formed the Southern Utah Wilderness Alliance (SUWA). It began as a grassroots organization with its headquarters in tiny Boulder, Utah. Kincaid and Johnson were promptly hung in effigy by citizens of Escalante, and Weed's home was vandalized. As the years passed, SUWA became Utah's most visible and vocal proponent for wilderness and a hated symbol for rural Utahns.

Something else happened in 1980. A couple of professional environmental lobbyists named Dave Foreman and Bart Koehler grew terminally frustrated with the endless bureaucratic entanglements and politically correct maneuverings that defined their jobs. They quit suddenly, left Washington, D.C., moved back West, and plotted their next move. Along the way they met up with Howie Wolke, Mike Roselle, and Ron Kezar. Around a campfire in the Pinacate Desert of Arizona, Earth First! was born.

A few months later, Earth First! gained the attention of federal law enforcement and the admiration and participation of Ed Abbey when they surreptitiously slipped a 300-

foot roll of Visqueen plastic over a security fence in broad daylight and unfurled it over the lip of Glen Canyon Dam. From the bridge, the tapered black plastic banner looked like a crack—the first crack—in the hated dam. Abbey offered a few words in praise of anarchy, confrontation, and direct action, while park service law enforcement rangers hovered uneasily in the background.

Ironically, I was on my way to Glen Canyon Dam at the same hour the Earth First! boys were unrolling their crack. But my travel plans had a totally different purpose. As a seasonal ranger at Arches, I had been required to receive law enforcement training and had even been sent to FLETC, the Federal Law Enforcement Training Center in Brunswick, Georgia, with a bunch of other half-baked seasonals like myself. Despite the fact our crime problems at small parks like Arches were primarily confined to illegal flower picking and unauthorized graffiti, the park service administrators thought we needed to be trained to deal with any situation. So, my buddies and I endured hours of lectures and live demonstrations. From "smoking dirtbags" to making said dirtbags "suck sand," we were expected to be cops when all we really wanted to do was goof off and explore the backcountry. But we received our commissions and were required to receive forty hours of refresher training each spring. In 1981 the course was at Page, Arizona, and the classes actually took place in the administrative offices of the Bureau of Reclamation inside the Glen Canyon Dam compound.

I'd heard rumors from my Earth First! friends that "something was going to happen at the dam," but I didn't know the specifics. When I showed up for class the next day, the park rangers and Coconino County sheriff's deputies were in a state of high agitation. Rumors of imminent arrests, undercover operations, and subversive threats flew recklessly like swallows on drugs. One overzealous deputy named Rex, who visited our classroom and was in such a state of excitement that I felt sure he'd soil his trousers, explained how he had dusted the entire 300 feet of black Visqueen for fingerprints. "We want to know *everybody* who was involved, and we're going to find them!"

I later became an Earth First! cartoonist and somehow danced the delicate line between my job as a seasonal park ranger and a radical artist. It still bewilders me how I was ever able to pen a hideously disgusting caricature of the secretary of the interior called "The Day All the Birds Crapped on James Watt" and then provide security to Watt as one of his park service bodyguards during a 1983 visit to Arches.

In Grand County, Earth First! staged one of its Round River Rendezvous near Arches, which stirred up the locals and made for some great letters to the editor of the *Times-Independent*. SUWA later opened an office in Moab, but in both cases, enviros' time and energy were aimed at the usual suspects—mining, oil and gas, cattle, and timber. At best, tourism in Moab was still a sideline that put a little extra cash into the pockets of a few motel owners, cafes, and river companies. Sometimes it was an annoyance. For me, a low-paid seasonal ranger, much of my job seemed tedious and exasperating. Only later did I see the humor, or even the glory, in it all.

I tended to the needs of the campground, which, aside from Moab itself, often represented the largest density of human beings in Grand County. At the Devils Garden campground, I spent a lot of time jiggling the toilet handles in our comfort stations to accommodate tourists in need. Disposing of human waste in its proper receptacle, I learned, is a universal human priority. I once spent twenty minutes with a woman at the Devils Garden trailhead who was concerned about "the lack of facilities" on the trail. The distressed hiker wanted me to confirm whether she could make it to Landscape Arch and back without using the facilities, as if I had a personal relationship with her bladder.

I became so familiar with the questions that I wrote the answers on the back of my trusty clipboard. If they asked, "Is it always this hot?" I could point to Answer No. 3: "It'll be hotter tomorrow." If they wanted to know about the biting gnats, I could refer to Answer No. 7: "They'll leave when they're full." When they asked, "And what about this damn wind, ranger?" I'd give them Answer No. 2: "Why, if it weren't for the eternal wind, these rocks would never have been shaped and sculpted in such a fantastic fashion. We should all be grateful for the creative spirit of the never-ending wind."

But despite the crowds and the banality, there was still time to be a ranger in the best sense of the word. We could still *range*, still wander into the backcountry and explore. In fact, it was my job to familiarize myself with the lesser-known parts of Arches National Park, and for two days of each work week, that's what I did. Sometimes a fellow ranger or two came along, but we rarely traveled in numbers more than three—the greater the crowd, the more diminished our opportunities to see wildlife—and it simply left too large an impact on the land. More often I hiked alone, and it was on those occasions that I made my greatest discoveries.

My boss, Chief Ranger Jerry Epperson, urged all of us to choose our backcountry days almost randomly, "Pick a spot, pull off the road, get out of the patrol car, and start walking. Let me know what you find."

We often told him what we found, but we were reluctant to say where. We learned that the most cherished and revered memories of the canyon country's treasures were the ones we'd made for ourselves. Somehow, discovering an old Anasazi granary, a cowboy inscription, or a new arch meant more if we discovered it on our own.

What makes something special? It's not just its beauty. Dandelions are beautiful, but most people despise them. If dandelions only grew along the rugged shoreline of a remote island off the coast of Newfoundland, the little yellow weed would be cherished and revered by people worldwide for its delicate beauty and perfect symmetry. Picking them would be a crime. We would celebrate Dandelion Appreciation Day. But because they are so prolific, most humans can barely tolerate them, spending countless dollars and endless hours digging them up and pouring poison all over their lovely golden petals.

I think it's the uniqueness of the place and the experience that gives it a special feeling. In nature, what often provides that uniqueness is its remote and unknown (to most) location. In a country of 300 million people, those secret places are dwindling at a rate that is difficult for many to fathom. For those of us who have lived in Moab for twenty years or more, there was an assumption that most of these desert gems could depend on their remoteness for protection far more than any wilderness designation or government legislation might protect them. Simply leaving them alone—and not talking about them—was our greatest gift to them.

At Arches, my fellow rangers and I understood and practiced this maxim. During my first season at the park, my good friend and fellow ranger Kay Forsythe came by the Devils Garden trailer after a backcountry patrol. She was hot, sweaty, and tired, but exhilarated from her long day in the canyons.

"Any chance I could get something cold to drink from you guys?" she pleaded. "I'm parched."

"Sure," we said. "Come on in."

Kay settled into one of our rat-turd-infested chairs, and I handed her a tall tumbler of iced tea.

"Where'd you go?" I asked.

Kay grinned. "I think I found a new granary. In fact, I'm sure of it. Even Epperson's never heard of it."

"Jerry's been all over the park since he became chief ranger," I said. "If he doesn't know about it, you're probably right. Where is it?"

She stared at me for a moment and drew another long gulp, "How hot was it today?"

"Not too bad. Hundred and one, I think. Kay . . ."

She held up her hand like a traffic cop at a busy intersection as she coaxed the last drop of tea from the glass. Then she looked at me and said, "I'm not telling."

"You're not telling? Not anybody?"

"Nobody."

"Well how do you know that Epperson hasn't seen it?"

"I don't for sure. I asked him if he knew where there were granaries in the park, and he said he only knew of one. I asked him where it was, and all he would do is point vaguely at the park map. But he pointed over here, and mine," she hesitated for a minute as she stared at our park map, "mine is sort of over here. That's all I'll tell you."

I gazed at the topo and nodded, "Well, that narrows it down to about 25,000 acres. You're all heart."

Kay said, "Someday you'll thank me for this. If you ever do stumble upon it on your own, it'll mean a lot more." I knew she was right.

Seven years later, on another scorching summer afternoon, I was hiking "sort of over here." Under an overhang, a mile from where I once imagined it might be, I found the mystery granary. There was no sign of recent human visitation. As far as I know, it still remains one of the secret places.

I never forgot that lesson from Kay, but perhaps I didn't learn it well enough. On a hot June morning, gloriously lost in a remote and seldom-visited section of the Fiery Furnace, my friend Reuben Scolnik and I struggled through a thicket of serviceberry and walked into a cathedral. I'd never seen anything in Arches quite like this stunning stone arch that clung to the edge of a 200-foot canyon. Across the canyon from our vantage point, the walls rose another 200 feet. From any angle I pursued, I couldn't see the bottom of it. We considered coming back with rappel ropes but thought better of it. We didn't *want* to know what lay below. We *liked* the mystery of it. And we assumed it would always be the way we found it on this bright hot morning. Later it occurred to me that this was the same arch that seasonal ranger Ed Abbey had alluded to in a 1956 monthly report. He had called it Cliff Arch.

But over the years, I failed to follow Kay's edict to the letter. Eventually I showed my future ex-wife and a couple of close friends. Others, who had been tantalized by my own vague description, set out to find the arch on their own, and they finally succeeded. I would wonder, years later, if my own indiscretions had made a difference. Still, my infrequent reunions with Cliff Arch never disappointed me. I assumed it would always be just like *this*. But nothing is eternal in a boomtown, and that is what Moab had always been. Moab would boom again, in ways we never dreamed of.

Moab at a Crossroads

In the summer of 1987, the economy of Moab and Grand County hit rock bottom. A few years earlier, as uranium prices plummeted, the Atlas Vanadium Processing Mill north of town closed its doors for good. The mill, which had at one time provided hundreds of jobs, now lay silent. It seemed as if the mainstay of Grand County's economy had vanished overnight, and Moab was ghost-town bound. Unemployment reached 20 percent. Empty homes and "For Sale" signs were everywhere. At one point as many as one in five homes was on the market. The story was that everybody moved to Elko, Nevada, where the mining industry was still viable.

Moab's politicians and promoters tried to stop the town's dwindling population and shrinking tax base, but Moab was hemorrhaging to death. For a while in the early 1980s, as the Department of Energy searched for a place to store the nation's high-level nuclear waste, a remote location in San Juan County, just 1000 feet from the boundary of

Canyonlands National Park, became one of the primary sites considered for the repository. The plan was to excavate a huge chamber in the massive salt domes, thousands of feet beneath the surface, and store the radioactive material in canisters. The subterranean vaults and the canisters needed to withstand the forces of nature for about 10,000 years. Considering this was a government operation, many of us were skeptical. In addition to the repository site, the associated infrastructure needed to deliver the goods would have been staggering. The Department of Energy proposed a railroad line that would go from Moab downriver to Lockhart Basin and along the base of the Needles Overlook to the site. The view at the overlook would have never been the same. But Moab, still very much a town with a mining mindset in 1982, voted two to one in favor of the repository in a nonbinding straw vote.

Moabites debated the repository at public meetings with the same amazing regularity and enthusiasm that we had devoted to other contentious issues over the years. Maybe there just wasn't anything else to do in those days but argue, but the meetings were well attended and participation remained spirited. Abbey's presence, either live or by proxy, may have boosted attendance. When Ed didn't feel up to the task, he often sent his young bride Renée to read his prepared comments. We usually preferred looking at her anyway.

But more often, the great debates were waged with remarkable civility at Moab's three greasy spoons, the Westerner Grill, Milt's Stop 'n' Eat, and the Canyonlands Café. Milt's was named for its creator Milt Galbraith, who built the Stop 'n' Eat in 1951 with $10,000 he borrowed on a handshake. Milt and his wife, Audrey, ran it fourteen hours a day, six days a week, fifty weeks a year until 1982, when they finally sold the Stop 'n' Eat to a new owner and settled into a comfortable, if not wealthy, retirement. The Westerner and the Canyonlands Café had origin stories of their own, but the cuisine at all three was similar. What made them so special was the seating arrangements. Even when tables or booths were available, they were few and far between, and most of us were thrown into the mix at the counter. You never knew who your dining companion might be on any given day. It made for interesting conversation.

The L-shaped counters at the Westerner and the Canyonlands especially encouraged animated cross-talk from all the customers. My favorite lunch partner was a former uranium miner named Neldon Lemon. The first time I met him, we'd been at the same meeting the night before, and I'd overcome my fear of public speaking to stutter a few words. Neldon wasn't pleased. When he sat down beside me and I attempted to introduce myself, he cut me off.

"I know who you are," he snarled. "You're one of them goddamn environmentalists that wants to lock everything up." He looked at me fiercely.

"Well, that must make you one of those uranium miners who wants to tear everything up."

Neldon squinted at me for just a moment and then shook his head and chuckled. "Ah, what the hell. I guess I can tolerate sitting next to you. What's the special today?"

That's the way it often was at the Westerner. Neldon and I became friends over the years. We chose to disagree on many issues, but we were able to acknowledge and even celebrate our common interests as well. We both chose to live a simple life away from the cities, we both loved the open space and freedom of the rural West, and we'd both chosen Moab. What else mattered, really?

Still, on one issue Neldon and I saw the changes in Moab very differently. By 1985 Moab was in a state of full economic collapse. For the old-time Moabites, the ones who had cut their teeth during the uranium-boom days of the 1950s, Moab's demise was an unmitigated catastrophe. It was inconceivable and heartbreaking to them that the party was over. For almost forty years mining had sustained the Moab community, and now it seemed as if the town had nothing to show for its past success except boarded up Main Street businesses and half-deserted neighborhoods.

For another part of Moab's dwindling population, however, the downturn in the economy offered an unexpected opportunity. Since the early 1970s Moab had become a mecca for a small but growing group of young pilgrims. We were searching for a different kind of life, away from the polluted, frenzied madness of urban areas. We thought we'd found it in Moab, Utah. Coming to Moab meant making some sacrifices. We knew we'd never get rich. We knew we had removed ourselves from cultural and social opportunities that we'd grown accustomed to in our old hometowns. We knew we'd probably always be a vocal but persistent minority in a very conservative part of the American West.

The end of the mining boom presented a disaster for some and an unexpected dividend for others. With the exodus of the mining community, housing prices plummeted. For the first time, all those seasonal rangers and river runners—the marginal citizens of Moab, like me—could suddenly afford to buy a home. Over the course of eighteen months, we went from being bearded hippies to responsible landowners.

I spent part of a day driving up one side street after another, stunned by the number of realty signs. Finally, I spotted an old stucco home with a big yard and a magnificent spruce tree in front. A catalpa tree grew next to the driveway. It was a sign from my grandfather, for sure, who loved the catalpa's spring blossoms but despised the seedpods. I decided to make an offer. But I had no idea how to buy a house. I didn't even know where to start, so I turned to Pete Parry, the superintendent at Canyonlands National Park, and asked for advice.

All he said was, "Go see Norma Nunn."

Norma was a paragon of energy and assertiveness, exactly what I needed to get me through this torture. I told her about the Locust Lane property, and she knew it well. The bank owned the house and had been sitting on it for five years, unable to unload it. When the house last sold in 1980, it went for $51,000. Now the bank wanted $23,000.

"We'll offer eighteen thousand and see what they do," Norma explained. "How much of a down payment can you make?"

I'd checked my pitiful savings account. I barely had $2000 in the bank, and during the off-season from Arches I was living on unemployment.

"Two thousand? They might take that," Norma assured me. "And be sure to list your unemployment compensation when you apply for the loan. That adds to your yearly income."

I thought she was crazy. "Are you sure, Norma?"

"The bank does not want to deal with all these empty houses. My guess is they'll unload it at the price you're offering."

She was absolutely right. The next morning, I drove to town and walked warily to her desk. I stared disbelievingly at the documents she'd left for me: "Approved." I was a landowner.

A few weeks later, we closed the "as is" deal. My new home was a wreck. No one had lived in it for years, and I didn't even know if the plumbing and wiring worked. As I stood in the backyard, I felt a bit dizzy, "What was I thinking?"

My doubts were pushed aside by a hard noise that sounded like a gravel crusher. But this was no mechanical clatter, it was Toots McDougald.

"Did you buy this goddamn house, or are you just renting it?"

She was leaning against the fence that separated my place from hers. She looked to be in her seventies. Toots was tall, angular, with not an ounce of fat on her. She combed her closely cropped hair straight back, like Valentino. A cigarette hung idly from the corner of her mouth.

"Well?" she repeated, "Did you buy this goddamn place or not?"

I nodded slowly. "Yeah. For better or worse, I bought it."

Toots shook her head, "Then I hope you paint those goddamn aluminum shingles up there on the roof. The glare from them shingles into my kitchen is just awful in the after-noon." With that she threw down her smoke, stomped it out with her tennis shoes, and walked back inside.

It became clear to me that painting the aluminum shingle might be a wise priority. As a result, Toots and I became lifelong friends. In the years to come she would feed me chocolate cake every time she wanted me to come outside and pull goatheads. She'd remind me that if she were thirty years younger, "You wouldn't be over there sleeping alone, honey." Toots told me of her adventures as a little girl in Moab, her long trail rides to Turnbow Cabin, the sorrows she'd endured and the joys she'd experienced over the years. She painted a picture of a Moab I had never seen.

But what about now? What was to become of Moab in 1987? With a dwindling population and few if any prospects for a brighter economic future, some thought Moab might literally dry up and blow away. But others saw Moab's economic slump as an opportunity to redefine our little community. It seemed as good a time as any to abandon our title of "Uranium Capital of the World." Moab had always been pushed and shoved along by a boomtown mentality. Maybe we could finally escape that kind of erratic life. But how to make a living, that was the rub.

In the waning days of the summer of 1987, Moabites began to realize how divided we still were on the subject. Rumors of a plan to build a toxic waste incinerator at Cisco, Utah, thirty miles upstream from Moab, reached the local cafes. The debate began.

As summer turned to fall, hard information began to replace the gossip, and the truth was disturbing. The Grand County Commission, made up of Jimmie Walker, Dutch Zimmerman, and David Knutson, had been working behind the scenes for six months with a corporation named CoWest, Inc. CoWest wanted to construct what they claimed would be a state-of-the-art incinerator on 180 acres of land in Cisco. But the land there was not zoned for that kind of use. In fact, there was no heavy industrial zone in Grand County at all. The county commissioners, seeing a way to dramatically boost the county tax base, thought they'd stumbled across a gold mine—or a high-tech toxic version of one, anyway. They were convinced that the residents of Grand County would support them.

Jimmie, Dutch, and Dave were all lifelong residents of Moab and survivors of the economic downturn. But none of them sensed how much Moab had changed recently. Just five years earlier, Moab residents had supported the proposed nuclear waste repository, despite the fact that the facility was to be built right next to Canyonlands National Park.

So the fact that the commissioners enthusiastically supported an industry that would incinerate a staggering variety of toxins, from benzene and paint thinners to pharmaceutical wastes, should not have surprised anyone.

But the community, or at least part of it, was enraged. No one predicted the extent of the anger. Was this just another vocal minority? Or were we seeing a fundamental shift in Moab and Grand County attitudes? We were about to find out.

By late October 1987, the incinerator was front-page news in the *Times-Independent*, and opposition was quick and fierce. A group calling itself the Colorado-Utah Alliance for a Safe Environment gathered 2000 signatures in just a few weeks from citizens in both states. But the petition had no legal standing, and Commissioner Walker dismissed the signatures out of hand. "Those signatures don't impress me at all. Ninety percent of the names came from Colorado." Walker and the other commissioners called efforts by the opposition "fear politics" designed to "scare the masses."

One thing was certain, though, the masses were definitely scared. Letters to the editor poured into the *Times-Independent*, mostly in opposition to the incinerator, and the Grand County Alliance was formed to consolidate Utah opposition.

The Grand County Alliance was born one night in Castle Valley. Andrew Riley had caught wind of the incinerator plans and shared this incredible tale with fellow residents Jayne Dillon, John Groo, and Dave Wagstaff. From that kitchen table, a strategy to combat the incinerator took root and the alliance grew. An attorney and lobbyist from Salt Lake City, Ralph Becker, offered hundreds of hours of free legal advice. Bill Hedden gave invaluable amounts of time, sifting through the scientific information. Kyle and Carrie Bailey worked tirelessly to organize and recruit new members to the cause, as did Lance and Larue Christie.

On the evening of December 2, 1987, a toxic waste information meeting was held at Star Hall. Commissioner David Knutson assembled a panel of CoWest officials, federal and state regulators, and private citizens. Almost 400 people crammed into the building for one of the most spirited gatherings in the town's recent history. Dean Norris, the president of CoWest, became an instant antagonist for incinerator opponents. Dressed in gray polyester and sporting a huge diamond-studded pinky ring, he barely tolerated the barrage of questions by angry residents that filled much of the evening. Many of us could not have been happier. Every cause needs a bad guy, and Norris played the role perfectly.

Nothing had been resolved when the shouting was over, and a showdown looked inevitable. The commission showed no sign of backing off, and Moabites continued to vent their anger through the letter's page of the *Times-Independent*. Finally, on December 17, editor Sam Taylor became so overwhelmed that he refused to print any more letters—pro or con—on the incinerator issue, "at least until the County moves into the public hearing process in the early part of next year."

Grand County residents kept scribbling anyway, but now they were signing their names to a petition that would put the issue on the November ballot. The Utah constitution provides a referendum provision to decide issues such as this. For an initiative to be placed on the ballot, it requires 12.5 percent of the total number of votes in the last gubernatorial election. In Grand County, that meant 418 signatures. After three weeks, sponsors of the initiative presented petitions to County Clerk Fran Townsend with more than 500 signatures. The petition demanded that "Section 2-5-12-C of Ordinance 134, passed by the County Commission on January 25, be referred to the people for their approval or rejection at the regular election to be held November 8."

Approval of the initiative would implement a new law that would restrict commercial uses in any Grand County zone. It stated, "No zoning ordinance in Grand County shall allow: the incineration or burning of hazardous and/or toxic waste; the storage of toxic waste other than that created as a byproduct of local business or industry; the manufacture of toxins and viruses; the manufacture of synthetic pesticides, herbicides, and fungicides; the manufacture of chemical or biological weapons."

In early March 1988, the commissioners announced that they'd put off any zone change on the Cisco incinerator site until after the election. Then in May they unanimously approved a heavy industrial zone for the land owned by CoWest, with the exception of an incinerator, leaving that decision to the voters. We wondered what that was all about, until, at that same meeting, Dean Norris was asked if he had any other plans for the I-2 zone. "Anything I can attract," he replied. The implication was clear: if CoWest failed to secure the right to build its incinerator, there were all kinds of other nasty things that could be placed in an I-2 zone. Jimmie Walker read the list of uses, and it was downright scary.

With heavy media coverage from Salt Lake City and Grand Junction, television viewers watched Jayne Dillon bolt over a table to present Commissioner Walker with a letter from a Salt Lake attorney who believed the commission's actions were illegal.

A weary Jimmie Walker replied, "I'm going to assume we acted legally unless told otherwise by a judge or jury."

As Election Day approached, Grand County was wound as tightly as a Warn winch. Coffee-shop conversations were tense and animated, but supporters of the initiative to stop the incinerator were feeling confident and the commissioners were beginning to look like besieged and outnumbered defenders of a lost cause. Still, with Moab's long history of mining and conservative politics, no one could be sure of the outcome.

When the polls closed at 7:00 p.m. on November 8, Grand County residents were glued to their television sets. But in Moab, there was no live local news. Thousands of us were staring instead at the Channel 6 weather scanner, waiting for the updates. The Channel 6 news director, Ken Davey, the "Dean of the Moab Press Corps," would videotape himself at the courthouse reading the latest tallies, then he'd sprint down Main Street to the studio and play the slightly delayed video.

Early on, though, it became evident that the incinerator was toast. By an ever-widening margin, Grand County voted in favor of the initiative and soundly defeated the project, ultimately by a margin of almost two to one. Most remarkable was the turnout itself. More than 80 percent of all registered voters went to the polls on November 8, 1988. It was a record then, and we have rarely come close since.

The incinerator issue died that day, and no one has ever seriously considered a similar project for Grand County since. The statistics that came out of that election are still remarkable, because the vote was so free of an ideological bent. While almost two-thirds of the population opposed the incinerator, in the presidential election Democratic candidate Michael Dukakis took a beating from the Republican George Bush. So liberal versus conservative, Democrat versus Republican didn't play a pivotal role. Instead, it was about our quality of life here in Grand County, and toxic waste incinerators did not sound like an enhancement.

To many of us, Walker, Zimmerman, and Knutson found themselves cast as the Darth Vader Trio, but it was hardly fair. None of them stood to profit personally from CoWest. Coming from lives spent in the extractive industries, the commissioners saw the incinerator as a quick way to increase the tax base in a depressed county on the verge of blowing away like a tumbleweed. Opponents of the incinerator celebrated. Had a new day dawned in Moab and Grand County? We all hoped and dreamed that perhaps we really could redefine our community and create something new and different, something to be proud of.

The winners and losers alike put the election behind us, and we moved on with our lives. But the question still remained—how to make a living in Grand County. A year before the referendum, in November 1987, the *Times-Independent* had run a small story in its second section entitled "Mountain Biking in SE Utah Is Becoming a Popular Sport." Hardly anybody noticed it.

Transformations

One day in 1984, Kris Allen and Bill Davis stopped by Arches to say hello. Although both had lived in Moab for years, they'd recently moved to California. Now they were returning as tourists. Strapped to the back of Bill's truck were two bicycles, unremarkable in most respects except they sported knobby tires and thicker frames. Kris explained that they were mountain bikes, and both believed that these bikes would revolutionize recreation in the canyon country.

"What do you mean, 'revolutionize'?" I asked.

"Mountain bikes can go anywhere," Bill said. "Anyplace a jeep can go, a mountain bike can go. And they're cheaper to run, I might add."

"Yeah," I said uncertainly. "Maybe they can go anywhere, but jeepers aren't going to give up their four-wheel drives for a bike."

"Maybe not the jeepers, but there's a market for this, believe me."

I remembered what a local rancher, Don Holyoak, had once said about the sport of bicycling: "Oh yeah, that's where you pedal your legs off to give your ass a ride. I'll keep my horse."

I thought Kris and Bill were both mad. The idea of mountain bikes swarming over my beloved slickrock like frenzied ants on a hot day disturbed me, but the idea seemed fantastic. I dismissed their prophesies with an uneasy smile. They climbed back in their Four-Runner and drove up the old highway for a premier ride on their mountain bikes.

Kris Allen and Bill Davis were early bike aficionados in Moab, but they weren't the first—not quite. The idea that our town could become the "Mountain Bike Capital of the World" first occurred to a most unlikely pair of brothers from Moab, who had both been laid off from the uranium industry.

Bill and Robin Groff don't *look* like mountain bikers. If they were riding Harleys, perched atop a chopper and decked out in black leather, that might suit a newcomer's first vision of the Groffs on a two-wheeled conveyance. They're big fellows with heads like hairy cinder blocks. Their wrists are as big as my thighs. A couple of Blutos might best describe them. Blutos who eat spinach. They take shit from no one.

Maybe that's why nobody had the nerve to advise them *not* to open a bike and outdoor gear shop in the fall of 1983, which is what they did, calling the place Rim Cyclery. At first they only sold road bikes. In fact, not many biking options existed, but they'd heard of the new sport of mountain biking. One day, a mystery biker known only as "Scott" appeared at their shop door. He had pedaled all the way from Santa Barbara, California, on what was a precursor to the modern-day mountain bike. It was a modified five-speed Ross, one of the early popular mountain bike brands, and soon the Groffs were Ross dealers. They also began selling a bike known as the Stumpjumper from a company called Specialized.

Robin put the new bikes through their paces, learning just what their capabilities were. He even helped herd cattle on them with his rancher buddy Deuce. It occurred to the Groffs that mountain biking could draw thousands of enthusiasts to the canyon country if they could just show them the many venues that were available. Robin scouted the backcountry for suitable trails and routes, and there were plenty of them to be found. The remnants of old jeep trails from the uranium-boom days were about to be revived. Old two-tracks would allow bicyclists to ride side by side through some of the most remarkable scenery on Earth.

But more than anything else there was the *slickrock*, the local name given to the vast expanses of raw hard sandstone that sometimes stretches for miles without interruption. The domes, channels, turrets, arches, and canyons provided every kind of recreational challenge imaginable for a hard-core mountain biker. In fact, the most extraordinary slickrock challenge already carried the name.

The Slickrock Bike Trail was created by dirt bikers, the motorized predecessors to the pedal-powered Stumpjumpers. Though the trail had received some early notoriety when it was first built on BLM lands above Moab along the Sand Flats, it had recently fallen into disuse. Robin and his friend Dan Hosco decided to test their bikes on the Slickrock Trail. As they did, lights came on inside their heads. This was it.

By the following spring, Rim began renting bikes and had teamed up with a new arrival, a tall lanky man named John Groo. The Groffs and Groo created Rim Tours and led small excursions into the backcountry around Moab. Bike touring started slowly. Early on, even one paying customer was enough to load up the bikes into an old pickup truck called "Old Green" and head for the trail.

Then, as it almost always happens, incomprehensible forces in the universe came together to create a recreational revolution. *National Geographic* was in Moab, and its photographer, Ken Redd, was shooting images of the spectacular red rocks when he began to notice the bicyclists. When the story appeared with a comment and several photos of the newly arrived sport of mountain biking, Hank Barlow, an avid biker from Crested Butte, Colorado, took note. In fact, he did much more than that.

Barlow had come to Colorado from Marin County, California, the place many call the

"Birthplace of Mountain Biking." Barlow and a group of fellow bikers had played with the idea of a magazine devoted entirely to the sport of mountain biking, and they wanted something extraordinary for its first issue. One glance at the pages of *National Geographic* convinced Barlow that Moab was the place.

Mountain Bike appeared on newsstands a few months later, but the bicycles played second fiddle to the incredible scenic backdrop. Moab dominated the first edition, and soon all roads led to Moab. The town and the surrounding countryside exploded. According to the Groffs, "It is said that in the realm of mountain biking, Crested Butte provided the 'spirit,' Marin County provided the 'tools,' and Moab provided the 'place.' The triad was complete, mountain biking had arrived, and Rim Cyclery was in the thick of it."

A year later, in late October 1986, Rim Cyclery sponsored the first Canyonlands Fat Tire Festival. Thousands of bikers arrived to experience the Slickrock Bike Trail for the first time. It was already world famous by the time their knobbies touched the rock. People began to refer to the influx of mountain bikers as a phenomenon.

Just a few years earlier Moab was "The Uranium Capital of the World," and now its citizens were utterly bewildered. This was the community that had been settled by ranchers a century earlier and had been one of the most remote backwater towns in the country until Charlie Steen put Moab on the map in the 1950s. For the last forty years, Moab had flourished or failed on the whims of the mining industry. No one imagined straying from that course, for better or worse. The men and women who lived here were predominantly conservative, hard working, and not prone to "nonmotorized recreation" (an expression not quite in the lexicon in the late 1980s) for its own sake. Recreation meant a day of four-wheeling while checking claims or fence lines. Other than the annual Jeep Safari and maybe hunting season, Moabites rarely saw people gathering for anything. The 1986 Canyonlands Fat Tire Festival changed all that.

Winter settled over Moab just a few days after the festival ended. The Big Tree on First South shed its leaves again, as it had each winter for more than a century. The skies turned gray. We retrieved our regular seats at the local diners. For all appearances, our little town had returned to normal. But there was an anticipation throughout those cold months—changes were coming that would affect our lives and our community forever. It seemed almost inevitable, and a nebulous sense of doom settled over some of us. But all we could do was fire up our wood stoves, sip our coffee, and wait for spring.

In Moab, winter can be especially cruel. Mild autumn weather often lingers into November, and we become seduced by the notion that maybe winter will simply pass us by this year. When winter brutally and suddenly appears, we are that much more unprepared to accept the bitter months ahead.

Moab's winters are exacerbated by its location and its bad habits. There is no more spectacular setting for a town than Moab, which lies between towering red sandstone cliffs. The West Wall rises more than 2000 feet above the Colorado River, and to the east broken ledges and cliffs lead to the Sand Flats and into the high country of the La Sal Mountains. But winter valley inversions love deep canyon towns like Moab. Under normal conditions, the temperature drops as you travel to higher elevations. But during an inversion, cold air becomes trapped in the valley by warm air above it. Then factor in the smoke from the wood fires that most Moabites used then to heat their homes and the acrid smoke that used to pour from the Atlas Mill, north of town, and the air was as foul as anything found in Akron or Pittsburgh. Driving into town from Arches, our nostrils could detect the shift from Atlas smoke to wood smoke, just as we passed the Grand Old Ranch House. Wood smoke, by comparison, smelled healthier.

While enduring all that, we'd wait for the colors of spring, like the iridescent glow of a mountain blue bird skimming across the sagebrush meadow near Sand Dune Arch or the first gaudy splash of Indian paintbrush poking through the rocks in Hidden Valley. Around town, folks carefully studied golden willows for a hint of green—always a good harbinger of spring. But in 1987, the color of spring assumed an entirely new meaning.

I was eating breakfast at the Main Street Broiler, homemade sourdough biscuits and fresh creamery butter if I recall, when Carl Rappe, the Broiler's soul proprietor, leapt from his seat and dashed out the door. He pointed toward Kane Creek Boulevard with a trembling finger and shouted, "They're here! They're here!"

It was the color I saw first. A hue so vivid and alive, it almost stung the eyes to look at it. But it wasn't the lupines that we'd longed to see, or a hint of violets, or even the locoweed that grew so prolifically along the roadsides. This was something else. It was a herd, a flock . . . a rash, perhaps, of mountain bikers, dressed in matching royal blue, skin-tight Lycra riding outfits. From my vantage point, they looked to me like a cluster of naked blue people.

"Aliens," I thought. "We've been invaded." Which in a sense was true. With hordes of naked blue aliens pedaling the streets and alleys of our quaint little backwater town, could Judgment Day be far behind?

Many Moabites were not quick to embrace the mountain bike phenomenon. Although local businesses geared to tourism were the first to see the benefit and tolerated the invasion, even if they weren't fully enraptured by it, Old Moab was not so generous. These guys had been wearing the same worn-out Wranglers, snap-front shirts, and weathered straw hats since 1952. To suddenly see their Main Street cluttered with men in tights—and royal blue tights, at that—rankled worse than an unshaved hippie. Confrontation was inevitable.

For a few years, the culture clash between Old and New Moab even grew violent at times. Moab teenagers, full of testosterone and beer, tried to amuse themselves at the hapless bikers' expense. Turned loose for the first time in their fathers' pickups and carrying an earful of their fathers' anti-bike rhetoric, the kids sometimes harassed the bikers, ran them off the street, and even collided with them on occasion. A few were arrested and charged. For a while, Moab gained a reputation for bicycle bigotry.

But the money was too good to even let prejudice and bad behavior interfere—and it wasn't just the tourist shops and restaurants that benefited. Again forces in the universe came into play with perfect synchronicity. Three factors affected Moab's destiny: one of them was a metaphysical notion and two of them were economic realities. One played off the other two, and what sallied forth from it is the Moab we see today.

First was that odd feeling that change was coming to Moab in unimagined ways. Something was in the air. We knew about the mountain bikes, and we'd experienced both the excitement and dismay that they caused. But we wondered how a few Lycra-clad bicyclists could alter the course of history.

Second, Moab was in a state of economic depression that spring. The Atlas Mill was shut down. Miners and their families had abandoned Moab in droves, in search of employment elsewhere. They'd left their homes behind, hoping a realtor could salvage at least a part of their investment.

Third, the vanguard of mountain bikers came from places like California and Colorado. Generally they were young urban professionals, extremely affluent, and always in search of a good investment. What none of them could fail to notice as they wheeled their way through the streets of town toward the Sand Flats or River Road was the extraordinary number of "For Sale" signs that lined almost every residential street. Sometimes it appeared as if the entire neighborhood was on the block.

Inevitably, one of those bikers came back early from a ride, looked up a local realtor, and inquired about prices. These out-of-towners must not have been able to believe their good fortune. Every kind of home was on the market, from modest one-bedroom cottages to luxurious five-bedroom mansions. But a small home that might have sold for $50,000 just five years earlier now could be had for less than half that.

Word spread like ticks on a reservation dog. In fact, it almost became a joke. Coloradoans and Californians, who traveled here merely to experience the new sport of mountain biking on some unique terrain, left Moab a few days later as new homeowners. And they rarely left with just one. Prospective homebuyers were so stunned by the rock-bottom prices they simply couldn't resist a great deal. Even some of the realtors were offended.

"They'd walk in here with their checkbooks in hand and a smug look on their face and ask, 'What can we steal today?'"

They stole quite a bit. It wasn't unusual to see someone buy four homes in a single day for under $100,000.

As always, the longtime unpropertied locals suffered the most. A few of us low-income types had managed to buy a house before Moab was discovered, but not everyone was so lucky. Many spent a few years scrimping to save enough money to make a down payment, only to have their dream snatched away by an out-of-town investor. One friend of mine, who had assembled her life savings to buy a small cottage on Fourth East, was outbid by a wealthy new arrival who actually went over the asking price, just to secure the property. It turned out to be his tenth home acquisition of the month, and he sold it three years later for a tidy profit.

By 1990 most of the steals had been stolen, and the sea of "For Sale" signs diminished. But many of the recently purchased houses remained empty. The new owners hired property managers to do a minimal amount of yard maintenance and waited for the market to drive prices up. It was a pork-belly housing boom in every sense of the word. Moab's cachet as a New West town began to have legs. The word was out: Moab had mojo.

New homeowners rode the pork-belly boom like a cowboy on a bucking bronco, spurring it from time to time with ridiculously marked-up prices. When a never-to-be-seen "neighbor" put a $70,000 price tag on a squat cinder-block shed of a house that we all knew had gone for $26,000 just two years earlier, well, we thought that was pretty funny. Even the realtors were stunned and tried to counsel their clients to show some restraint. But the new owners knew more than the professionals, who failed to grasp the situation. These people were in no hurry to sell. They'd bought the homes outright. The taxes and insurance were modest. Upkeep was fairly simple. What was the hurry? They'd simply wait for the market to come to them. A year later, the owner of the cinder-block shed got his asking price. (In 2005 it would fetch $175,000.)

It wasn't just housing speculators who were watching Moab mojo with increased inter-est. As if things weren't bad enough already, as if we weren't feeling the hot and heavy breath of the real world on our necks with each passing day, in 1989 rumors began to cir-culate that a clown with orange hair and a red nose was checking out the property once occupied by Charlie's gas station at the corner of Main Street and Kane Creek Boulevard. The clown was Ronald McDonald, and I haven't been able to stomach a Big Mac since.

I felt particularly nostalgic about Charlie's gas station and about Charlie. He was the only state safety inspector in Moab who would consistently pass my 1963 Volvo when the registration was due.

"Ah hell," he'd shrug. "Who needs two goddamn windshield wipers anyway? As long as one of 'em works, that's ok with me." If it hadn't been for Charlie, I would have spent most of my time walking.

Years later, Charlie gave up the station and retired to his home in Castle Valley. Dis-abled by emphysema and unable to do much of anything but wait for death, Charlie got tired of waiting. One morning he decided to take matters into his own hands. He shoved a .45-caliber revolver under his chin and pulled the trigger. The blast blew off the bot-tom part of his jaw and knocked him across the room, but, incredibly, he was still alive and conscious. Evidence at the scene indicated that Charlie dragged himself across the room to the revolver, turned it toward his chest this time, and fired again. Finally, after all that, Charlie found peace.

Charlie's lot sat empty for years, and I had somehow assumed it would never change. McDonald's threw up (literally) one of its cookie-cutter restaurants just a few months after the Ronald rumors began, and the local café culture started to crumble. It was as if every national junk food chain in America was waiting for the McDonald's go-ahead. If Big Mac said the demographics were right, it must be right for everyone. Within a couple years, several chains were established on Main Street, and both the Westerner Grill and the Canyonlands Café closed their doors forever. Only Milt's survived the changes.

In one winter alone, seven new motels were built. Part of the urgency was the incredible opportunity Moab's city government had provided them. Hookup fees were ridiculously cheap, impact fees didn't exist, water costs were minimal, and all of these motel owners saw a good deal when it licked them in the face. Moab had been completely transformed in thirty-six months.

▬▬▬ ▬▬▬ ▬▬▬ My own life was changing as well. In the late 1980s, after almost a decade, I quit my seasonal ranger job at Arches National Park. There were some who thought I'd never leave, and even I had my doubts from time to time. I had lived in the Devils Garden trailer for most of those years, and I could not imagine a time when I would not be its caretaker and custodian. But, finally, the place wore me down.

The tourists didn't help. I thought at some point that if one more park visitor knocked on my door at three in the morning and asked me if the campground was "really full," if I had to jiggle the toilet handle in the comfort station one more time to restore a proper flush, if I had to explain to a man with a hammer and chisel that carving his name in a rock over petroglyphs left by Anasazi Indians 1000 years ago was not only different but wrong, if I had to endure one more day wondering why these people had ever bothered to come here in the first place, I would lose what was left of my mind.

But ultimately it was the National Park Service itself, the federal agency once honored as a beacon of integrity in a bureaucratic sea of incompetence and corruption, that sent me packing. The park service has always been plagued by a dual mandate that is conflicted enough to make anyone a bit schizophrenic. The service was instructed to "protect the parks" in the United States, while "providing for the enjoyment" of all its citizens in them. The sorry human history of negative impacts on pristine wildlands is well known. Yet, the National Park Service has always done everything in its power and its budget to make parks more accessible to more humans and at a staggering cost, financially, environmentally, and spiritually.

Of course, this is not a recent phenomenon; it was an issue that Abbey first addressed in *Desert Solitaire*. But in the late 1980s, plans were already being processed in Washington and funds being sought in Congress to pave the last gravel road in the park, the one to Delicate Arch, dramatically expand the visitor center, construct many new toilet facilities, and replace the old Devils Garden trailer with a permanent structure. They even planned to install heaters in the campground toilets. At one point, they eventually built cut-stone staircases in the Windows section of the park at a cost of $500,000.

But the number of seasonal interpreters hadn't changed in a decade. (In fact, fifteen years later, it still hasn't.) Any opportunity to educate the public about the fragile desert environment always took a backseat to flush toilets and asphalt. The National Park Service felt that instead of educating visitors, it made more sense to just regulate them to death. That's why the law enforcement budget always pulled more funds than interpretation.

During my last year at Arches, we were instructed to wear our sidearms whenever we were on duty. Most of us balked at the notion, but we were admonished, "Remember there's a big difference between a ranger who wears a gun and a gun who wears the ranger." Still, tourists were alarmed at our armed presence, and the best way to tone down the look was to conceal our .38s altogether. But when the park service began hiring former big-city cops to fill law enforcement positions, there was a grain of truth to the "guns wear the ranger" admonition.

I knew it was time to leave when I was briefly partnered with a new ranger, fresh from a twelve-year stint with the Topeka Police Department, where he'd shot and killed two suspects in five years. His last park service assignment had been as an undercover narcotics agent at Yosemite. He infiltrated a clan of known potheads in the valley, befriended them, and became part of their family. On the night they threw him a surprise birthday party, a squad of heavily armed rangers descended on the camp and arrested the bunch. The hardest drug found was hash, and Todd told me that later he "almost felt bad."

"Yeah, I have to admit, they were pretty nice people. But then I thought to myself, 'Fuck 'em.' They knew what they were doing."

The National Park Service was still teeming with dedicated if extremely frustrated rangers and naturalists. Hand wringing was a common practice among many of us. One chief ranger, with more character and integrity than she could ultimately endure, began writing letters to the chief ranger (that is, to herself) under an assumed name, protesting the very policies and decisions she had been forced to implement. That kind of inner conflict finally killed her.

For me, it was time to leave. After a decade living at the end of the road, I was now ensconced in my own little home, just 100 yards from Dave's Corner Market, almost within sight of the Big Tree, and next door to the infamous Toots McDougald. Just as I moved into town, Moab was already being transformed, but I'd have a ringside seat for the knockout.

A year after my departure from Arches, I signed on with a local rag called the *Stinking Desert Gazette* to do some cartoons and write a few stories. The *Gazette* was pure satire at its silliest and finest, and I'll always be grateful to its publisher, Robert Dudek, for the opportunity he gave me to explore my skills as a writer.

In late 1988, with the toxic waste incinerator vote upon us and a sense that Moab wanted to shape its own destiny, the idea of my own publication began to take shape. It would cover stories that the local weekly missed or avoided. It would try to be fair and balanced, but it wouldn't be afraid to express an opinion either. I'd interview the county commissioners each month, and I'd ask tough questions, regardless of their political leanings.

I struggled to find a name. For a while its working title was the *Slickrock Journal*, then the *Canyon Courier*, but neither were very inspiring. Then one day, as I drove down Mill

Creek Drive to get a coffee at Dave's, the word *Zephyr* came to me, the *Canyon Country Zephyr*. That was it.

I stopped worrying. The name gave me confidence, and I was convinced I couldn't fail. Of course, I had no money and no equipment, but my attorney, the irascible Bill Benge (a.k.a. Willie Flocko) lent me the use of his computer and his typist, I convinced 100 of my friends and family to buy a ten-dollar annual subscription, I coerced some of my new advertisers to pay in advance, and I went forward with the first issue.

In late November, I circled a day on my calendar, March 14, 1989, my target date for publication. I began to assemble a list of story ideas, and I set about finding writers. In December, Ed Abbey came to town, reluctantly promoting his novel *Fool's Progress* and enduring the fools who came to see him. I watched Ed wearily answer questions at Ken Sleight's bookstore for three hours.

When a woman asked him to sign her copy, she beamed, "You know, Mr. Abbey, I'm a writer, too. I'm working on my first novel."

"Is that so?" Ed said through clenched teeth.

"And I've always wanted to ask you. How long do you think a novel should be, Mr. Abbey?"

"Three hundred and twelve pages," he replied without hesitation.

"Thank God," she sighed. "I'm almost done then."

Ed glanced at me and lifted his arms in surrender, "And this is only Moab. Imagine what Denver will be like, or Chicago."

When I told Ed about the *Zephyr* he heartily embraced my plan. In fact, he wanted to be a part of it. He pledged an original story to the premier issue and made me promise I'd remind him. But two months later, without any prompting at all, a package arrived in the mail from Abbey, along with an unexpected apology.

"I had wanted to send you a story, written specifically for the *Zephyr*, but I'm afraid a looming deadline for *Hayduke Lives!* has kept me busier than I anticipated. As soon as

I can get this book done, I'll send you something special." What he had mailed me was an original short story called "Hard Times in Santa Fe," never published in the United States, about his misadventures with his longtime buddy, the artist John Depuy. It was perfect.

As the deadline approached, I finished the layouts and prepared to go to press. On March 14 I drove 120 miles to Cortez, Colorado, to see the first issue of the *Canyon Country Zephyr* come to life. Larry Hauser, the head pressman, labored through the morning, shooting negatives and transferring them to plates. They started the press at noon, and by one o'clock we'd bundled and loaded 2000 copies into my '63 Volvo. On the two-hour drive home, I wondered what the reception to this new publication would be, wondered if it would survive a year. And I wondered what Abbey would think of it.

I had just shut off the motor and was unloading the first bundle from the trunk when a friend of mine, Jean Aken, stopped suddenly in the street and slowly approached me.

"Did you hear about Edward Abbey?"

I shook my head.

She looked at me warily and paused, "Abbey died this morning."

In the weeks and months that followed, all of us tried to adjust to a world without Ed Abbey. Bill Benge and I drove to Tucson the next week to attend a private memorial service at Saguaro National Monument. In late May, Ken Sleight proposed and a few of us helped him organize a service for Abbey on a high stretch of slickrock near Rough and Rocky Mesa, overlooking his beloved Arches. A thousand friends (whether they'd met him or not) made their way from all over the country to attend the sunrise service.

Of all the speakers, Abbey's old pals John Depuy and Ken Sleight perhaps knew him best. Depuy, the crazed abstract painter from Taos who had been Ed's *compañero* for thirty years, was too overwhelmed to speak. He'd let his brushes and paints speak for him, John said, and he sat down, shattered.

Sleight, who first met Abbey near Glen Canyon Dam in 1967, had been with him on more river and pack trips than Ken could recall. He tried to speak of his memories, but he was ultimately overcome by the loss.

Ken said, "Ed, your sudden leaving on this great journey caught me unprepared, as I'll not be able to see you for a while. You left us a lasting legacy. I'll never forget what you've done for me. Never has any man had such thoughts and ideals. I admire you greatly. Ed, why did you have to leave us now, my dear friend, Abbey, when it seems that we need you most? How can we manage without you? You came to this land suddenly. You made your mark. And you departed just as suddenly. May we always appreciate what you have done for us. We shall now proceed onward with the tools you've given us. I just wish you were here."

Abbey had called Moab "the center of the universe." Now Moab was changing, and its strongest defender was gone. We wondered what lay ahead.

Warnings and Premonitions

From the beginning, it was all about getting high. I like to get high. I've always been like this. Even as a kid in Kentucky, I couldn't stand being a lowlander.

In those days, I used to paddle my canoe on the Salt River as it wound its way through the Fort Knox Military Reservation. Entering the army property was apparently illegal, and large signs along the river read, "Warning: Impact Area! Do Not Enter! Day and Night Firing!" The exclamation points gave me some pause, though ultimately they did not deter me. By afternoon, I'd grow tired of watching live ammunition fly over my head and explode in the open meadows east of the water, so I'd bring the boat ashore and fight my way through the tangle of wild grapevines and poison ivy to the top of Buzzard's Roost, 300 feet above the river, and observe the military fireworks from on high.

But I just couldn't get high enough. I felt absolutely stifled in the closed-in and smothering green forests. I needed a change of scenery, and, of course, the West provided me with that. My first view of the Southwest came after an all-day, all-night drive in a Chevy Impala from Louisville, Kentucky, with my parents and little brother. It was one of those thirteen-day, 7000-mile vacations guaranteed to create lifelong family animosities by the time it was over. We drove through the night on Rt. 66 through Oklahoma and across the Texas panhandle. When the sun came up, we were in Tucumcari, New Mexico. I thought it was the most beautiful spot on Earth.

As we raced across the vast desert toward the Grand Canyon, my brother and I noticed black patches dotting the barren landscape. "What are those?" we asked each other. I thought perhaps they were burned sections of desert charred by a brush fire. Then we noticed that the dark splotches were moving—they were shadows cast by the clouds. We'd never imagined such a sight could exist, that land could be so wide and open that it might allow us to see the shadows of clouds as they floated above, scudding across these brilliant Southwestern skies. Once I'd seen this, I knew I could never live without it.

Since then, I've been seeking out the high and wide-open places. In time I realized that it was more than just the view. It was more than getting high. It became a humbling experience for me, a way to remind myself just how insignificant my presence was and should be. At the same time, it was gratifying and reassuring to see, in one long sweep of a 360-degree horizon, how vast, wonderful, and eternal a place this home of mine was.

I started climbing mountains from time to time. None of these ascents was the kind that could make an adrenalin junkie happy, for I've never much cared for the technical aspects of climbing. All that rope and hardware was just too intimidating, and I'm scared of precipitous heights. Just watching someone else at the edge of a cliff makes me queasy. In fact, I've never even particularly liked walking uphill. As my old friend, former uranium miner Joe Stocks once said, "Why would anyone in their right mind *enjoy* carrying a fifty-pound pack on their back and walking all day?" Joe did that in Vietnam, and it was all the serious hiking he needed for a lifetime.

Still, I reluctantly use my feet, sore and blistered as they may become, to get to where I want to go. Once I reach my viewpoint, I am more than content to just sit there along the ridgeline, the top of the mountain, or the edge of the canyon and stare blankly at the scene beneath my feet, spit sunflower seeds, and sip water for the better part of an afternoon. I've frustrated many a fellow hiker who, as part of their aerobics workout, insisted that we maintain a high pulse rate for a designated period of time and demanded we keep moving. I couldn't be budged.

"Jog in place," I suggested. "Or abandon me, for that matter."

Just don't ask me to move once I've settled into my new viewpoint. All that I ask is the right spot facing the right direction where I can reach my pack without disrupting my gaze. At that moment, I am as content as I ever can be.

But what is it about such a view? From that height, the scene is mostly static. Nothing below seems to move. From up there, if I squint just so, if the light is with me, if my imagination is willing to play a few tricks, I can see all the country I love, the way I want it to be: unspoiled, silent, even forgotten. Being born fifty years too late doesn't bother me when I'm up there, because as far as I'm concerned it *is* fifty years ago.

I first experienced mountaintop time travel years ago. I was wandering the foothills of a favorite mountain of mine, first in my VW Squareback on old jeep roads, then on foot, with no particular destination in mind. In the process of not knowing where I was going, I stumbled upon the most extraordinary campsite I have ever seen.

On an exposed point of ground, with an unobstructed view, I came upon a cluster of granite boulders each as big as a house. They had been sculpted by wind and rain over countless millennia into fantastic shapes, creating alcoves, caves, and shelves of every size and form imaginable. On the northern side of the big rock, the faded remains of two pictographs, a human figure and a bighorn, still clung tenaciously to the weathered stone. Nearby a cowboy had left an inscription and a date that left more of an impression on me than the ancient rock painting. It was the date that caught my eye: December 6, 1941. What this cowboy was doing in the high country on that Saturday afternoon is long forgotten now, but the date he left behind had more significance than he could have known.

The next day, the Japanese launched their attack on Pearl Harbor and thrust the United States into World War II. Everything that has happened to us since then goes back to that morning. It was one of those watershed moments in history when one era closes and another begins. Even in southeastern Utah, in what was the most isolated section of the United States, the race to build an atomic bomb before Hitler's scientists could annihilate us eventually led to the uranium boom, a rush of people to the area, and the construction of thousands of miles of roads and jeep trails. Where would recreationists be today without Tojo, Hitler, and J. Robert Oppenheimer?

Whoever the cowboy was that hunkered down in that shady alcove and scratched his initials in the rock, he looked out over the same land that I beheld for the first time so many years later. But to see it and to *feel* it the way he did, I really had to squint. And that's what worried me. There was a gnawing fear deep down in my gut, even then, that squinting might not be enough. There were signs of things to come that I knew I'd ultimately be unwilling and even unable to bear. "Black revelations," a friend called them, and I was to have a few of them.

A few weeks after my encounter with the cowboy inscription, I was back there with my friend, Buck Fortknocher. We'd barely made it to the nearby pass because I'd had to splice the tail pipe back together with an orange juice can and some wire when a rock ripped it from the manifold. Buck and I were halfway up the mountain, when we decided to pause by a remnant snowfield for rest and reflection. The wind blowing from the north was ferocious on the far side of the ridge. But here, facing east, it howled above us while we contemplated the scene below. The air was sparkling clear, and our visibility was unlimited. My eyes scanned the horizon from north to south—the Book Cliffs, Eagle Park, and the Devils Garden at Arches, the Sand Flats, the La Sals, Grand View Point, Elaterite Butte, Lisbon Valley, the Blues, the Bears Ears, Dark Canyon, Navajo Mountain—the wild places that lay beyond. Above us, the sun shone like a diamond in a sea of blue that was darker and purer than I had seen in a long time. It was a perfect moment.

"Stiles," grumbled Fortknocher, "I don't think this duct tape is holding up."

The soles of Buck's shoes had split open several weeks earlier, and now faced with flipping and flapping his way to the summit, he turned to his old friend, duct tape. A few wraps appeared to do the job, but the sharp granitic rock could be brutal.

Fortknocher, a frequently out-of-work musician and an old friend of Abbey's, had joined me at the last moment on my yearly ascent of my favorite peak. There was some concern that we'd kill each other before the trip was over. While no one is more sensitive to the environment than Buck (he claims he's never littered in his life), the man whose stage name is Swarthy Jardine could at other times be a god-awful slob (although he claims my anal-retentiveness is the problem). We'd barely left Moab, and a pile of garbage began to accumulate at his feet on the passenger's side of the car. Salsa trickled off the dashboard of the Squareback and pooled inside the glove compartment. The rest of it clung stubbornly to his scraggly beard.

As Swarthy agonized over his feet, my eyes drifted over his shoulder to the talus slope that lay ahead. To my surprise and indignation I saw another hiker coming down the scree from the summit register. Stylishly attired in mauve and teal and carrying a graphite hiking rod, the man appeared to march, more than hike, down the mountain. He stopped briefly and perfunctorily to speak with us, as he looked disdainfully at Buck's duct-taped boots. He asked us if we'd ever been up here before, and he inquired about access to the pass from the east during the spring—factoid stuff. In a minute, he said, "I must continue my walk now." He turned briskly and moved off at a very measured and efficient clip toward the saddle.

Buck eyed him suspiciously as he left, "He's in an awful damn hurry. What's his problem?"

I shrugged and reached for my pack. Buck squinted again and said, "I wonder if he's that Kelsey guy, the one who writes all those damned guidebooks."

"Why'd you say that?" I asked.

This time it was Swarthy's turn to shrug. He'd never been introduced to Kelsey. He'd never seen his picture. It didn't matter. Buck pulled on his own pack and we both trudged onward. Twenty minutes later, we were on top. A large pile of rocks and a trail register marked the spot. Inside, a tattered book kept the names of everyone who had scaled the mountain since 1963. Flipping through the pages, I found the names of old friends—Dave Loope 1974, Dick Robertson 1985, Joan Swanson 1985, Michael Salamacha 1989—a lot of water under the bridge. I'd climbed this mountain every June since 1986. When I turned to the most recent entry in the register, I was stunned.

"Buck, look at this!" I yelled.

Fortknocher leaned over the book, squinting in the bright sun, and read the signature. "I'll be damned," he said. "I'm a son-of-a-bitchin' psychic."

The name read, "Michael Kelsey, Provo, Utah."

I couldn't believe it. Buck never struck me as particularly intuitive. In fact, on several occasions I'd been concerned that his upper brain functions had ceased completely. Yet, there it was. The signature in the book had been foretold a full thirty minutes earlier by my swarthy buddy with duct-taped boots.

Michael Kelsey has been prolifically writing guidebooks for more than twenty years about seldom seen areas of the Colorado Plateau. Like other guidebook writers across the West, Kelsey provides detailed information on roads, distances, conditions, things to see, available services, historical and archaeological descriptions, travel times, in essence, data. It's an attempt to make exploring more efficient. When Buck and I first encountered Kelsey, fifteen years ago, his succinct comment in the trail register said something about his style. After his name, he simply wrote, "45 minutes from Bull Pass [*sic*]." He'd clocked himself on the race up the mountain. Our chat with him on the way down must have upset his timetable.

I don't know Michael Kelsey personally, except for our brief chat on the peak, and I've never seen him since. He may be a kind and caring man, a loving son. But even then, I feared what his guidebooks were doing to the last blank spaces on the map. He and many others of his guidebook ilk find remote, infrequently visited places, then grid and dissect them, write up the "how to, where to, when to" details that define what a beautiful place is these days. Then they desktop publish the results and distribute the book in every bookstore, drug store, grocery store, and curio shop within 500 miles of the target area. Mass marketing brings results.

Kelsey didn't invent guidebooks, and when it comes to finding my way around cities and urban areas, I've always found them helpful. But the secret-places guidebook phenomenon has been expanding in the last three decades. Many years ago, when I made my first descent into the Grand Canyon, backcountry hiking was almost unheard of. I walked into the South Rim ranger station and asked what was required to hike to Phantom Ranch.

"Nothing," the ranger said. "Just make sure you have the energy to come back up."

When I reached Bright Angel Creek, there was nobody around. The pool at the ranch was full of water but empty of tourists, and I never saw a ranger. I loved every moment. But the backpacking craze would change all of that, almost overnight. Three years later, the Bright Angel and Kaibab Trails were overrun with hikers. Phantom Ranch became a madhouse. They drained the pool and filled it with sand. Park rangers got nasty. I looked elsewhere for solitude.

I discovered that there were a number of unmaintained, primitive, but passable trails that led from the South Rim to the Tonto Plateau and usually down to the river. Trails like the Hermit's Trail and Grandview Trail were rough in sections, but wonderfully remote and full of history and surprises. I felt as if I'd been given a treasure that I should share with a very few. Let the masses trudge past the pissing mules on the Kaibab. Who needed them? I kept my vow of silence and looked forward to returning to the old trails and exploring some more unknown canyons that had no names.

But when I did return several months later, I was shaken to see a new book for sale near the park's visitor information desk, *A Guide to the Primitive Trails of the Inner Grand Canyon*.

"Tell me this is a bad dream," I thought.

I walked to the desk and asked for a backcountry permit for the Hermit Trail. The ranger shook his head and smirked, "You've got to be kidding," he said. "That trail has a five-day waiting list. Take a number." (Today the waiting list is measured in months.)

Take a number? Could this be the same lonely trail I hiked barely a year earlier? Reluctantly, I realized the trail was the same; it was the *world* that had changed in the blink of an eye. Today those so-called primitive trails are heavily traveled. Designated campsites have been established. Rules and regulations have been imposed and are strictly enforced by eager rangers.

Elsewhere, the pattern was the same. Use of established trails doubled, tripled, quadrupled, thanks in part to the ubiquitous guidebooks. When cramped hikers sought refuge in lesser-known areas, willing writers were there to fill the void. A recent review of guidebooks in area bookstores boggled my mind. Included were detailed volumes about the High Uintas, the San Rafael Swell, the Colorado Plateau (the broad stroke), the Paria and Escalante Rivers, the Grand Canyon, Mount Timpanogos, the Wasatch Mountains, the Great Basin, Dinosaur, Desolation Canyon, the San Juan Mountains, and the Wind River Range.

I wondered how many of those dwindling blank spots on the map could survive an onslaught like this. Can we leave anything for our imaginations? Does adventure exist in its purest form, or must we structure, organize, and sanitize our adventures to make them safe enough and comfortable enough for us? Does anyone have an interest in *not* knowing what lies around the next bend? Maybe not, but I know for a fact that my most memorable experiences were the ones I hadn't planned.

I remember traveling north into Utah from the Grand Canyon one summer afternoon many years ago. As I approached Blanding for the first time on old Highway 160, I saw a sign that indicated a road junction a mile ahead with State Highway 95. The road led to places I'd only heard about, and I thought, "Why not? I'm in no hurry." I checked my road map and decided to give it a try. The little paved road wound its way through the pinyon-juniper forest, always climbing slightly on its way westward. Abruptly the pavement ended. Beyond lay a dirt track cutting through the trees. Was it like this all the way to Hanksville, more than a hundred miles away? The map was no help, and thank God I didn't have a guidebook to make me be logical.

I remembered a passage from a slim volume of wonderful words called *On the Loose* by Terry and Renny Russell: "Well, have we guys learned our lesson? You bet we have. Have we learned to eschew irresponsible outdoorsmanship, to ask advice, to take care and to plan fastidiously and to stay on the trail and to camp only in designated campgrounds and to inquire locally and take enough clothes and keep off the grass? You bet we haven't. Unfastidious outdoorsmanship is the best kind."

I decided to give it a try. The road was rough and dusty. I climbed in and out of ravines, but always kept gaining ground. Finally, the world opened up, and I found myself on the brink of Comb Ridge. The old road snaked its way to the wash below, where clear water trickled between towering cottonwood trees. I hadn't seen a soul. The air was still, quieter than anything I'd ever experienced in my life. I stretched out by a pool, chewed on a blade of grass, and watched the clouds float past the crimson sandstone cliffs above me. It was on that day, at that moment, that I knew I had to find a way to make Utah my home. Now I have to wonder, if someone had written a guidebook about old Utah Highway 95 (before they paved the whole damn thing in 1976 and completely ruined it), would warnings about loose sand, chuckholes, unbridged washes, and an absence of services have intimidated me into staying on the designated roadway? I'll never know.

Today, guidebook writers are more prolific than ever. There is scarcely a piece of *terra incognita* left on the Colorado Plateau. Our favorite guidebook writer, Mr. Kelsey, is still right out there on the cutting edge. He seems determined to turn the phrase "a secret place" into an anachronistic bad joke. In his book *Hiking, Biking, and Exploring Canyonlands National Park*, Kelsey set out to give detailed route descriptions of those few and far-between gems that the general public had not yet stumbled upon and over.

For instance, he had this to say about a seldom-visited part of the park, whose name I leave out here, "[Blank] was always impossible for cows to get into, therefore it was never grazed. The NPS considers this to be a special place because it was left more pristine than any other such place in the [area]. They have never promoted it in any way and will not mention it to you, unless you mention it to them first. They have never put it on any maps either, so few people know about it." In the very next sentence, he gave a detailed description of the route. "The rangers might tell you it's difficult," he warned, adding, "But it's not." You bet, Michael. Any damn fool can get in there, as long as he has your trusty guidebook along side.

According to then Canyonlands National Park Chief Interpreter Larry Frederick, the subsequent degradation to the park was obvious. "Backcountry use is increasing," said Frederick, "and very definitely Kelsey's book is contributing to the damage that's being done." Of course, Kelsey doesn't see it that way. In 1987, when the Zion National History Association refused to carry his books at the Zion visitor center, Kelsey made his feelings known to the park superintendent in a fiery letter: "National park rangers are a bunch of city kids," Kelsey complained, "who are totally inexperienced as to the ways of the wilds. . . . Yet they continue to give advice to hikers, as though they were." Furthermore, Kelsey added, "To set the record straight, I've traveled in 129 countries of the world, and have climbed mountains in most, making this climber the most experienced in the world."

The most experienced hiker in the world. He really said that. At least we know he can count to 129.

Kelsey is only one of many who make a nice living by revealing what little is left of what was once the wild and uncharted West. What can you do to stop these rip-off artists? It's quite easy: don't buy their books. You may say, "If I don't, someone else will."

Fine. Let the shame fall on someone else's shoulders. But don't we need to know where we are, where we've been, and where we're about to go? Why? What difference does it make? If you don't know where you've been, you can't be forced to tell anyone else, and you'll be contributing even more to its preservation.

Do this. The next time you decide to take a hike, arbitrarily pick a number to determine how far you intend to drive. When you've driven that number of miles, pull over, get out of the car, pick a direction, and just *go*. Let it be a surprise. Treat yourself to the unknown.

▬▬▬▬ ▬▬▬▬ ▬▬▬▬ After our climb down from the mountain, Buck and I discussed the problem as we bounced along a rocky section of the road near Copper Ridge. The problem was, we agreed, that *anybody* who writes, photographs, paints, or sings about the West is exploiting it to a certain extent. Our friend Abbey rued the day he ever mentioned the Maze in any of this books. He felt responsible for the rapid increase in visitation. Even here, I've felt the need to mention a place or two by name. Can hypocrisy be measured in degrees? I pulled my ragged copy of *On the Loose* from a satchel and read the line about "unfastidious outdoorsmanship" to Swarthy. The problem is, we concluded, with so many people descending on the West, this myriad of rules and regulations is becoming ever more necessary to control the impacts that the masses are creating. Buck and I hate rules.

"These idiots should just stay home," Buck concluded, and I heartily agreed.

"But doesn't that make us elitists and hypocrites?" I asked.

We both shrugged and looked at the scenery. A few minutes later, as we drove across a bone-dry Bromide Wash for the fifth time, I looked over at Fortknocher. He was eating tuna out of a can with his fingers. The fish juice kept spilling on the seat, and when he tried to open his wing window, Buck smeared the glass with his greasy hands.

"Swarthy," I complained, "Look what you're doing to my car. You're making a mess out of it."

Fortknocher gave me the eye. Then he winked, smiled, and patted me on the back with his tuna-smeared hand.

"You know, Stiles," he grinned, "that's the problem with you."

"What's that?" I asked.

"You're too . . . fastidious. You want some of this tuna? After all, it's dolphin free."

He had a point. I suppose I could be a bit anal at times. Secretly, I'd always longed to be a slob like Buck, but I could never quite pull it off. I cringed at the thought of being labeled "fastidious," of all things. Perhaps spilled tuna juice wasn't so bad after all.

And Terry Russell was absolutely right, of course, when he talked about "unfastidious outdoorsmanship." The disorganized, spontaneous search for beauty is the only justifiable and honest way of seeking it. The search for solitude, beauty, and all things remote and mysterious must be random. To be more organized is to risk commodifying beauty itself. But there were clear warnings, even in the early 1990s, of more things to come. Our encounter with Kelsey was one of them, but more rude awakenings were lying in wait. They weren't hiding in the tall rabbitbrush by the side of the road. They were parked quite stylishly in air conditioned BMWs and Saabs.

▬▬ ▬▬ ▬▬ When the Utah Department of Transportation paved the old dirt road that ran from Blanding to Hanksville in the late 1970s, there was only one silver lining to the sleek new road. While realigning the highway, UDOT abandoned much of the old road and allowed it to crumble. That was particularly the case at Comb Wash, where the old Dugway still snaked its way down the side of Comb Ridge and into the shadows of giant cottonwoods that grew in the wash below. The road was empty then, as it was most days.

Feeling a little nostalgic one morning about a decade ago, I made a sentimental journey (most of them are) to the top of the Comb Ridge Dugway. Flash floods had washed out the old road to vehicles years ago, and standing on the same boulder at the top of the Dugway felt familiar and comforting. On this particular morning, the air was clear, the birds were singing, and I had the place to myself. Or at least I thought I did.

I'd walked several hundred feet down the old road when I heard something strange. Only the crunch of my footsteps and the song of a canyon wren had disturbed the silence of this lovely morning, when I thought I heard the sound of laughter and applause. I took a few more steps, and I heard it again. The noise was definitely coming from Comb Wash, almost a mile away. I looked through my field glasses and saw a confusing sight. It appeared to be . . . an audience. I estimated between fifty and seventy-five people, dressed in a wonderful assortment of pastels and earth tones, all of them clapping and laughing enthusiastically for . . . well, I couldn't see *why* they were clapping, actually.

I was annoyed, puzzled, and indignant, so I decided to go down there and find out who this well-appointed mob of people was and why they chose this sacred location to gather. I made my way back to the new road, drove through the cut in Comb Ridge, and turned onto the dirt road that led to their camp. Close up the sight was even worse. A big Ryder truck provided support for the cooking operation, which had come prepared to feed a small militia. Handsome young men and women with appropriate outfits chatted pleasantly with each other as they loaded their cars with state-of-the-art camping equipment.

I walked up to a man who looked to be in his thirties. He was shaking the sand out of his Timberlands, sitting on the tailgate of his Toyota Landcruiser.

"Excuse me," I said.

The man looked up and nodded serenely.

"Yes," I said, "I was just wondering, who are you people? I could see you from the top of Comb Ridge. I could even hear you. Is this some kind of group?"

He smiled. "Not exactly," he replied. "We are a gathering of individuals."

I shook my head blankly. "Huh? What does that mean?"

He cleared his throat and said, "We're all here together trying to develop a more positive attitude about ourselves."

"Excuse me?" I said.

"We're trying to get to *know* ourselves better," he explained, mildly exasperated that I even had to ask. "Maybe you should talk to our leader," he added and pointed vaguely toward the cook tent.

Eventually, I found the man in charge, or, to be exact, he found me. I had begun to draw stares as I snapped photos and grumbled just slightly under my breath. I think I got reported.

Jim Muir (apparently no relation to John) was the logistical coordinator of this event, operated by a for-profit group called the Garden Company of Sand Point, Idaho. He was a pleasant-enough fellow and eager to alleviate my concerns. Muir explained the purpose of the gathering. Apparently the Garden Company was founded by a man named Kendrick Mercer, whose talent—his *shtick*, if you will—is to enlighten people, to awaken them, as the young fellow said to me earlier, to help them know themselves.

Muir and the logistics people did all the grunt work, though it wasn't as much as you might suspect. He explained that the participants had to provide their own transportation to the gathering point, then they traveled en masse to Comb Wash. They brought their own equipment as well. On the first evening, Mercer appeared on a rock before and above his paid disciples and spoke inspirationally for a few minutes. Then Muir and his team provided a splendid meal, and everyone retired to their tents to be alone with their thoughts.

The following morning, however, it got ugly. Support trucks picked up each of the customers at 6:00 a.m. They were not allowed to bring anything but a liter of water, six matches, and the clothes on their back. At long intervals, the Garden Company's drivers deposited their victims along the four-wheel-drive trail in Arch Canyon, where they would be required to spend the next thirty-six hours totally alone.

"I'm sorry," I said, "but I just don't get it. These people don't look like they've ever spent a *day* alone in the woods, or even an afternoon, much less a night."

"Precisely," Muir replied. "Look, these are professionals, doctors, lawyers, CEOs. You're right, too. Some of them have never camped out a day in their lives. This is giving them a whole new way of looking at this planet and their own lives. We are increasing their consciousness."

"Sure," I nodded. "But at what cost? They can't be taught environmental ethics in thirty-six hours any more than they can be taught self-reliance. Or *enlightenment* for that matter," I snarled. "And what about the fragile nature of the desert itself? They'll be stomping through cryptobiotic soil and snapping branches off junipers and making a nuisance of themselves." Fifty hungry, scared doctors, lawyers, and CEOs roaming the canyon, lost in what was once a sacred place, for thirty-six hours. I shuddered at the thought of it.

Muir was patient with me and even tried to be empathetic, saying things like, "I can certainly understand how you feel" or "I can sure see your point," but ultimately he felt the program was a good one.

"When we pick them up tomorrow afternoon, they will have had all this time to reflect on their lives, their livelihoods, and their loved ones. It will have at least created questions, if not answers. They'll relax for a few hours in the evening, we'll feed them a spectacular meal, and then Mr. Mercer will try to put it all in perspective for them. Believe me, it will be worth every cent they spent to be here with us."

"And how many cents is that, Jim?"

A shadow crossed his face, but just for a moment. He smiled softly and said, "It's not about the money in the end, it's about who we are."

I thanked Muir for his time. He invited me to stick around for Kendrick Mercer's finale, but I declined. He had been kind enough to at least listen to my tirade. As I walked back to my car, though, it occurred to me that we had taken a significant step in marketing the very beauty of the land. We'd gone beyond promoting a recreational sport that requires equipment and an outfit. We had now found a way to market the very spiritualistic aspect of the outdoor experience. The "meaning of life," produced, packaged, and *sold*. So, you want to increase your consciousness? The next Mystery Tour leaves in fifteen minutes.

When I got back to Moab, I called directory assistance for the Garden Company in Sand Point, Idaho. A soothing voice on the other end answered the phone. I explained to her that I had by chance met this wonderful group of enlightened people in southern Utah. How could *I* be a part of this learning experience?

"Easy," she schmoozed, "that particular gathering only costs eighteen hundred and fifty dollars for the three-day experience. Would you like to get on our waiting list? There is quite a demand at this time."

I told her I'd think about it and inquired further about Kendrick Mercer, "What if I just wanted to spend some one-on-one time with Mr. Mercer, what would that cost?" I could almost feel her reaching for my credit card through the phone line.

"Well, Sir, of course that is considerably more expensive, but I assure you the benefits of time spent with Mr. Mercer cannot be measured. A full day with him is only thirteen thousand dollars."

Suddenly the future became very clear to me. It was like an epiphany. Later, when the Garden Company produced its own Web site, I was able to understand their motives even more clearly—I just had to read carefully. First, the Garden Company explained, "One of our highest values is individual freedom. Unfortunately, in our culture most of us are trapped: in our work, in our relationships, and in ourselves. We often get into situations to trap ourselves or use others in order to trap us, and then claim we cannot get out. The Garden Company supports people in realizing they are free to create their life anyway they want."

Yes, create the life you want—by handing the Garden Company your Gold Card. But what's the bottom line here? Why should you really take a course with Kendrick Mercer? Here are the benefits, in the order they're listed on the Web site: "Increased profitability by overcoming obstacles to making money; working less with better results; improved sales acceptance—before the Mountain Experience many people are afraid of rejection, afraid to say how much their product or service may cost; enhanced business administration, leadership, and management skills."

So, according to the Garden Company, seeking enlightenment for any kind of altruistic reason is a sham. It's the money. It's always the money. Gain your freedom. Make a buck. Wreak havoc on Arch Canyon in the process.

▬▬▬ ▬▬▬ ▬▬▬ I can trace the demise of another secret place to commercial exploitation with absolute precision. It's the sad case of Antelope Canyon. In the late 1970s I saw a photograph in a calendar that was as surreally beautiful as anything in nature I had ever seen. It depicted a narrow and convoluted slot canyon, bathed in an otherworldly light. I had never seen anything quite like it. The caption on the photograph identified it only as a "sandstone gorge in northern Arizona."

Good, that's pretty vague. That should keep the slot-baggers busy for a while. In fact, I decided at that moment that I would make no attempt to learn the identity or location of this lovely place myself. The photograph would inspire others to seek it out. My absence would at least diminish the crowd by one. Yet, somehow, I think I knew what was coming. The photographer and the calendar publisher, my old pal Ken Sanders at Dream Garden Press, had the sensitivity to keep the place fairly anonymous and I appreciated his efforts. I hoped that the canyon was inaccessible enough to save it. Still, I worried and wondered how such a sculptured masterpiece could remain that way.

A couple of years later, I mentioned the picture to a ranger friend of mine.

"Sure," he replied, "that's Antelope Canyon. I haven't been there but it's down by Lake Powell near Page, I think. Not too many people know about it."

"Near Page?" I exclaimed. "Near Glen Canyon Dam and the power plant?"

"That's it," my friend sighed.

A few months later, I saw another picture of the secret canyon, this time identified by name. Over the years, I heard of others who had gone there, and I learned that the Navajo Nation had even considered building a marina on Lake Powell at the reservoir's terminus with the canyon. Though the marina has never been built, Antelope Canyon continued to gain recognition. I started to hear rumors that the canyon was beginning to show signs of overuse. For the first time in a million years, Antelope Canyon had a litter problem; hikers started to notice candy wrappers and film canisters.

Then one summer day, about ten years ago, I was driving past the Navajo Power Plant near Page when a large hand-painted sign caught my attention: "Antelope Canyon. Access into Premises with Permit Only. Permits Can Be Purchased Here." Unbelievable.

There must have been thirty cars in the lot on this hot, windy June afternoon. Discouraged but not surprised, I took a picture and headed home. Five hours later, I reached Moab. Hot, tired, and dusty, I pulled a Popsicle out of the freezer and plopped down in front of the boob tube. I wasn't paying much attention; in fact, I was much more engrossed in consuming my quiescently frozen raspberry confection, but something caught my eye as I glanced at the flickering screen.

There was that actor from the movie "Cocoon," the big guy who was the alien being . . . Brian Somebody. He was talking about a new acid indigestion remedy, Zantac 75, I think. He said it was "the last word" in stomach pain relief. With a voice as confident as God's, Brian assured the viewer that a Zantac pill would provide instant relief and last up to eight hours.

He was making his sales pitch from the bowels of Antelope Canyon. As the sculpted sandstone walls glowed like amber, Brian talked about the effects of spicy foods and the miracle of these little tablets. Why the makers of this product thought Antelope Canyon provided a perfect backdrop for a stomach pill commercial is beyond me, unless they thought the canyon itself resembled an inflamed esophagus. But there it was, and there it goes, from secret place to backdrop for a Zantac commercial in less than twenty years. Just watching it gave me acid indigestion.

A year later, almost a dozen French tourists were swept away and drowned by flash floods as they toured this once secret and unknown piece of paradise. The tragedy was reported worldwide by the media, and I can only guess that in the wake of this awful event business has never been better. Years later, some tour operators would agree.

▬▬▬ ▬▬▬ ▬▬▬ That was a decade ago. The commodification of nature was gaining strength, and not just the industrial-strength tourism that Abbey described in 1968. This was something different, something more than obscene. It was taking the purest form of nature and bastardizing it for profit. For all of us who preferred our adventures free and unfettered, the changes in recreation were ominous.

Among the dissenting voices, none has been so persistent as Scott Silver's. Headquartered in Bend, Oregon, Silver's Web site (www.wildwilderness.org) has relentlessly dogged both government and private entities who threaten the free-roaming existence of wildlands. Years ago, Silver offered "Three Visions" for the future of wildlands in America. They're worth remembering.

> VISION 1: The Traditional—You bounce down a wash-boarded forest road for what seems like an eternity until you come upon your favorite lake. Once there, you are treated to a magnificent setting, a pit toilet, a few rustic tent sites and maybe a hiking trail that leads into the backcountry. The lake itself is totally peaceful and so pristine that you can easily imagine this is how it's

always been. That afternoon you'll do a little fishing from your canoe, or maybe go for a swim, or a hike, or simply enjoy a picnic while you marvel at the setting. Later that evening you'll set up your tent, get out your cooler and camp stove and prepare for a night under the stars and a rare opportunity to become one with the Great Outdoors as nature provided them.

VISION 2: Industrial Strength Recreation—You race down a freshly paved forest road in your $150,000 RV to that same lake; having first made reservations for a premium site at the new KOA campground. The old tent sites have all been freshly upgraded and turned into pull-through ribbons of concrete, complete with water, sewer, electrical and internet hookups (which you'll use to make your next night's reservations). Once you've leveled your motor home, you unhitch the trailer, unload the ATVs, put on your helmet and go for a look around. Perhaps later on you'll play a quick round of golf before enjoying cocktails at the marina. You might even rent a jet-ski for an hour before returning to the RV and microwaving a quick dinner. After dark, if you've the energy, you may visit the amphitheater and listen to Ranger Rick's wilderness presentation.

VISION 3: Industrial Tourism—You cruise down that same paved road, this time stopping frequently to explore hardened nature trails and to learn how active forest management creates wildlife habitat and maintains healthy ecosystems. After several stops you'll reach a parking lot and pay $19.95 to take the monorail to the lakeside visitor's center. At the center you'll purchase reserved seats for the 3:00 p.m. showing of "The Lake." While you wait you'll visit the gift shop, eat in the restaurant, capture a few Kodak moments at the Kodak Photo Stop and perhaps look at still more interpretive displays. Years later even with your memories, photos and home videos to remind you of that wonderful visit, you will note with sadness that nothing can begin to compare with having seen "The Lake" in person, on the giant IMAX screen.

Silver warned, "If you want Vision 1, be prepared to fight for it." I thought the fight from our side would be unanimously waged. But what surprised us, even then, was the docile way many environmentalists were watching this recreational shift. Even ten years ago, alarms were going off in my head. I'd hoped that my intuitions were wrong, but they weren't.

The Invasion of Moab

Biker Insanitaire

Sometime in mid-February, usually, Allen Memorial Hospital's emergency room accepts its first injured mountain biker of the year. He or she would have probably taken a spill on the Slickrock Bike Trail or maybe Poison Spider Mesa—someplace sexy and dangerous, though, to be sure. As I understand it, this new tradition now officially kicks off the tourist season in Moab, and each year the excitement and anticipation rises to new levels of intensity.

Spring isn't what it once was, at least not in Moab. When the throngs return, I lose my enthusiasm and leave expressions of uncontrolled joy to my pals at the Moab Chamber of Commerce or the Travel Council. Even before life went totally out of control here, I avoided the teeming masses. For forty years, Easter Week had always meant Jeep Safari and the arrival of several hundred four-wheel-drive enthusiasts, determined to conquer some hellishly and impossibly steep rocky sandstone talus incline. They came for a few days, destroyed their expensive vehicles, spent a lot of money in town, and went home happy. I could hardly fault them or the merchants for that.

When it came to springtime festivities, I'd become downright unpleasant over the years, causing some people to wonder if perhaps I would be happier living somewhere else. Some people even *suggested* it. One realtor buddy of mine, Joe Kingsley, offered to buy me a ticket to Central America.

"Round trip or one way?" I asked.

"What do you think?"

I have toyed with the idea of abandoning this hectic life for the serenity and simplicity of an island called Funafuti. There the tourist trade is nonexistent and the water is unsafe to drink; instead, the native population depends on fresh and sometimes fermented coconut milk for liquid nourishment. The people of this paradise have celebrations called *fiafias* in thatched pavilions called *falafones*. Yes, someday I hope I can go to Funafuti, where I can go to fiafias at the falafone.

But Funafuti would have to wait. I was still here, with the 1990s' explosion of thousands and thousands of motorized and nonmotorized recreationists of all sizes and ages coming to Moab to frolic on the same land at the same time. It was almost more than a paranoid curmudgeon like me could tolerate.

Still, my conscience and others begged me to be kind, to be tolerant, even accepting, even joyful of this glorious diverse enclave of new friends that blessed our small town during a few critical weeks with their cash and credit cards. Or, as one of my friends said, "At least shut your goddamn mouth for a few weeks and stay away from us."

For a while I decided to do something about my bad behavior and tried to extend a helping hand to hapless visitors, but I didn't really have what it takes to be a good will ambassador of Moab. I lacked the patience. After all those years in the National Park Service answering dumb questions and directing tourists to the nearest toilet, I knew

I could never go back to that life. Consider the following incident, which I absolutely swear happened to me many Spring Breaks ago.

I was driving down First North on my way to the post office, when I noticed a young man walking across the street in front of me. He was moving slowly, almost shuffling, as he crossed my lane from the left. He was not inside a crosswalk of any kind, and I believe it would have been within my legal rights to run over him. But, what the hell, I figured, what's the rush? I was in a magnanimous mood, so I braked to let him pass by.

The young man, who was perhaps in his late teens or early twenties, rather gaunt, and looking very grim, raised his right hand to me, like a traffic cop might gesture to an oncoming auto, and stepped slowly by my front bumper. But instead of proceeding to the other side of the street, he came around to the side of my car, reached for the handle, and opened the passenger door.

"Hey, dude," he said, "like, my feet are killing me. Could you give me a ride?"

I'd never laid eyes on this guy in my life.

"Uh, well, I'm sort of heading home," I explained a little uneasily. My new friend was already moving things off the passenger seat so he could climb in.

"I have blisters on my feet, and I need a ride to Rim Cyclery," he said. "My bike's down there, dude. Like, I'm gettin' new tires. So I've been walkin' and, like, *look* at this."

He pulled off his Tevas to show me an oozing blister on the ball of his right foot. It did look pretty gruesome, but then so did my situation.

"Oh, I see," I replied. I would have offered to drive him there, but by then he was already in the car. He slammed the door, pointed, and sort of grunted, as if to say, "Let's go."

I drove down First North, past my original destination, and stopped at the interminably long stoplight at Main.

"So, where are you from?" I asked, making conversation.

"Indiana. And I have blisters on my feet."

"Really? I'm originally from Kentucky," I said, trying to find common ground with this visitor to our area, trying to be a good host. Either he didn't hear me or he loathes people from Kentucky, because he didn't say a word. He seemed to be concentrating on his feet. We drove on.

I pulled up to the front door of Rim and stopped near the door. "My bike's in the back. I can probably walk the rest of the way."

"Are you sure? I can't bear to see you suffer like this," I said, as I smiled ever so sincerely.

"Like, you rock, dude. Thanks," he said.

He turned to open the door, and, almost as if this is the way he always exited a vehicle, as if it somehow propelled him, my new buddy farted. Loudly. He broke wind right there on the front seat of my car. I don't even think he noticed. He slammed the door and I roared off, rolling down all the windows as I went. The memory lingered.

Despite the farting tourist, I was doing alright. After enduring the overwhelming tourist onslaught for years, I was determined to improve my attitude. It was time to put an end to these dismal apocalyptic predictions. After all, I convinced myself, this madness only lasts for six or eight weeks. I could survive that. Ask anyone, for a while I could be a pillar of hope and optimism to my friends and acquaintances. By June, I assured myself, the temperature will rise into the hundreds, the biting gnats will come out, and the throngs will go away. I had found a level of inner peace and contentment that I knew would allow me to survive these difficult days of spring.

But Easter 1993 was a turning point, a seminal moment. I was run over, flattened, in mid-bliss. I had never seen anything like it in my life. It surpassed anything that anyone in Moab had ever witnessed or endured (until 1994 and all succeeding years since). In spite of my pledge to be cheerful, I knew that my friends and I had just witnessed the end of civilization.

Estimates varied on the number of people who converged on Grand County, but here's how I figured it: There were something like 1200 jeeps registered for the Jeep Safari, but another 200 jeepers probably tagged along who never signed up. Assume that each registrant brought three family members along (a conservative estimate by anyone's standards) and that gives us 5600 souls.

I didn't even want to *think* about the Slickrock Bike Trail and the Sand Flats campers, but I could hardly ignore them. One BLM estimate placed the number of cars up there at 1100. That's triple the vehicles counted at the previous year's event. Figure three to a car, and we have 3300 marauding bikers on the Sand Flats.

Along the river corridor, both upstream and downstream from Moab, another 3000 campers fought for space and the right to enjoy the great outdoors, amid blowing garbage and ever-increasing quantities of human excrement. Farther north, on access roads that intersect US 191, additional large groups partied down. One gathering of 150 recreationists partied under a giant Bud Light banner that one of their group had suspended from an adjacent sandstone pinnacle, which probably attracted another 1000 people. If only the rocks could speak.

▬▬ ▬▬ ▬▬ I took some comfort from an article in *Newsweek*. In it, Dr. Irwin Goldstein, an impotency expert from Boston University, issued a grave warning to men who regularly ride bicycles. His studies showed that when men ride bikes with a standard seat, the kind that looks like a mutated black banana, his body weight flattens his main penile artery. This artery is essential for an erection. And, from a man's perspective, what could be more essential than that?

Goldstein suggested that riding a bike and putting that kind of pressure on the penile artery over time can irreversibly damage the vessel. The worried doctor was seeing several new patients a week. Among them was Ed Pavelka of *Bicycling Magazine*, who described his ordeal. He complained that his years of intense marathon bike riding had left him "as soft as an overcooked rigatoni." Not exactly a macho biker pick-up line.

Dr. Goldstein said that a better-designed bike seat may alleviate the problem but didn't think any of the new, more heavily padded seats being offered would make much of a difference. He said the perfect men's bike seat would "look like a toilet seat."

But what was bad news to bikers cheered me considerably. With a world in which science and technology have removed the "survival of the fittest" concept from the population growth formula and with the world population exploding with each passing day, the mountain bike dilemma is a modern-day miracle. With penile arteries getting hammered flatter than prairie dogs on I-70, population stabilization and even shrinkage (if I can say that with a straight face) is within our grasp. We shouldn't be fighting the extreme right over free distribution of contraceptives. Planned Parenthood should not waste its time distributing free condoms. Instead, why not provide complimentary mountain bikes to all males over the age of fifteen? The future could take care of the biker problem simply through attrition.

In 1993, however, relief was not in sight. With 13,000 temporary residents trampling the land as fast as they could get to it, I found myself asking several questions. First, had Moab's tourist promotion strategy been an unqualified success, or what? But, more pointedly, would it be possible now for our great chamber of commerce, the travel council, and other funding entities to quit worrying about the prospects of Moab turning into a ghost town? Could we stop spending so much money on promotion? Or was it already too late to save at least a *little* of "old Moab"?

And, finally, . . . are we still having fun? That's what Moab used to be about—it was fun to live here, even if half of us were broke. Moab had been full of people who loved our town when it went dead in wintertime. We *wanted* to be part-timers. We looked forward to the prospect of unemployment and reduced responsibilities. But now the Moab Chamber of Commerce and the Travel Council were looking for ways to "build up the tourist season shoulders." Were they trying to take away our fun? I received no answer from the funding entities.

As to the environmental damage, ironically the jeepers, at least the ones who were part of the Jeep Safari, were about as respectful of the land as a group that large can be. The Red Rock Four-Wheelers still go to great efforts to reduce impacts and to assure that their event comes off with a minimal amount of environmental damage. Trail leaders relentlessly remind their groups of the threat they pose to the sensitive environment, and peer pressure alone has everyone trying to "do the right thing." But here in the desert, the sheer magnitude of the numbers can make the best intentions meaningless. Outside the organized realm of the Red Rock Four-Wheelers, jeep and ATV damage is staggering, causing most responsible four-wheelers to shudder. They realize that reckless off-road behavior reflects on them all, but few are willing to criticize their peers.

On the Sand Flats, peer pressure assumes an entirely different meaning. The 3000 or so people who occupied the area surrounding the Slickrock Bike Trail were, for the most part, the Spring Break crowd, high school and college students in search of relief from the academic grind. If Daytona Beach were not so far away, they would have gone there. The Spring Break mobs take along their surfboards when they head for Daytona, just as they bring along their mountain bikes when they come to Moab. But they don't make these pilgrimages in search of the perfect wave, to test their endurance on the trail, or to listen to the sounds of nature. They do not come here to contemplate the meaning of life and their role in the universe. They come here to consume massive quantities of beer and to explore the edges of insanity.

During one particularly rowdy Spring Break, students ignited several trees with white gas rather than go to the trouble of actually gathering kindling. The mobs of teenagers surged forward in the night toward the burning pyres, as if about to offer human sacrifices to the Great Sprocket God. That year the Grand County sheriffs wisely retreated from the Sand Flats, leaving the students in command of the field.

As Sheriff Nyland explained later, "It was a hell of a lot easier to just wait and arrest 'em later when they was passed out."

I advocate the massive consumption of spirits and other adult beverages from time to time, so that consumers can make utter fools of themselves, throw up all over their friends, and have a terrific hangover the next day—just so they can appreciate the sheer joy of recovering from such an ordeal. You can never fully appreciate how wonderful it is to simply feel normal, until you've poisoned your body with enough alcohol to pickle a large horse.

I'd rather see the county open up the rodeo grounds for the week and make it an "anything goes" zone. When the party is over, Fire Chief Corky Brewer can come in with his high-pressure pumps, hose the kids down, and send them home happy.

But year after year, the land absorbs the abuse, and I wonder how much more misery it can endure. Twenty years ago, environmentalists worried about range damage from overgrazing; now I missed local rancher Don Holyoak's cows. Predictably, the government's response has been to "stabilize" the Sand Flats with designated hardened campsites and a mandatory fee. What better way to remove damaging scars to the land than to just pave over them? Some scientists worry about the threat by recreationists to cryptobiotic soil, that fragile crust of lichens and mosses that binds the desert together. On the Sand Flats, forget about trying to save the cryptogams, *all* living things are at risk. Blackbrush, cactus, yucca, juniper trees, and, of course, anything that moves. Most of the critters have sought refuge someplace else. No self-respecting Moabite will venture up to the Sand Flats. The only wildlife that survives is the kind we all hope faces immediate extinction.

▬▬ ▬▬ ▬▬ But, am I being unfair? Specifically, have I wrongly stereotyped the mountain bike community and turned them into thick-browed Neanderthals? Is there a redeeming quality to this biker phenomenon?

I was walking out of Dave's Corner Market with a cup of coffee one afternoon when I felt a rush of wind and heard the whine of gears and chains cranking furiously. Dave's sits at the corner of Mill Creek Drive and Fourth East and is situated in a direct line with US 191 and the Sand Flats. Mountain bikers descending from the nearby Slickrock Bike Trail often choose to avoid the T-intersection, where they'd actually have to stop and obey traffic laws, and cut across Dave's lot. It's like riding the hypotenuse of a right triangle at about thirty-five miles an hour.

My lightning reflexes pulled me out of harm's way as the neon blur pumped by, and most of my coffee stayed in the cup. I lifted my cup in the air and said, "Have a nice day," or something along those lines, but the guy was well out of earshot by then.

About an hour later, the high Wingate sandstone walls around Moab reverberated with the wail of sirens. It was, yet again, the Grand County Ambulance crew on its way to the Sand Flats to retrieve another fallen biker.

"I just hope it wasn't that fellow who almost ran over me this morning. Although we didn't have a chance to talk, he seemed like one hell of a nice guy," I said to myself.

The hostility that ebbs and flows in the hearts and minds of Moab's citizens on both sides of the bicycle issue has already been acknowledged here. But during the 1990s, the anti-biker sentiment was palpable. Under-the-breath comments at the post office, snide remarks at City Market, and pickup trucks swerving into the bike lanes were all indications of what one biker described to me as "an ungrateful community."

"Ungrateful?" I said. "You must be joking. Why I literally shed tears of joy each and every spring when I see that first flash of Lycra," I explained to my royal blue friend.

"This is no time for sarcasm," he snarled. (These guys are *so* damned serious.) "Tell me, have you ever actually done it?"

"Done what?" I asked.

"Mountain biked. Have you ever actually climbed on a mountain bike and experienced the sport for yourself?"

"You mean put on the outfit and the helmet and . . . the whole deal?" I asked incredulously. "There's no way."

"You don't *have* to wear all this gear if you don't want to, but have you ever biked a trail?"

"Well, no," I conceded.

"There!" he proclaimed triumphantly. "You admit it! How can you criticize something you have never experienced? I don't want to read one more negative comment about bikers in your paper until you've experienced mountain biking on a personal level."

"But it's spring. I've got to finish my taxes, and there's the next issue to get out!" I cried, as he tugged at the strap on his helmet.

"The choice is yours. I'll be watching," he grinned and pedaled away.

Not many people knew this at the time, but I actually owned a mountain bike. One of my organically grown friends persuaded me to buy her old Schwinn. She suggested that I would learn to love my new bike as much as she had. I was skeptical, but she only wanted a hundred bucks for it. So I figured, what the hell.

I rode it about six times, if I recall correctly, and only around town, never a true mountain bike experience. I'm not mechanically inclined, and I had problems shifting gears from the outset. Plus, I kept getting glares from cowboys in pickups and startled looks from my friends. Once, the dumbstruck stare of a familiar passerby almost resulted in an accident. I strapped a sign on the back of the bike that said, "Local, Lycra-free," but I still felt uncomfortable. Finally, the bike was relegated to the porch, where it served me well as an all-weather clothesline and an interesting conversation piece. Well, until that morning.

With the sun just breaking behind the La Sals, I rolled the bike off the porch and loaded the Schwinn into the back of my car. As I backed out of the driveway, I wondered if I was embarking on an adventure that would ultimately and forever alter the way I view my life and the world around me. Had I been operating from the darkened halls of ignorance all these years? Was I about to see the light?

There's an old jeep road just outside the Arches park boundary that is seldom used and offers a variety of mountain bike opportunities. This was the place, I decided, to test my wings.

Before departing, however, I consulted my copy of *Above and Beyond Slickrock* by the former dean of fat-tire biking, Todd Campbell. I took note of his helpful hints on bicycle care and maintenance and paid particular attention to the "Techniques" section. This, I figured, would be critical to a good day's ride.

With this knowledge and the thrill of anticipation pounding in my chest, I crept out of town, bathed in the warm glow of a brilliant spring morning. I turned off the highway at the appointed spot and headed east into the sun until I reached my destination. Parking the car in the shade of an ancient juniper tree, I unloaded the bike, strapped on my fanny pack, and climbed on. It was all downhill after that.

Actually, it was all uphill. My plan was to follow this jeep trail from a wash bottom crossing through an area of broken rock and ledges to a large expanse of slickrock, pedal to the top, and then coast back down. I pedaled across the wash, encountered the ledges on the other side, and immediately fell off the bike.

I pulled out Campbell's book and reread the passage that pertained to this particular mishap. According to the text, "To avoid small obstacles, actually aim at them when approaching and you'll be better able to avoid them when the time comes to pass." I thought that was what I'd done, although it seemed sort of masochistic to me. I aimed my bike right at the ledges, and ended up here on the ground, sucking sand. I read on, "Balance, tenacity, and proper gear selection all play roles in dab-free climbing."

"Dab-free?" I didn't even know what it meant, but thirty seconds after beginning this little adventure, I had already been dabbed. I had lost my dabness. I was not a dab-virgin anymore. Actually, I was in pain.

But Campbell said that *tenacity* was critical to a successful ride, so I got back on and pedaled east. Things went swimmingly for a while. The road was fairly smooth and only climbed modestly. I played with the gears, even doing a little "thumbtip shifting" as described in the book. I can say that I rode my bike with the confidence and skill of a professional for the better part of 200 yards before another obstacle confronted me. I found myself in a dry wash and I remembered Campbell's advice on sand, "If you begin to auger in, downshift before there is too much stress on the chain."

I augered in. I crawled out from under the wheeled monster and thought, "To hell with stress on the chain, what about me? I hadn't been this stressed since I once lost the *Zephyr*'s subscriber list in the computer. It had to get better.

With the slickrock looming ahead, I again sought comfort and advice in the book. But what I read only terrified me more. I learned that "pedal-gouging can send you sailing" and that failing to use the proper technique can result in "the dreaded crotch-split." With these confidence-builders spinning in my brain, I got back on the bike and *went* for it. With grim determination, I gripped the handlebars, concentrated on the terrain in front of me, and sallied forth into the unknown.

I had hiked much of this country over the previous fifteen years. I love the broad vistas, that beautiful contrast where the red rock meets the blue sky, where only the sound of mourning doves breaks the stillness of an otherwise silent and peaceful day. But now, now I developed an entirely different intimacy with the land. I developed a special interest, an obsession almost, with the land that exists exactly three feet in front of my bike. Sometimes it was difficult to discern all the subtle changes in the rock because I was bouncing so badly that my vision was blurred. Still, I just couldn't take my eyes off that tiny piece of real estate that I saw just before I ran over it.

In an effort that I considered almost miraculous, I reached the top of the slickrock summit and paused briefly to congratulate myself. The view, as always, was incredible. I could see most of the Colorado River drainage, from the Blue Mountains on the south to my beloved Henry Mountains on the western horizon. But I had no sense of how I'd gotten here. A *hike* from point A to point B allows me to see the changes that occur between those two locations. I see the effects of last week's flash floods on the dry washes, and I see the tracks of a solitary coyote that passed by when the flooding had subsided. I see that little patches of Newberry twin pod are already trying to bloom, even as cold March winds scour the sandstone. I see two rusty bean cans left under an old pinyon pine by a cowboy fifty years ago. Maybe sixty years ago, who knows.

But now, I stood on the brink of this sandstone massif, feeling like a transcontinental jet traveler who knows nothing of the land he has just flown over. I could see my car gleaming in the noonday sun, three miles away. What stories lay between here and there? I couldn't tell you.

I got ready for the ride back to the car and consulted Campbell's book one last time. For downhill "posting," he recommended that I "pinch the saddle between my thighs." I think not.

After a momentous downhill, out-of-control descent that would take too long to describe and would be too painful to recall, I reached the safety of my car, stashed the bike in the back, and spent the rest of the day using my *feet* to explore the country instead of the seat of my pants. When I got home that evening, I concluded that biking is more like rock climbing than hiking. It is personally challenging, it tests one's strength, endurance, balance, and skill. Mountain biking is a test of one's equipment as well. Having submitted myself to this test, I still don't see what the deal with the royal blue tights is, but I'm only a beginner.

Now that I'd become familiar with the dreaded crotch split, subjected myself to this grueling ordeal, and experienced biking "on a personal level," I did have a better sense about myself. I knew I belonged in a very slow lane, one slow enough to stop and smell the cliff rose, slow enough to feel the breeze instead of "a rush," easy enough to find faces in the clouds instead of jarring blurred images. Let others auger in. I'll just watch, if you don't mind.

What Hath God Wrought?

Located seventy-seven miles south of Moab in San Juan County, Blanding, Utah, is Moab's Bizarro World. Populated mostly by Mormons and Navajos, Blanding chooses *not* to be everything that Moab is—or at least that's the plan. I have to wonder if all that tourist money will someday be too much for the locals to resist, but for now, the familiar and oft-repeated Blanding refrain is, "If we end up like Moab, shoot us." So far they're in no danger of a bullet between the eyes.

One hot summer day a few years ago, I was hiding out and being fairly successful at it, when I realized I was running low on spicy peanuts and Dr. Pepper, two important components of my current bachelor diet. So I drove into Blanding, the nearest town, to stock up. When I pulled into the lot at Parley Redd Foodtown, I was struck by the lack of customers. In fact, I appeared to be the *only* customer. On closer inspection, though, I was stunned to see that the place was closed on Sundays.

It didn't occur to me that *any* supermarket closed on Sundays anymore. Surprised, but not defeated, I drove to Blanding's other supermarket, the one that had just opened a few weeks ago. Surely, they would be open on the Sunday of Labor Day weekend. No way. The sign on the door said they'd be locked up tight until Monday morning.

For a moment, I was greatly annoyed. I'd driven twelve miles for nothing. How could I go an entire day without a Dr. Pepper? But as I sat there in the truck, my anger passed. I realized that Blanding, just seventy-seven miles down the road from my hometown, had not yet become a slave to tourism, greed, and the Brave New West. For the first time in my life, I was proud of Blanding, Utah.

Blanding has its faults, for sure. Its politics are pure Rush Limbaugh. It's home to Neil Jostlin's *Blue Mountain Panorama*, cheerfully called by liberals "The Paranoia," a very right wing weekly that often lumped Bill Clinton with the likes of Adolf Hitler and Josef Stalin. Its residents are not quite sure they even belong to the United States, or at least its government, and they certainly don't want to. A Blanding resident was once bitterly complaining in very broad terms about the state of the country to my friend John Hartley, who owned a business there. Shaking his head sadly, the man pointed toward the clearly visible peaks of the Sleeping Ute Mountains in Colorado and muttered, "Yessir, things are sure a mess *out there* in America."

Perhaps because of its conservative bent, Blanding was still a pretty quiet little town in the mid-1990s, and it remains so even today. Meanwhile, during that same Labor Day weekend, the enlightened New Moab was booming as usual. The contrast was striking.

In 1995 alone, the fruits of Moab's labor included a new Denny's Restaurant; the King World Waterpark, named for an old Moab hermit who died in an insane asylum in the 1930s after being abandoned by the town; a Wendy's Old Fashioned Hamburgers; an Arby's Roast Beef; and a Dairy Queen, which we all know is "Scrumpdelicious." Since then, both the Arby's and the Dairy Queen have gone broke, but they were quickly replaced by other tourist-based enterprises. Those nationally franchised restaurants were only one year's additions to the Main Street strip, an area that used to be the heart of the community, not a strip at all. Main Street now serves as a gateway of sorts for the million-plus tourists that pour into Moab each year. The changes on Main Street since 1990, when McDonald's broke Moab's franchise food barrier, can only be called stunning.

In addition to the changes that were occurring to the business district, the development of residential housing projects accelerated in the mid-1990s, driven by a market that could never seem to be satisfied. All the vacant houses that had been gobbled up for pennies on the dollar in the late-1980s by savvy investor/mountain bikers from California and Colorado now created a housing shortage in a town that had only recently become hip. Not only did the price of existing real estate skyrocket, ground was broken on one condo development after another, with names like Solano Vilejo, Mill Creek Pueblos, Coyote Run, Orchard Villa.

"Daddy, why do they call our home Orchard Villa?"

"Because, son, there used to be an orchard here."

"What's an orchard?"

Most ominous of all were two huge developments along the Colorado River on Highway 128. Multimillionaires Colin Fryer and Robbie Levin purchased the Tommy White and Bill Boulden ranches with long-term plans to create high-end, top-dollar resort hotels. By 2005 most of their plans were complete, and the hotels were up and running. Fryer's Red Cliffs Lodge and Levin's Sorrel River Ranch are both luxury resorts on a scale never before seen in southeastern Utah. In the beginning, Levin solemnly promised that he would plant enough trees to hide his multimillion-dollar lodge from the Colorado River, which is used throughout the summer by thousands of tourists on daily river trips. Everyone knew he was lying, but you can feed a planning commission practically any wild story and they'll swallow it, especially when most of its members are developers, too. Later Robbie Levin became a member of the Grand County Planning Commission himself, which made winking and nudging even more expedient.

About the only aspect of Moab that didn't change was the Big Tree. It still dominated First South and could be seen for blocks. Its trunk measured more than six feet in diameter, and the magnificent branches shaded half the neighborhood. The city had recently made road improvements, and the Big Tree blocked their plans to extend a curb to the corner. But, for once, the road crews deferred to nature, and the road went around the tree instead of through it. Someone suggested that extreme pruning of the tree—basically cutting it back to a stump—would be good for its long-term health. But many residents, me included, couldn't bear to see the tree topped so severely, and the idea was dropped. With Moab in upheaval mode, the Big Tree gave me comfort and a continuity that was getting more elusive all the time. Otherwise, Moab was under assault.

As the town grew, many of us wondered—what is it about unlimited, uncontrolled, never-ending economic growth that is so appealing to some people? Is it all about the money? Is it the power? Is it a bit of both? What is the thrill in taking a horse pasture and turning it into a parking lot? Both Fryer and Levin came to Moab wealthy. Are they two rich guys searching for a legacy in concrete and stucco? Among the promoters of economic development, surely some of them are earnest citizens who feel a robust expanding economy is always a benefit to the community and that it offers the promise of a stable future by providing an ever-expanding tax base. To think otherwise is blasphemy to most capitalists.

A few years ago, the Grand County Council, in conjunction with the Nature Conservancy, proposed to use federal grant monies to purchase a lovely parcel of land called the Mayberry Orchard along the Colorado River. They hoped to save it from possible development and ultimate destruction. At a public meeting to discuss the plan, I watched one prominent member of the community after another rise up to condemn the proposal. The lament was always the same: by quashing development (a commercial campground and convenience store, in this case), the county government was shrinking its own tax base and increasing the tax burden of Grand County's citizens. The council ultimately secured the land, and the Mayberry Orchard was saved.

A decade later, though, developers and some citizens still complain about another lost opportunity to expand the tax base. May God forgive them for their ignorance. An increased tax base in small rural communities rarely reduces individual tax burdens. The exact *opposite* is more likely to occur. This is my mantra: "An expanded tax base rarely reduces individual tax burdens. An expanded tax base rarely reduces individual tax burdens. An expanded tax base rarely reduces individual tax burdens. An expanded tax base rarely reduces individual tax burdens." How many times do I have to say it?

Small towns across America have often come too late to the same conclusion. According to the American Farmland Trust, for every $1.00 paid in property taxes, the average U.S. urban resident uses $1.36 in public services, while the average farm uses only $0.21 in similar services. That's a remarkable gap.

According to the U.S. Census Bureau, in St. George, Utah, for every $1.00 generated in tax revenue per housing unit, each house consumes $2.70 in municipal services. Similar comparisons in the Yampa Valley in Colorado and the Madison Valley in Montana produced similar results. It's happening all over the rural West, and that's because we never confront these changes until it's too late.

In the mid-1990s, Moab saw an exponential increase in residential water and sewer bills, and citizens foamed at the mouth. What did everyone expect? Did Moabites think that all these new franchise restaurants and modular motels, both massive water consumers, were somehow going to lift a giant financial burden from the town's shoulders?

In the end, it's simply a matter of different visions, different dreams. About fifteen years ago, Tom Shellenberger, a transplanted realtor and developer from Park City, Utah, told a writer for *Salt Lake City Magazine* that I "had a closed mind when it comes to progress." He concluded that Moabites probably define the word differently, and he felt that the *Zephyr* picked on him for his pro-development views. But Shellenberger was right in one respect: when it came to progress, Moabites do define the word differently. There is a difference between progress and development, although it's surely a subjective distinction. I can only speak for myself, but this is how I separate the two.

When I think of progress and what it means for a town and its surroundings, I think of a community in which its citizens can earn a decent living, pay the bills, and have something left over at the end of the month. But it's progress only when those citizens also realize the value of the intangible qualities that make our town unique and enrich their lives. Qualities like the beauty and solitude of the canyons and mountains that surround us and the friendship, compassion, and trust of our neighbors are, to me, just as important as the bottom line on a financial statement.

Progress is maintaining our small-town atmosphere, while recognizing that *some* change is inevitable and that change can sometimes even be an improvement. Development is when the greed of its citizens allows uncontrolled growth that destroys all the qualities of small-town life, the very things that brought many of us here.

Progress is a business that flourishes and expands to meet a growing demand, while still maintaining the quality that created its success in the first place. Its success is due to the owners' talent and hard work; expanding the business is the reward for their efforts. Development is an out-of-town investor who sees there's money to be made and throws up another fast food franchise, taking business and customers away from the local cafes that had flourished for decades.

Progress is the effort by local citizens to stay loyal to those well-established restaurants. Development is locals abandoning them in droves for the franchise chains in order to save a few cents.

Progress is a business that comes to town and offers a new service or product that we truly need and could not obtain before. Development is another T-shirt shop with an absentee owner.

Progress is suitable housing for all its citizens. Development is another tacky condo development for wealthy out-of-towners looking to invest in a second home and hoping to turn a tidy profit.

Progress is the Grand County Council and the Nature Conservancy saving the Mayberry Orchard. Development is seeing most of Grand County's other orchards turned into subdivisions.

Progress is appreciating the value of the spectacular view we all enjoy of the West Wall each day. Development is a chairlift running up its sandstone flanks.

Progress is we humans recognizing the value, the absolute *necessity* of preserving what's left of our wild pristine country. Development is seeing it bulldozed under or, perhaps worse, seeing those special places trampled under the feet of hordes of well-meaning people who claim they *do* recognize the value of wild lands but don't recognize that their sheer numbers are destroying it.

Progress is the mountain biker who gets tired of staring at his knuckles, the handlebars, and three feet of ground ahead of him and stops and looks around, overwhelmed by the silence and the beauty of the canyons. Development is painting more white lines on the Slickrock Bike Trail so nobody *has* to stop and look around.

Progress is appreciating the fading light on the slickrock palisades above the valley. Development is ridgeline housing.

Progress is moving to Moab, wanting to be a part of the community, and wanting to contribute something *to* it. Development is moving to Moab and seeing what can be taken *from* it.

In short, progress is Moab the community, whereas development is Moab the population center. What's the difference? It's everything.

███████ ████████ ████████ It's not the tourists who transform a community like Moab, it's to what lengths the citizens will change to accommodate unlimited numbers of those tourists. The residents of towns like Moab, the people who don't just live here but who have made their *lives* here, must deal with the changes every day of the year, while tourists, for whom the changes were made, are in and out of town in a matter of days.

When Moab first embraced tourism as the core of its economy, the town rose to the task of providing the kinds of goods and services that tourists seek. For a while, the economy did well. Even if the growth was limited to restaurants, motels, and Southwest jewelry stores, these businesses filled a need and prospered. But it's still a boomtown economy in many respects, and that kind of success never goes unnoticed. In the same way the 1849 California gold rush created a stampede of treasure hunters, eager to get rich quick, the same mentality applies now in the booming Brave New West.

So Moab was flooded by speculators, out-of-town investors—carpetbaggers really —who were much better financed to exploit the situation. They opened more restaurants, motels, bike shops, and convenience stores, and the established business owners began to feel the effect. When the ever-increasing numbers of restaurants, for example, outpaced the increase in tourist visitation, all the businesses saw their slice of the economic pie decrease. Often the new arrivals were better equipped to ride out a dip in the economy than their established competition. Ultimately, the business community demanded even more tourist promotion, eager to see the size of the pie grow again.

But it's a vicious trap. Moab did promote itself with a fury in the mid-1990s, and the numbers rose. Life seemed better for a while for the struggling economy, until even more out-of-town speculators took note of the rise and brought even more of the same redundant shops and stores to town. You'd think somebody might have one original idea.

Why do the agencies and organizations that are allegedly most concerned about the welfare of its business community work so consistently to undermine them? If a town's chamber of commerce or its travel council is primarily devoted to the existing businesses, why do they continue to promote more economic development, often from outside the business community, to compete directly and unfavorably with its own members? Why wouldn't a chamber send a clear message to potential new carpetbaggers that we have enough motels, taco stands, and hamburger joints? Are these agencies really working for the community as it is, or do they have an agenda for the future? Consider Telluride, Colorado, for a moment, our mountain cousin to the east.

My friend Sam Taylor, the long-time publisher of Moab's weekly *Times-Independent*, suggested in an editorial a few years ago that Telluride really hadn't changed much in twenty years. He noted that there are no malls in Telluride, no McDonald's, and not even a stoplight. Even its population has stabilized around 1300.His information came from the Telluride Chamber Resort Association.

The reason the population has remained static for twenty years is because hardly anyone can afford to live there anymore. A modest home that might have sold for $30,000 in 1975 was selling for $500,000 in 1994 and passed the $1 million mark in these brave new days of the twenty-first century. Perusing the real estate listings in a recent *Telluride Style Magazine*, I found: "The Cashman Retreat/Aldasoro Ranch: Gated 12-acre site high on a sunny ridge of Aldasoro Ranch, 11,676 square feet of gracious living space. Five bedrooms & five and a half baths, extensive patios & two outdoor hot tubs. . . . Views of all the region's southern peaks. Named by Barbara Walters' 'The View' as 'The World's Finest View!' Offered at $14,900,000."

Not many of the people who lived in Telluride in 1975 still reside there. Annual property taxes now dwarf the amount they paid for the home. Still, in his editorial Sam Taylor warned the Moab Travel Council to maintain its promotion budget instead of allowing funds to be used for other needed county services. He said, "You can grow and still maintain quality." For him, Telluride was a shining example of that admonition.

But I also remembered what Grand County Councilman Charlie Peterson said ten years ago, "We want a town that is as nice to live in as it is to visit." But how should we have done that? What would have been needed to save a town like Moab? What steps could the governing bodies of our city and county councils have taken to preserve some of the small-town values that we took for granted for so long and that we now seem destined to lose? How much of a sacrifice to the pocketbook would the citizens of this county endure to assure Moab's future as a decent place to live?

I decided to ask my fellow citizens, and I was impressed with their originality. Here are some of their suggestions:

- An ordinance that would not allow the absentee ownership of commercial or private property in Grand County. If you want to buy here, you've got to live here.
- An anti-Wal-Mart ordinance that would limit the size of commercial buildings that can be constructed within the county.
- An ordinance that would require any *new* business that hires more than a certain number of employees (maybe five or ten) to provide housing for those employees.
- New motels should be required to pay the single-family dwelling rate for water use in each unit of the motel.
- Lobby for the right to use transient room tax revenues for dealing with impacts from tourism. Or simply eliminate the tax, and do away with the travel council.
- Use some of the transient tax to purchase vital green space within the city limits and in adjoining developed parts of the county.

A decade ago, the Moab City Council had a chance to apply the last of these ideas at bargain-basement prices, but it allowed the opportunity to pass into history. The horse pastures and bottomland across from Dave's Corner Market had long been a favorite place to watch the arrival of spring. It seemed that each April the cottonwoods leafed out at the same time the mares gave birth to their foals. Sitting on one of Dave's benches, sipping hot coffee, and watching the pastures early in the morning was just about perfect. The land belonged to Venice Denny, a longtime resident of Moab and a man who, in the early 1990s, was contemplating retirement. Venice needed to sell the property but couldn't bear to think of the pastures being developed, so he went to the city with an offer. In 1991 I pleaded with the council members to consider Denny's proposal in a *Zephyr* editorial:

> The City Council has an opportunity right now to do something visionary. Moab has always been blessed with a lot of green space. We've taken

for granted the fact that within the city and right around its perimeter, we have orchards, and alfalfa fields and pastures—sights that we've grown accustomed to. But all that is likely to change as more and more out-of-town speculators buy up relatively cheap acreage.

One such property is a six-acre parcel on Fourth East, across from Mill Creek Drive. The owner has recently proposed to lease this property to the city with an option to buy after 10 years. During that time, the owner would continue to pay property taxes. It is one of the loveliest spots in Moab and adjacent to the Mill Creek Parkway. But if a developer gets a hold of it, condos and apartments loom just over the horizon. It would cost each citizen of Moab about $2.75 a year for a decade to preserve and protect this valuable "green space." That's less than $30 in ten years. . . . This could truly be a People's Park—a piece of yesterday that we've set aside. Talk to your councilperson; there's still time, but one of these days, if we don't act now, that land will be sold, and then it will be too late to do anything but kiss it goodbye.

But the city council did nothing. Not one council member would even make a motion to bring the subject up for discussion. Venice, who had only asked $125,000 for the parcel, finally sold it to a private individual who held the land for three years and resold it for a healthy profit. A couple years later the land sold again, for an even higher price. Finally, a developer purchased the property, bulldozed many of the trees, and built a few dozen condominiums. Not a trace of that pasture or the joy it evoked in Moabites survives. And it never had to happen.

It was my old pal, aging hippie and philosopher Carl Rappe, who first defended junk as the "last bastion of defense against rich weasel Yupster developers" and a means of controlling growth and keeping property taxes at a reasonable level. He believed that no urban upper-middle-class American would be caught dead living next to a shabby trailer with pigs in a wallow out back, every car they've owned since 1957 parked out front, and a healthy portion of old refrigerators and discarded batteries tossed about for good measure.

Rural Westerners have always coveted their junk, long before it became a tool to discourage new neighbors. Perhaps because the distances are so great in the West (or were, at least), getting replacement parts for just about any appliance or vehicle could be costly and difficult, and when located they might take weeks to arrive. So, if the family car went kaput, it made sense to store it in the weeds and see what use it might provide in the future. After all, just because the engine threw a rod didn't mean there was a thing wrong with the transmission, the differential, or any number of other still-functioning parts. The next car just might be able to use some of those parts. If their new car wasn't compatible with the junked one, a neighbor might have a use for it. Soon nobody threw away anything. That's why miles of black pipe and conduit, brass fittings, washing-machine motors, swamp coolers, and practically anything you can imagine that once performed a task for rural Westerners could be found in their backyards. Maybe they're even a touch sentimental.

But it was Carl, known locally as Uncle Meat, who saw the connection between all that lovely junk and maintaining a rural culture. To hold the line against out-of-town investors, condo time-share holders, and other ne'er-do-wells, he proposed that the governing bodies of our community needed to take immediate and drastic action. Specifically, Carl wanted a city and county ordinance that *required* the presence of junk in every Grand County resident's yard. I believe his plan called for at least one prominently displayed inoperative vehicle on cinder blocks, three doorless refrigerators, and 500 square feet (minimum) of waist-deep weeds, preferably noxious, per front yard. Backyard junk was optional because it wasn't always clearly visible from the road. Uncle Meat also mentioned tax incentives for homeowners who maintained smelly farm animals in small pens.

At first glance, this idea might strike some as unusual, and to others it may seem downright extreme. But this is Utah after all. In other communities across my beloved Beehive State, city councils and county commissions have endorsed and approved all kinds of far nuttier ideas. Some have passed ordinances that mandate the wearing of firearms, for example. In one community, the city council voted to require a sign in every resident's yard condemning the United Nations. By comparison, a pro-junk ordinance would have been quite mild, even tepid, by Utah standards.

But Carl's vision never came to pass. Instead we were all slowly outnumbered by an influx of new Grand County residents with an urban past. They had a habit of buying land next to junky yards or farm animals, knowing the junk or the smell was there, supposedly accepting and even embracing life in Moab the way it was. Then weeks or months later, they would get annoyed, then angry, then hysterical about the offending view or odor. It was the same story.

The new neighbor might try being perfunctorily pleasant the first time, "Uh, excuse me, but the odor from your pigs are really making it impossible for me to enjoy my dinner. Could you do something about that please?"

When the farmer looked at them blankly, shook his head, and walked away, the newcomers might ratchet it up a bit with a letter to the health department. Usually, that didn't work either. All the new resident could do was wait for a demographic shift that would allow anti-junk ordinances to be passed by the city and county councils. In places like Moab, it didn't take long. Today, Grand County moves forward to implement new anti-junk ordinances, the antithesis of Carl's dream, by offering to pay for the removal instead of threatening fines. Even many of the old-timers, tired of fighting what feels like inevitable restrictions on their old lifestyle and seduced by exploding real estate prices, have figured out that junk-free yards get a better price. They know their days are numbered, so they might as well take the money and run.

Spanish Valley Drive was once a funky mishmash of trailers, homemade cabins, and rundown ranch-style leftovers from the uranium boom. Today they're giving way to high-density planned urban units, built out of cheap wood, polyfoam insulation, chicken wire, and stucco. The developers squeeze as many of them to the acre as the planning commission will allow and call them homes. Nobody knows their neighbors, everyone locks their doors, and burglar alarms are standard equipment. And if you need a spare tie rod end for a '73 Buick, don't count on anyone to help you out.

Some will argue that the explosive growth of small towns like Moab is inevitable. It's happening all over the rural West. To fight it is a hopeless waste of time and energy and ultimately will cause heartbreak and disillusionment. Yet, no small town has ever shown more courage and determination than Moab when it wanted to. Moab is the living proof that we citizens could have stopped what's happening to it now.

After Grand County passed a referendum to stop the toxic waste incinerator in 1988 and tossed out the rascally commissioners who had proposed it, its citizens found themselves facing yet another crisis. The lame-duck commissioners found a way to hold onto at least some of their power and a lot of funding as well. As lame ducks, Jimmie Walker, Dutch Zimmerman, and David Knutson created the Special Services Road District, appointed themselves to its board and one of them as its paid administrator, and then applied for federal mineral lease money to finance them. Because the law stated that the district must be autonomous of county government, they assumed that, once again, they were free to do as they pleased.

The road board planned to spend the money on one of the biggest pie-in-the-sky boondoggles this part of Utah has ever seen. In conjunction with their Vernal County neighbors to the north, the board proposed to build a seventy-five-mile highway from I-70, over the rugged and remote Book Cliffs, to Uintah County and us 40. They said they could build the road for $10 million, but everyone knew they were nuts—$100 million was a lot closer to a realistic estimate. The state constitution suggested that the mineral lease funds could be used for other needed county projects like the landfill and the hospital, but Walker, Zimmerman, and Knutson insisted the funds could only be used for roads. Two years later, another election put a majority of the county commission on the road board's side. The new county commissioners, working closely with the road board, announced that they were untouchable. The commissioners turned down all requests for interviews with the *Zephyr*, claiming that our interviews "confused the voters." One commissioner added ominously, "You can't even impeach us in this state. All you can do is shoot us!"

But that wasn't quite right. A friend of mine had been reading the Utah statutes, looking for ways to get rid of the commissioners without using a gun. He found something interesting, and his idea began to catch fire with other Moabites. In a subsequent *Zephyr* editorial, I wrote, "A possible solution lies within the Utah State Constitution. The law provides specific ways of restructuring local government to make it more responsive to the citizens it serves. And the citizens have the opportunity to decide which restructuring options suit their needs best. It is the best example I have seen of government *by* the people."

Incredibly, Moab and Grand County citizens did it again. In 1992, for the second time in four years, a petition drive was organized by a diverse group of county residents and enough signatures were obtained to put the issue to a vote. Did Grand County want to scrap its three-person county commission in favor of a seven-person council? After a difficult and rancorous campaign, the referendum won with 56 percent of the vote. Three months later, a special election was held to fill the new council seats. Every newly elected member, save one, voted to disband the road board and the Book Cliffs highway died quietly a few weeks later. Again, the citizens of Grand County showed the kind of grit that convinced many of us Moab wasn't an ordinary town.

But the euphoria didn't last. Even as the votes were being counted, more change was in the air. Taking on one big toxic incinerator company or three county commissioners was one thing, but trying to deal with steady but incremental speculative growth was something else. The tourist economy was on fire, and the unexpected side-effects—new businesses with absentee owners, the rash of new condo developments, a pork belly housing market—were difficult to get a handle on.

Again, as strange as it seemed to me, the environmental, social, and political impacts created by this upheaval went unnoticed by the Utah environmental community. What was happening here? It took me a while to understand.

Tourists in the Vortex

Sitting helplessly and innocently in the center of this ugly debate about the future of the rural West is the hapless tourist himself. Maligned and beloved, praised and condemned, urged to stay longer and encouraged to leave sooner, he stands at the Moab Information Center, bewildered, confused, and wanting the answer to the one pressing question that matters most, driven by the most painful of all agonies, the distended bladder and a place to relieve it.

Most tourists are oblivious to the uproar, divisiveness, and controversy their mere presence creates. It never occurs to them that, in fact, a tourist town is ultimately designed and constructed to appeal to *them*, not the residents who live there, those who work, raise children, and pay taxes. They roll into town, check into a motel, wander the streets in search of trinkets and T-shirts. They schedule a river trip on the Colorado for the following day or a drive to Arches and Canyonlands. Then they return in the evening for a hot meal and a beer or two, stumble back wearily to the motel, and rise early the next morning for the next long driving segment of their marathon two-week journey to do the West.

There was a time when tourists in Moab seldom thought to even venture off Main Street to see what lies beyond the shops and stores. For many, it was like a no man's land.

"What's back there, Daddy?"

"Nothing, honey. We don't want to go in there. People live there."

In Moab, of course, that indifference changed in the late 1980s when affluent out-of-town visitors discovered the incredible real estate bargains to be gobbled up for peanuts. Moab's subsequent ascendancy to Brave New West Yupstertown made real estate shopping as essential a part of the trip for some tourists as "doing the daily" float trip on the Colorado River.

It feels at times as if the world wants to move to Moab. In truth, though, the vast majority just want to get in and out as quickly as possible, with as little difficulty as possible, and with the hope that they'll see some lovely scenery and have experiences they can share later with their friends back home. Most Americans rarely take the time or find the opportunity to do anything memorable and unique. These days vacations are intended to convince the traveler that he still lives an interesting life, even if the experience he seeks is not at all spontaneous. Tourists seem to assume that since they're on vacation, they'll escape the cruel realities of the life they left back home. It never occurs to them that cruel reality lurks everywhere.

Because being a tourist is only a part-time job, he never has an opportunity to develop any real tourist skills. Practice really is everything. So, imagine millions of humans out there on the highway, total novices at the tourist game, and they've all chosen to leave their coping mechanisms at home. It's a recipe for chaos, for disaster.

It took a long time to reach the current frenzied state of tourism gone bonkers. For most of Moab's history, tourism was merely a sideline. From Ringhoffer's discovery of

Tower Arch in the early 1920s and the creation of Arches National Park in 1929 until a decade past the close of World War II, most rural Utahns regarded tourism as a tolerable way to make a few extra bucks. Though farming, ranching, and mining still dominated the local economy, there were a few notable exceptions. The *Times-Independent* editor, Bish Taylor, and longtime tourism booster J. W. "Doc" Williams were both fervent supporters of expansions at Arches National Park. As active members of the Moab Lion's Club, Taylor and Williams actively embraced subsequent promotions they both hoped would bring more tourism to this remote corner of America. But the Depression and World War II did little to create a tourist boom. In the early 1940s, most of the rangers enlisted and left their park assignments behind. The CCC crews that began construction on an Arches entrance road in 1940 left, too. Hardly anyone in America was sightseeing in the early 1940s. With war's end and a booming peacetime economy, however, change came rapidly—too rapidly for some.

New Mexico native Bates Wilson came to Arches in 1949 and stayed until his retirement in 1972. He saw visitation at Arches grow from just a few thousand when he arrived to almost a quarter million when he left to take up ranching in Professor Valley. Wilson's tireless campaigning led to the creation of Canyonlands as a new national park. His expansive personality was destined to make him a legend in his own time.

When we weigh the polarization that exists between special interest groups now, it's difficult to imagine one man managing to bridge the animosities that existed fifty years ago, but nobody didn't like Bates Wilson. He repeatedly found common ground, simply because he chose it for himself. He never thought too highly of himself, despite the way he introduced himself to strangers, "I'm so glad you got to meet me." Wilson didn't think much of hierarchy, and he was known to show up unannounced at a work site simply to get familiar with new rangers and maintenance men alike. If a trail crew was doing maintenance, he'd grab a shovel and help out, and he'd often reward the crew later with one of his famous Dutch oven dinners.

Wilson was as tolerant a man as any of us could hope to find or try to be, but he did not suffer fools gladly. His exasperation with graffiti scribblers made its way into the old monthly reports in May 1956, when he wrote, "The increasing desire by fools to carve their names in public places has reached the highest level possible in Arches at Delicate Arch." Later, graffiti vandalism got worse.

Another entry in the monthly reports conceals the frustration and grief with green, inexperienced tourists that Wilson must have felt, particularly in this case. In June 1959 Leroy Black, a sixty-seven year old from Bethlehem, Pennsylvania, was hiking at Natural Bridges National Monument, 100 miles south of Moab, and failed to return to his car. Wilson organized a search and determined that Black had missed the trail to Kachina Bridge. Black had instead continued downstream through White Canyon. He hiked fourteen miles and for three days before search parties caught up with him. It was June, so water was plentiful in potholes and the stream itself, but apparently Black was concerned with issues of water quality and would not drink from it. His dog meanwhile was having a grand time and probably failed to miss an opportunity for a swim and a drink. When Wilson found Leroy Black he was suffering from severe dehydration.

Wilson reported, "He was found on June 28 at 3:00 p.m. still alive, but in very poor condition. As there was not sufficient time to remove him from the canyon, he was made as comfortable as possible in a sleeping bag and fed small quantities of water and broth. By 10:30 p.m. he appeared to be much stronger, but around midnight he died." Most tourist fatalities are particularly difficult to accept because they're often so senseless and easily avoided.

Bates Wilson played an integral role in the creation of Canyonlands National Park. He was once on a reconnoitering trip, one of his celebrated horse pack trips into the Great

Red Unknown with Secretary of the Interior Stuart Udall. Bates hoped to persuade Udall that the magnificent Canyonlands needed federal protection. If anybody could convince Udall, it was Bates Wilson. Joining them was another park service administrator, Bill Briggle, and one of Bates's dearest friends, Arches heavy equipment operator Dutch Gerhardt. Gerhardt wasn't schooled to be a diplomat. He was a man who said what was on his mind, clearly, succinctly, and bluntly, qualities that Wilson admired. It was the reason they were such good pals. But not all park service managers appreciated candor, and Briggle was one of them.

They had been riding all day, and as the sun dipped below the canyon rim, the group decided to make camp. As Wilson unsaddled his horse, he turned to his old friend and said, "Gather up some firewood, Dutch. I'm going to be needing it pretty soon for supper."

Gerhardt squinted at Bates for a moment with icy disdain and said, "Go to hell, Bates. I'm off the clock now. Go get your own goddamned wood."

Briggle sprang to his feet, bristling with officious indignation, stepped between the horses, and practically bumped noses with Gerhardt. Gerhardt didn't move. With a man just six inches away and breathing heavily, you'd think Gerhardt didn't even see him. He looked bored.

"Mr. Gerhardt!" Briggle sputtered. "Mr. Wilson is the superintendent of this park, and he is your supervisor. When Mr. Wilson tells you to do something, you don't question his instructions, you don't ignore them, and you certainly don't act like this! You *do* it! Do I make myself clear?"

Briggle's face was the color of a crimson sunset. The veins bulged at his neck and temple.

Gerhardt looked deeply into his eyes. "Fuck you, Briggle," he said. He turned to his supervisor, "Fuck you, Bates." And then he turned to the secretary of the interior of the United States of America and said, "And fuck you, too, Udall, and the mules you rode in on."

Gerhardt spit softly on the ground, gave Bates a wink, and lumbered off to take a nap. Some say that Briggle was never the same man again. But a year later, Udall announced his unconditional support for the creation of Canyonlands National Park. Congress approved the legislation in 1964.

███████ ███████ ███████ Forty years later, many of us aren't sure if the park creation was such a good idea after all, but in those days, park status seemed to be the only and best way to protect the land. In order to sell the idea of a park to local politicians and the citizens they represented, the National Park Service promised much more in the way of new roads and developments than anyone should ever have committed to. It left a bad taste in rural Utahns' mouths for many years.

But road building did come to the parks, even if the scale wasn't as grand as some had hoped for. The old Arches entrance road near Seven Mile Canyon was abandoned in the late 1950s, when a new paved highway was completed. By 1963 more than twenty-three miles of pavement were laid, and at one end of the park workers put the finishing touches on a visitor center. At the far end of the road, the Devils Garden campground opened. It was part of a federal spending program called Mission 66. The idea was to upgrade the parks to provide for the ever-increasing numbers of tourists. But what the National Park Service did, by building thousands of miles of new park roads nationwide, was to provide far easier access to them. As a result, tourists came to the parks in numbers that exceeded anything they ever dreamed possible. The park service has been playing catch up ever since.

Abbey was there, of course, to disapprove of everything he saw. He wrote in his journal, "The tourists drift in and out of here like turds floating through a sewer. The simile could be extended in several directions. And I? I am a watcher of turds."

He lived in a trailer near Balanced Rock for two seasons. I was one of the last people to see Abbey's trailer intact before it was taken from the old park service boneyard and sold to the Mesa County Road Department in Grand Junction, Colorado, for salvage. It was later junked for the axles. Before they hauled it away, I stole the "#1" sign from his front door. Today, I could sell it on eBay and retire. Ed and I had revisited his trailer site years before and discovered that the old septic tank cover was still there along with some of the leach field lines. We contemplated taking the pipes, cutting them into three-inch sections, and mounting them on cheap wooden plaques with the message, "Edward Abbey's Shit Passed Through This Pipe." Abbey would autograph and authenticate it, I'd handle the marketing, and we'd both be rich. Somehow we never got around to it, but there was money to be made.

Of course, making money is what tourism is all about, but it's more complicated than that. Embracing a tourist economy means being willing to tolerate, accommodate, even grovel to the most insipid, helpless human specimens ever to point at a map and say, "Where are we?" Bless their pointy little heads.

Years ago, I met a woman from New York at Moab's old Westerner Grill. She looked fatigued, worn out, defeated.

I asked her what was wrong, and she replied, "You people around here really hate tourists, don't you?"

"What?" I exclaimed. "Certainly not! Tourists are the life blood of the community," I schmoozed.

"Well then, explain this. First they got mad at me out at that Arches Park because I told them they should really provide toiletry kits to visitors using the rest rooms. Then, at the post office, I suggested that tourists should be able to go ahead of other people because we're in more of a hurry. And, finally, at the gas station, I'd meant to buy the unleaded regular but put the supreme in my car instead. When I asked them to pump the expensive gas out and replace it with what I wanted in the first place, the man just stood there and stared at me. I mean, what was *his* problem?"

I just stood there and stared at her.

"Well, say something, young man."

"You're right. You are absolutely right. We do hate you. You'll be lucky if you get out of town alive. In fact, I have a good mind to throttle you myself."

She fled for the door and was never seen again.

This little story illustrates that, while tourists fear being bitten by rattlesnakes and scorpions, tourist towns have a bite all their own. And there's no bite like a Moabite's. It's a defense mechanism, for we must strike or be struck. The residents of tourist towns, "locals" we like to call ourselves, feel as if our towns are *occupied* by people who don't live here. As the occupied, our resentment doesn't come from any seriously imposed oppression by our brightly dressed invaders. No, instead, our resentment comes from a long-held attitude by locals, a bias if you will, that most tourists are genetically and environmentally inferior. It's shameful and unfair, it's bigotry at its worst.

Having been a tourist myself in places where *I* felt like a floundering fish out of water, I realize that tourists simply need a helping hand. A recent trip of my own to New York City reminded me just how stupid I could be when away from my native stomping ground. To be sure, we all need some guidance occasionally, and tourists are no different.

So a few years ago, I tried to reach out to the tourists and offer a few subtle hints that might keep visitors from making total fools of themselves. I wanted to help. I wanted to impress upon my tourist cousins that, in order to survive, they must not only learn how to deal with Mother Nature, but how to deal with *us* as well. I prepared a survival guide of sorts for tourists, which I published in the *Zephyr*.

After years of first-hand analysis, I thought I'd found the key. I realized that the difficulties tourists encounter are often related to the methods they've chosen to convey themselves. What I mean is, the ways a tourist can incur the wrath of a local when driving a thirty-eight-foot motor home are very different from the ways that riding a bicycle can annoy us, for instance. Consider some possibilities.

The Mega Motor Home

Mocking the Winnebago is almost a cliché now, but clichés are wrapped in truth. Tourists who travel in large mechanical monsters have public opinion working against them at the outset, because size *does* matter. Some locals despise motor homes.

Many of the wheeled palaces I've seen are bigger and certainly more ostentatious than the modest homes we common folk live in all the time. I recently saw a diesel-powered, deluxe forty-five-foot motor home that I learned had a sticker price of $300,000. The opulent owners towed a Mercedes-Benz SUV behind it. It made me nostalgic for a vintage Airstream trailer.

So, to you wealthy weasels in mechanical, high-tech mansions, all I can advise is that you not make things any worse than they already are. If you can, try not to draw attention to yourselves. When you pull into a crowded grocery parking lot, don't park your rig diagonally across eight or nine parking spaces, forcing the rest of us to park at the back of the lot. *You* park at the back of the lot. The walk will do you good.

If you're in a national park campground, don't fire up your Briggs & Stratton generator and ask the ranger to help align your satellite dish. Rangers are now heavily armed. Many of them are extremely unstable and on medication or are very bored with their jobs and on medication. The two conditions are interchangeable.

Do not twist off and get crazy just because a campground doesn't have a dumping station. Never aim your raw sewage hose at the ranger. It won't change the situation, and he has a limited clothing allowance.

Do not activate the loudspeaker system on your motor home and broadcast, from one end of town to the other, Lawrence Welk's greatest hits.

If you and your wife are the proud owners of a large RV, and you, like many other large recreational vehicle owners, prefer to wear matching royal blue Mickey and Minnie Mouse jump suits when traveling, and you want to take a drive into the La Sal Mountains in the autumn to look at the colors, *don't* do it. Hunters in the area may see the flash of royal blue, mistake you for Lycra-clad mountain bikers, and shoot you with high-powered rifles. Play it safe. Show off your outfits in the relative safety of a KOA.

Finally, be humble.

Europeans Who Tour America in 1975 Ford Station Wagons

For some reason, many European visitors have recently taken to buying beat-up old station wagons when they arrive in New York or Los Angeles and use them to tour the country or until they blow up. But the station wagon is how I've learned to spot our European friends. In any case, the foreign tourist offers a completely different set of challenges to the intolerant local. If you are from a foreign land and you are concerned about international relations, here is what you can do to improve them.

If you are at the grocery store and you're ready to pay for your goods, remember, you have to go to the back of the line. It's a silly custom we have here, but you can't go to the front of the line when there are already people *in* the line. If you violate this custom, it's called "butting in line," and Americans despise a line-butter.

If someone points out your error to you and suggests you do something about it, like move to the back, don't excuse yourself by saying, "It is alright, vee are German." Don't do that. As the former assistant superintendent of Canyonlands National Park and one of my early heroes, Tom Hartman, once said, "We whupped you twice, and we'll whup you again."

Der Kampingplatz ist voll! Ubernachten ist verboten! That's all the German I know; it means, "The campground is full! To stay overnight is forbidden!"

If you are a guy and you intend to mingle with other people in public places, put some clothes on, please. Most of you gentlemen don't have the physique for it anyway. You look ridiculous walking around town with nothing on but a Speedo, a gold chain, a scrubby goatee, and a cowboy hat. Most of you don't even have a tan. Have a heart.

Thank you, and be humble.

The Yupster/Boomer Couple with the Obnoxious Kids in the Back of a BMW

Well, you waited to have kids until you were financially secure. First came the Beemer, then Beavis and Butthead. Now you want to show them the American West, recreating the great trip you remember taking with *your* parents almost thirty years ago.

But you spoiled the little buggers rotten, and now they rarely look up from their Gameboys and PlayStations to check out the scenery. When they do, they articulate the experience as best they can, "This sucks."

Sure, you'd like to kill them. So would we. Even if you think it's the best thing for yourselves, for us, and the future of civilization, you cannot take them down to our world famous Colorado River, put them in a pillowcase, and throw them in the water, the way some Moabites have been disposing of their excess cats for decades. Well, you *could*, but as Richard Nixon once said, "It would be wrong." Besides, you parents spoiled the little greedy monsters in the first place. If anyone should "do the daily" in a pillowcase, it's you.

I am not a parent, but you all must surely agree with me that some of these kids need to be conscripted into military service. If you've brought the kids on vacation, take away their electronic games. Remove from their clutches the personal cell phones. Make them get out of the car and look around. But don't turn them loose on our streets, because we have enough of a gang problem already.

At night, when you've gone down to McStiff's for a wheat ale, don't leave them in the motel room to watch cable television. Get them a copy of *Desert Solitaire* and tell them if they don't read it, you'll bring them over to my house and I'll read *to* them. In fact, I'll read the complete works of Edward Abbey over and over and over until they get it.

Teach your children (and yourselves) humility.

"Our Economic Salvation," the Mountain Biker

If you're a mountain biker, do not tell us you're Moab's economic salvation. You may get a response from some locals like, "Salvation *this*, you bubble-headed Spandex freak!" Some of the old uranium miners carry grudges for many years.

Please keep in mind that, although Moab has been designated the "Mountain Bike Capital of the World," probably less than 20 percent of Grand County's population actually ride a bicycle. Some of us still ride pickup trucks, dip snuff, and spit out the window. A few of our elected officials still think wilderness is a commie trick.

Yet, on any given day in our town half the men seen on the street are wearing brightly colored tights. If you ever feel the desire to blend in, slip a pair of Levis over your Lycra, complain about all those damn espresso shops, and say ugly things about Hillary Clinton or something. The old locals will embrace you and invite you home for supper.

Here's another tip: When you're sitting around the campfire on a Friday night up on the Sand Flats and some of our local boys drive by in their pickups and shout thoughtless epithets at you, don't respond by giving them the finger or mooning them. If you perform such gestures, you need to remember we have some teenage boys in this county who are almost as stupid as you are, and life is cheap out here in the wooly West. The things they'd like to do to your titanium frame bikes defy description.

Like our Speedo-clad European friends, don't wear Lycra if you don't have the body for it. This is true for men and women alike, although men are by far the greater offenders, especially when they have no butt. Have you ever seen a guy with no ass wearing Lycra, with his drawers all droopy in the back? Yes, I am a heterosexual male, and I try not to notice, but it's like police photos of a bad car wreck—you're disgusted, but your morbid curiosity gets the better of you. If you are a buttock-free person, try overalls.

Finally, don't tell us you saved our economy. Be humble.

Miscellaneous Tips

Try to avoid asking stupid questions. Actually, there's one question you should always ask *yourself* before you pose another one to someone else, "Can I figure this out on my own?"

For example, before you ask for directions to the bathroom at the Arches Visitor Center, did you actually make an attempt to look yourself? Did you rotate your head from side to side and look for the international symbols? If you didn't and asked the ranger anyway and she glared coldly, you have no one to blame but yourself.

Have you ever asked, "What time does the wind stop?" There is not a meteorological table that provides that kind of information. It's not like the sunrise and sunset or the tides, Okay?

Unless you want to die an early and painful death, don't ask Pat at the post office if she's posted tomorrow's mail yet. It's doubtful if she'll post tomorrow's mail today. She'll probably post it *tomorrow*. Get it?

Here's another one: Don't go into a Moab restaurant, take over a table or two, and then tell the waitress you don't want to order anything because you brought your own food and merely came inside to get out of the weather. "You know, we're having our picnic inside. It's not *our* fault. No one would tell us when the wind would stop."

Be Humble

This is the key to everything. If I have sounded harsh or somewhat intolerant of tourists, you've misunderstood my intentions. I know how dopey tourists can be because I become a dopey tourist every time I leave home. I've humiliated myself from one end of this country to the other and beyond, in ways I didn't think were possible. I'm only now beginning to appreciate the true value of groveling. Practical experience has taught me that humility is a beautiful thing, and it takes the sting out of stupidity. Humans will forgive damn near anybody for being stupid, if they'll just admit it. It's *arrogant* stupid people, the deadliest combination of all, that make my blood boil.

So the next time you invoke the ire of a Moabite simply because you were confused or just because you've put your brain on hold during summer vacation, do what I did when my own confusion angered a cab driver in New York City. He was about to toss me out the door, when I said, "Look I'm screwed. I'm an idiot. I'm from *Utah!*" His mood changed, his eyes almost glowed with compassion, and he never uttered another harsh word.

With a few modifications, you can save your butt, too. That is, if you have one.

The Greening of Wilderne$$

I was just a kid when I first heard the word *wilderness*. Being a good Methodist in those days, it came to me in its purest religious sense. While I have a knack for recalling trivia, I must admit my Biblical knowledge fails me on most counts. Still, stories of Moses leading his people into the Wilderness or Jesus spending forty days in the Wilderness, being tempted by the Devil himself, sounded intriguing and mysterious, even to a five year old.

Just a year or so later, when we moved from our downtown apartment to one of the first suburbs of Louisville, Kentucky, I thought I'd found my own wilderness right in my backyard. Glen Mead Road poked a solitary asphalt finger into what had been farmland for almost 200 years. Of course, the country had already been drastically altered by early white settlers in the late eighteenth century. Kentucky was once dense with ancient

Jim Stiles
©1987

hardwood forests, and between these magnificent trees endless canebrakes stretched for miles in all directions.

By the time we moved to Glen Mead, the virgin forests were all but gone, but their descendants were still strong and tall, sporting diameters of four feet or more. Cane-brakes still clung to the edges of the forests and made perfect thickets through which to cut trails from one hideout to the next. Behind our house, a wheat field yawned across an eternity of space, bright and golden in the summer sun. Beyond the field, beyond the reach of any five year old lay a forest as dark and impenetrable as any fortress nature could construct. We called it "The Woods."

No matter how old I live to be, no matter where I may travel on this planet, there will never be a place so full of mystery, excitement, and adventure as The Woods was to my friends and me. The stories and legends that grew out of those trees still rekindle power-ful feelings, even after all these years.

We knew the place was haunted. An old cemetery, consumed by grape vines and poi-son ivy, was a perfect breeding ground for spirits. My friends and I were sure that a rem-nant population of bears still resided deep within the forest. Never-before-seen bottom-less swamps teemed with slime, dead bodies, and poisonous snakes. Most frightening and exciting of all, reports of a hobo camp in The Woods, led by the notorious Big Lips Louie, sent chills up and down our spines when we discussed the possibility of running into them.

This was wilderness. It had no designated boundaries, and in our minds it went on forever. Wilderness was more than the sum of its parts. It was unexplainable. It was a mystery.

▬▬▬ ▬▬ ▬▬ It troubles me that the word *wilderness* has come to repre-sent a political and bureaucratic designation, that it rolls off the tongue of some like a four-letter word, that it has become an angrily chanted battle cry for those who support wilderness. Perhaps the greatest insult is when it becomes a legalistic game, a maneuver. Show me the passion and the mystery in an injunction.

Wilderness was supposed to inspire us. But somewhere we lost the poetry, or at least we misplaced it. Wilderness wasn't originally intended to create such contentiousness. More than boundary lines on a topographic map, wilderness is a state of mind, a feeling, an emotion. Wilderness is *any* place where we find silence and solitude or adventure and surprise.

As I drift back to my days as a kid and my journeys into The Woods, I realize I can still find that same mystical connection to the land when I'm picking through the ruins of an old mining cabin in the Yellow Cat, north of Arches. I look up through the darkness to the exposed rotting rafters and find myself eyeball to eyeball with a great horned owl who never blinks, outstares me, and backs me out the door with his fierce glare. Isn't that a wilderness experience? When I'm walking down the wash-board road between the Bears Ears and suddenly the oak brush in front of me rustles. A form begins to emerge from the leaves, and I'm stunned to see a beautiful, sleek mountain lion, whose muscles ripple in the sunlight as she walks silently in front of me. She stares deeply at me for just a moment, and then vanishes into the ravine below. Isn't that a wilderness experience? When I sit down to watch the sunset from the summit of Tillie's Nipple, Windy Point, Nasty Flat, UFO Hill, or a thousand other quiet forgotten places, and I sit there for hours and all I hear is the wind, the swallows, and the humming of my own brain, isn't that wilderness?

Wilderness is anywhere we find things wild and free and solitude that is long and unbroken. All these places deserve our respect, our reverence, and our concern, or they will not survive. Not all the places I've mentioned (most of the names I invented) are considered "wilderness" by anyone. They don't meet the official criteria. But I worry that congressionally designated wilderness will somehow suggest to the world that the remainder of the land is unworthy of any respect at all.

All land is sacred. We need to remember that, especially as the beauty of the land itself becomes the product that fuels the every-growing and powerful tourism industry. It's not enough to be a recreationist. People come here to play, but this is not a playground. The day we treat *all* of these lands with the reverence they deserve is the day we won't need wilderness designation at all.

Unfortunately, that time has not arrived. In fact, not that long ago, none of this rancor and debate existed because none of the land in question was wanted by anyone. Barely a century ago, the *Deseret News* of Salt Lake City described the lands of southeastern Utah as "one vast 'contiguity of waste' and measurably valueless, excepting for nomadic purposes, hunting grounds for Indians, and to hold the world together."

Ranchers in the nineteenth century discovered the tall grasses in the La Sal Mountains and ran their herds there and on the tablelands and deserts below. By the early twentieth century, they'd left much of the rangeland burnt to a cinder. But ranchers and later uranium miners would have laughed (or shot) an environmentalist right out of the country. Land was to be used, not looked at, and certainly not preserved. Land could only be appreciated if it could be assigned a dollar value.

Wilderness possessed intangible values that transcended all that, or at least it was supposed to. That is why we needed wilderness designation and why the Wilderness Act was passed by Congress in 1964. Then and now, we need it for the right reasons, for *all* the right reasons. In the twenty-first century, those reasons are more complicated than even the most dedicated professional environmentalists are often willing to consider.

███ ███ ███ Twenty years ago, nothing in the red desert of southeastern Utah seemed as ugly or intrusive to me as a seismic truck and a goddamn cow. During my seasonal ranger days at Arches National Park, I watched helplessly and grumbled as monstrous seismic vehicles, loaded with tons of high-tech equipment, crept ponderously but surely across the valleys and mesas adjacent to the park boundary looking for oil and gas. My partner-in-crime, known only in these pages as "The Salamander," and I once crawled on hands and knees in full National Park Service uniform to pull a half-mile of seismic survey stakes that came closer to the park boundary than we deemed reasonable and proper. It was our duty. But the seismic crews replaced the stakes and the ribbons and eventually crushed everything in their path. The result decades later, there and elsewhere, is a patchwork of intersecting roads that begin nowhere and end nowhere. Future civilizations may wonder just what in the hell we were doing. Perhaps they'll think they were alien landing strips. Or perhaps Erich Von Däniken was wrong about mysteries like the Nazca Plain of Peru—all those confusing lines were simply the handiwork of Inca seismic trucks during the planet's last industrial incarnation.

Cows wandered frequently into Arches. They fouled the water in Courthouse Wash. For reasons I could never explain, cows faithfully and regularly made their way up the park road (always on the right side) to Balanced Rock, where they seemed to congregate near the viewpoint until local rancher Don Holyoak came up with his truck and removed them. It was the park's responsibility to fence the cows out, but never-ending budget constraints made that task nearly impossible. So, for years, the cattle shuffled in and shuffled out. I grew to loathe them.

Environmentalists in southeastern Utah, as elsewhere in the Intermountain West, viewed the battle to save its dwindling wilderness lands in very black-and-white terms—and with good reason. Twenty years ago, the rural West was still a vast, mostly unpopulated expanse of deserts, mountains, and prairies. The region was dotted with tiny communities that had changed little in a century, that depended mostly on the extractive industries for survival, and that might, at best, get a small boost from tourism during the summer. Even in tourist vortexes like Jackson, Wyoming, gateway to the Grand Teton and Yellowstone National Parks, the tourist season barely lasted three months. They called the long off-season in Jackson the "cocktail hour." It was that quiet.

Tourists, of course, could be a terrible annoyance, but their impacts were temporary and their visits were limited. Although their numbers seemed overwhelming at the time, they had the decency to leave. Even in desert recreation meccas like Moab, the crowds had thinned to a trickle by October, and the canyon country had time to recover. The lands didn't need management for tourist impacts, they simply needed to be left alone.

So, environmentalists devoted their time, energy, and resources to fight the threats to wildlands they thought were most persistent and enduring—mining, timber, and cattle. In partnership with big business, the Reagan administration's Secretary of the Interior James Watt came to represent everything environmentalists feared from a government that saw land as simply a commodity to exploit for its natural resources. We protested the accelerated energy exploration programs of the 1980s, the extensive chaining of thousands of acres of pinyon-juniper forests to expand rangelands for ranchers, the destruction of forest lands in the mountains that saw the construction of new roads and the loss of wildlife habitat. We thought that if these lands could be spared further degradation by these huge industries, the West would simply be left alone. Our assumptions were tragically wrong.

In the late 1980s, the conflict between the rural and urban West came more clearly into focus. Here in Utah, SUWA changed its strategy and began to abandon its local emphasis. Wilderness, SUWA argued, was not a local issue. The BLM wilderness lands in Utah were owned by all Americans, and consequently all Americans deserved a greater voice in determining how those lands should be used. SUWA's membership skyrocketed, jumping from 2000 in 1985 to 20,000 by the mid-1990s. SUWA argued that New Yorkers, Californians, and Floridians had just as much of a stake in the future of Utah wilderness as a fourth-generation rancher in Escalante. Never before had the argument been so polarized. But it would get so much worse.

In the 1980s, the idea of wilderness needed no justification for most of us—it was simply the right thing to do. We believed that there should be places on this planet spared from the Hand of Man. Wilderness should be saved for the rocks, the trees, and the animals that inhabited those lands. If wilderness offered a recreational benefit, an economic advantage, or even spiritual enrichment, those opportunities were secondary achievements. Beyond the legal designation of wilderness areas, environmentalists strove to raise the level of sensitivity to all lands.

Rural Westerners recoiled at the idea of wilderness designation, as nonmotorized recreational tourism increased and small Western towns felt the economic impact. Wilderness proposals were met with anger and fear. If large tracts of land were shut down to any mechanized vehicle, as the Wilderness Act mandated, they believed the collapse of the rural West was inevitable. Although the economics of the West was always a primary concern, there was more to it than just the shutdown of public lands to extractive industries like oil and gas. Rural Westerners feared the loss of a lifestyle that not many urban Americans can understand, much less appreciate. The rural Westerners may not have appreciated the dynamics of cryptobiotic soil communities or the sexual habits of a blackfooted ferret, but they understood another component of wilderness far better than most members of the Sierra Club. Rural Westerners understood solitude.

City dwellers cannot fathom the isolation and remoteness of most rural Western towns or comprehend just what the people who reside in these communities *do*. For the better part of a century, rural Westerners basked in the emptiness and solitude of the American West and loved it. The onslaught of forces dedicated to saving the very places they had assumed would always remain empty and mostly untouched seemed impossible. By 1990 the rhetoric had been ramped up on both sides. "They want to lock it up for the elite few!" was the battle cry of most rural Utahns at the turn of the decade. That spring, anti-wilderness advocates publicly presented a study paid for by the Utah Association of Counties, which attempted to prove that wilderness designation would have dire effects on the state's rural economy. The study's author, Dr. George Leaming, concluded in his report that designating 5.1 million acres of BLM lands as wilderness in Utah would cost its citizens $13.2 billion over the next twenty-five years. His assumptions were extraordinary. Leaming's estimates were based on the notion that without wilderness, 80 percent of all speculative minerals would be recovered and sold by 2015, and that with wilderness designation, *all* grazing, mining, and recreational visitations would cease completely.

The Leaming Report was easy to dismiss, and other studies clearly showed that the numbers were extravagant. Three years earlier, Republican Governor Norm Bangerter created the Resource Development Coordinating Committee to consider the impacts of wilderness, and the committee could find no sign of economic disaster waiting in the wings. Their report noted, "It is unlikely that exploration or development would occur in most wilderness study areas even without wilderness designation."

But wilderness proponents were compelled to take the argument a step further. Supporting wilderness offered certain economic advantages that environmentalists believed should not be overlooked. They pointed to a 1987 study by the University of Idaho that compared economic growth in rural Western counties that contain federal wilderness versus the growth of counties without such lands. The study concluded, "Counties which contain or are adjacent to federally designated wilderness are among the fastest growing in the United States."

As Lance Christie wrote in a 1991 *Zephyr* article titled, "Wilderness Economics: Boom and Bust Baloney," on behalf of the Utah Chapter of the Sierra Club, "Studies done on the economic impacts of wilderness on local economies consistently support the idea that designated wilderness in an area acts like an advertisement that says: 'Here is a treasure house of environmental amenities! And, they'll be here tomorrow because some treasure hunter with a bulldozer can't come and tear them up.' This advertising attracts people economists call 'amenity migrants,' causing twice the economic growth in rural areas with designated wilderness than in areas without wilderness." Christie concluded, "The migrants responsible for this growth are younger and highly educated and move in to enjoy environmental amenities rather than because of economic opportunities. . . . Once there, these energetic and educated people develop their own economic opportunities."

SUWA weighed in on the issue. It asked the question, "What is the economic impact of wilderness designation?" SUWA had a ready answer, "Rural Utah counties that have booming economies, such as Grand and Washington, are growing because the public land, open space, and scenery provide the setting for a healthy tourist industry with an influx of people who want to live in such a spectacular setting. The future of Utah's economy lies in preservation of its wildlands and quality of life, as opposed to promotion of an economy based on the extractive industries."

The economic message from almost all environmental groups was bewildering and a bit duplicitous. While environmentalists suggested that the economics of wilderness would benefit rural Utah, their wilderness economics strategy would never augment or benefit the rural citizens who already lived there. Ranchers and oil-field workers didn't have the money, skills, or inclination to invest in tourist-based businesses. What was being proposed and embraced by the environmental community was a new economy that would simply destroy the old lifestyle of the rural West and replace it with a new one. Where would the rural Westerners go? Perhaps they could get jobs at McDonald's or the Motel 6. Environmentalists were vague on the fine points.

And what of these "booming economies" in places like Moab? Did the explosive growth in the numbers of "amenity migrants" carry its own environmental risks? By the early 1990s, places like Moab had indeed exploded. Visitation in nearby national parks had doubled in five years, and the adjacent BLM lands were hardest hit. Visitor use jumped from about 130,000 in 1985 to over 1 million in a little more than a decade. Many of us environmentalists kept waiting for the same kind of resistance from our side that had met ranchers and seismic trucks, but the professional environmental community said little of these new kinds of staggering impacts and the exploitation that brought them.

But Lily Mae Noorlander said something. Mrs. Noorlander grew up in Moab and lived through good times and bad. She reveled in the quiet days when Moab was a sleepy orchard town. She watched Moab come alive in the 1950s, only to see it go bust in the 1960s. She had seen it all. But Lily Mae had never seen anything like this. To her, recreational exploitation was the mother of all obscenities. In a letter to the *Deseret News* in 1994, Mrs. Noorlander wrote:

> Long-forgotten ranches, abandoned decades ago, are now front page fare in the full-color marketing pieces of this lucrative industry. . . . Some of the direct consequences of their promotional activities, aside from generating profit from calendars, hiking exposés and membership dues include: more foot trails, bike trails, garbage, human waste, instructional signs, regulations, law enforcement patrols, costs to local government for crowd control, and a general loss of peace and serenity to the plaid clad, waffle stomper crowd. . . . The spirit of wilderness, has already been stolen by those who profess to be its savior, but who have, in fact, trampled the life out of its essential serenity and solitude in an orgy of self-indulgence.

A few months later, as if to confirm Mrs. Noorlander's greatest fears and suspicions, a letter titled "There's Money in Wilderness" was published in the *Salt Lake Tribune*. The author was Randall Tolpinrud, president of Groupwest Properties Corporation in Salt Lake City.

> As a real-estate developer and homebuilder in Utah, I have a very strong interest in maintaining the long-term economic foundation of this region. . . . Because of this conviction, I am concerned over the wilderness proposal suggested by our congressional delegation.
> I support the Utah Wilderness Coalition's proposal for 5.7 million acres [in 2006 the proposal is over 9 million acres] of wilderness primarily because of the long-term economic potential which wilderness designation will provide this state.

The West is changing dramatically. Lands from Montana to New Mexico are rapidly being developed by people like myself in response to growing migration and population. . . . We must look years and decades ahead. Wilderness designation will grow to represent a powerful economic opportunity as the West's open spaces shrivel from development. Utah, with its unique beauty and abundant national parks, could be positioned to reap significant economic rewards from masses of people seeking solitude in a wilderness experience from their fast-paced lives.

It was an extraordinary letter. In effect, Tolpinrud was saying, "Look, people like me are going to develop most of the West's open space. If you can save what we developers *can't* get our hands on, we can make money from *that* as well." There was something contradictory about his image of "masses of people seeking solitude in wilderness." How long would it take and how large would the masses have to become before the purity of those wildlands was so degraded they could no longer be called wilderness?

I expected some sort of response from at least one of Utah's environmental organizations, but there was none forthcoming. In their quest to run up their membership rolls, especially as the cost of lobbying Congress grew increasingly expensive, groups like SUWA were hard-pressed to refuse the support of anyone, no matter how tainted their reasons for supporting wilderness. What mattered was money—and lots of it. It wasn't a matter of environmentalists gone greedy or corrupt. They simply saw no other way to push their wilderness agenda than to play the high-dollar game. But the danger was in becoming just like the other guys.

Meanwhile, the impacts from millions of those well-meaning amenity clients became more obvious with each passing season. As far as thirty and forty miles from Moab, resource damage from hundreds of thousands of bicyclists was clearly changing the landscape of Grand County. And it wasn't just the bikes, it was the vehicles that brought the bikes and bikers. It became a bit embarrassing to praise the nonpolluting aspects of non-motorized recreation when most bikers drive their suvs hundreds of miles so they can pedal for ten.

There were cultural and social impacts as well. In Moab and Grand County, the housing boom that began in the 1980s continued a decade later at full steam and with no sign of a pause. Much of the agricultural lands in the valley seemed to disappear overnight. The vast numbers of people coming to build in the canyon country posed a greater threat to the surrounding wildlands than anything else imaginable.

Habitat encroachment and a permanent human presence drive wildlife to the edge. How many times have we heard the same story? An affluent urban family wants to get closer to nature and builds a home in the midst of it. They're thrilled and excited to see the deer browse from their picture window, but when a coyote carries off the family poodle, attitudes change rapidly. Two years ago in California, a cougar attacked and killed two bicyclists pedaling through an area that had been too isolated to enter until recreational trails were built and the teeming masses from nearby Los Angeles sought refuge in it. The cougar was promptly shot by wildlife officers, and not one environmental group objected, proving that environmentalists will defend the rights of wild animals until they start eating their members.

Environmental organizations in Utah stayed silent about the impacts of the amenities industry. For example, suwa contributed regularly to each issue of the *Zephyr* for more than ten years. In that decade, suwa wrote tens of thousands of words about a variety of impacts affecting the canyon country. They wrote scores of articles about cattle, mining, oil and gas exploration, and atvs. But the stories devoted to nonmotorized impacts or the ever-growing amenities economy numbered just two. Either suwa refused to acknowledge or simply hadn't noticed that the rural West was changing in ways they themselves had predicted and perhaps even wanted.

Rural Westerners, alarmed at the sudden influx of urban immigrants, reacted angrily and fearfully. For better or worse, they had enjoyed carte blanche on public lands for a century. As one old cowboy said, "I could feel the saddle turning under me. Everything was changing."

There was an irony here. Many of the third- and fourth-generation ranch families who had lived in these small Western towns were the descendants of the original settlers, who had come west in the last half of the nineteenth century. They had played a decisive role in driving the buffalo to near extinction and had all but obliterated Native American culture. In 1876 white settlers could not find a single redeeming aspect of Native American life. As General Philip Sheridan once said, "We took away their country, broke up their mode of living, their habits of life, introduced disease and decay. And it was for this and against this that they make war. Could anyone expect less?" But Sheridan also said, "The only good Indians I saw were dead."

In the twenty-first century, the great-great-grandchildren of the white people who showed so little tolerance for a culture they didn't understand, and thus feared, face a certain kind of extinction themselves. Although this onslaught is certainly not as brutal as the "justice" their ancestors meted out against the Indians, in terms of maintaining a way of life, this influx of strangers is just as terminal.

Whether they somehow deserve to pay a price for the sins of their forefathers has nothing to do with their threatened existence. In fact, the reasons for their endangered status are not that different from the Native Americans' plight a century ago. Rural Westerners are simply in the way. They impede the march of progress. The Brave New West wants their land, just as their ancestors wanted the Indians' land.

Opportunities for reconciliation and resolution are just as rare now as then. Rural Westerners have responded passionately but often irrationally, and the New Westerners don't seem to be interested in a dialogue at all. Are Old Westerners getting so frustrated by the silence that they've become destructive? Or is it the irrational violence of Old Westerners that keeps New Westerners from sitting at the same table in the first place?

For instance, some off-road-vehicle fanatics with an anti-wilderness bent have gone so far as to deliberately enter proposed wilderness areas for the sole purpose of doing enough environmental damage to disqualify them as wilderness lands. We've all seen the destruction that unrestricted ATV use can cause in the fragile desert landscape. For many people, including a majority of ATV users, the wanton destruction is inexcusable. It creates stereotypes that only deepen the chasm between the two sides. Yet, responsible motorized recreationists refuse to criticize their destructive peers, lest they be accused of acting like their adversaries, the environmentalists.

Anti-wilderness forces have clung to the century-old federal law RS 2477, which allegedly gave the states legal right-of-ways across public lands. Using this law, Utah has claimed thousands of miles of access as a way of stopping wilderness designation. That battle is still being fought in the courts.

Environmentalists display their own stubborn streaks. Not only do they refuse to discuss the future of public lands with their opponents, they keep dramatically raising the stakes. In the early 1990s, "5.4, Keep It Wild" was the battle cry of the wilderness movement in Utah. It referred to the 5.4 million acres that enviros believed existed on BLM lands in the state. Utah politicians thought 1 million was about right. The bureau's studies came in at 3.2 million acres. In 1995 SUWA and the Utah Wilderness Coalition upped that number to 5.7 million, and it stayed there for a long time. The battle lines were drawn, and the wildlands of Utah were where the fight would be waged.

In 1999 the Utah Wilderness Coalition conducted a new citizens inventory. Hundreds of volunteers were sent out to examine these BLM lands close up. The numbers they came up with were stunning. Now they'd found 8.3 million acres. Then the number jumped to 8.8 million, then 9.1 million. Even I was puzzled by the increases. Environmentalists have been saying for two decades that wildlands in Utah were under perpetual assault and were shrinking daily at an alarming rate. How, then, could we have overlooked 4 million acres of wilderness that had apparently been there all along?

Roads are at the heart of any debate about wilderness. Roads, or actually the lack of them, is what defines wilderness. The Wilderness Act requires that wilderness be a roadless area no less than 5000 acres in size. Trying to determine when a route is a road has always been a subjective argument. Ultimately, it came down to usage. If a jeep track could be proven to carry fairly regular vehicular traffic, it was a road. If an old two-track left over from the uranium days was barely used at all, environmentalists thought they could include such a remnant in proposed wilderness. But a rereading of the Federal Land Protection Management Act a few years ago changed some preconceptions, and even many ardent environmentalists still don't realize it.

According to SUWA's Web site, "The word 'roadless' refers to the absence of roads that have been improved and maintained by mechanical means to insure relatively regular and continuous use. A way maintained solely by the passage of vehicles does not constitute a road. The key word in this definition is 'maintained.'" SUWA added, "We will sometimes exclude a vehicle route from our wilderness proposal if we feel it looks like a 'road' to a hypothetical typical American, or if it serves some important purpose . . . such as unmaintained 'two track' jeep roads that receive moderate to high recreational use."

If they mean what they say, then SUWA and other members of the Utah Wilderness Coalition believe they have the legal right to demand the closure of every jeep road in Utah, unless it receives heavy use and it was constructed in the first place, with a road base and culverts. There's no other way to read their interpretation of the law. In their minds, the fact that they don't actively seek such closures is a measure of their generosity.

Not long ago, dozens of Moab businesses attached their names to a full-page ad in the *Salt Lake Tribune*. Paid for by SUWA, the ad's aim was to call attention to the damage being caused to public lands by excessive and abusive ATV recreation. No one but the blind and the stupid can argue that the damage was not extraordinary. Bill Burke, a professional tour operator from Colorado and a long-time advocate of environmentally responsible four-wheeling, sent an angry email to his peers after the 2005 Moab Jeep Safari. "What I saw last week really sickened me," Burke wrote, "and makes me wonder why I continue to be aligned with this sport." Burke was "afraid that the actions of the uncaring, indolent, boorish imbeciles will drive the general public and land managing agencies to start pushing for road closures and more government interference."

While I was talking with a business owner who sponsors SUWA, he mentioned the angry emails he'd received from ATV enthusiasts and their boycott threats. "I just don't understand why these ATVers aren't content with the roads they already have. There's hundreds of old jeep roads left over from the uranium prospectors. How much more do they want?"

Even though he was a member of SUWA and had attached his business name to the SUWA advertisement, he was unaware of the alliance's relatively recent revelation on the definition of roads. Nor did he know that the acreage in the Utah Wilderness Coalition's wilderness proposal had nearly doubled since 1994. Like so many other environmentalists, he was oblivious to the facts.

If there was any room for dialogue between the two entrenched and warring factions, no one took advantage of it. Road crews from rural counties defiantly bladed and bulldozed some of the contested roads, as if to say, "You didn't think it was a road before? Well, it sure as hell is a road *now*." Jeepers and ATV users seemed to go out of their way to create even more damage. It reaffirmed in environmentalists' minds just how ignorant and insensitive rural Westerners could be when it came to protecting natural resources on public lands. Rural Westerners were even more convinced that environmentalists would use any ploy, run any legal maneuver to keep them from the land they'd used for a century. Old-timers tolerated bad behavior from their own side, if it meant maintaining a united front against enviros.

Meanwhile, environmentalists defended and even supported the economic exploitation of wilderness lands that were sure to eventually cause impacts of their own. They looked for legal loopholes to expand wilderness designation, convinced that legal restrictions were the only way to protect public lands.

Lost in the melee was wilderness itself.

Going to Extremes

It had been several years since I'd paid a visit to Cliff Arch, the haunting stone window Abbey discovered many years ago in an obscure part of the Fiery Furnace. In fact, it had been twenty-five years since my own discovery of the arch, and I decided a reunion was overdue.

The hike to Cliff Arch requires a scramble through a mazelike series of fins. After so many years away, I got confused for a moment, but I eventually found my way to the top of the spires and towers and walked south through a blackbrush meadow. Less than a quarter mile from my destination, I encountered footprints, many of them, emerging from the main part of the Fiery Furnace and moving in my intended direction.

"Not again," I thought.

I dropped into the dry wash that led to the arch, still following the tracks, and took my last steps toward what had been one of the best-kept secrets in Arches National Park.

I'd missed the crowd, but their detritus was still there, hanging from an old pinyon tree. Wrapped around the trunk was a climbing anchor, complete with webbing and carabiners, all of it attached to a rope that crept over the sandstone fin in front of the tree.

This was the canyon that had meant so much that years earlier Reuben Scolnik and I had refused to explore it. The canyon had been a mystery. Now it was a route.

I wondered who the rigging belonged to and considered removing it, but instead I reported my find to the park rangers. In the weeks that followed, I learned that the presence of the ropes and slings were far more ominous than anything I'd considered. This wasn't a one-time descent for a group of climbers. This was part of a commercial operation, a regular tour.

The climbing ropes belonged to a recent Moab arrival, Matt Moore, owner of Desert Highlights. Moore began his enterprise in 1997 and continues to operate daily tours at several locations in Arches National Park. His tours are all cross-country and off-trail, and they lead visitors into sections of Arches that, as recently as 1996, saw perhaps 100 visitors a year. Moore insists that his trips are not for adrenalin junkies, and he offers a natural history lesson along the way. But take out the key component of the trips, the 150-foot free rappel, and my guess is that his business would plummet like a failed belay.

Arches is a front-country park. The paved roads and the 800,000 visitors a year who travel them are already a major disruption to what was once a remote and pristine environment. But there was always some comfort in the fact that one park administration after another saw the wisdom in keeping the backcountry remote and relatively untouched. The National Park Service's conflicted dual mandate—to preserve and protect the land and to provide for the enjoyment of the people—has always been a challenge. At least *something* was being preserved at Arches. Pressure by some groups to develop a backcountry trail system consistently met with resistance by the park service. There was some balance there.

So it's difficult to understand, much less accept, the benign way park service officials have responded to commercial enterprises like Moore's. Since 2000 Desert Highlights has conducted more than 500 off-trail tours into the Arches backcountry for thousands of paying customers.

In 2001 then Southeast Utah Group Superintendent Jerry Banta called the Arches climbing policy one of the weakest he'd ever seen, and Moore's climbing hardware was confiscated by rangers when it was discovered he was operating without a permit. Local river companies and four-wheel tour companies have been operating in the national parks for decades. They are heavily regulated and have to jump through a plethora of hoops to maintain their permits. The companies are very restricted as to where they can go. But these new canyoneering companies discovered that, by keeping their trips limited to one-day outings, they could slip through the regulatory cracks with very little red tape at all. The Arches staff suggested he apply for an incidental business permit.

The following spring, I reviewed the permit application paperwork, via a Freedom of Information Act request. Among the documents was the Environmental Screening Form (N-16), a part of the permitting process. Included in the form was a checklist called, "Section B: Mandatory Criteria." It asked questions about the short- and long-term effects of the proposal: "Would the proposal, if implemented, (1) Have highly controversial effects? (2) Be directly related to other actions with individually insignificant, but cumulatively significant, environmental effects? (3) Establish a precedent for future action or represent a decision in principle about future actions with potentially significant environmental effects? (4) Have the potential to be controversial because of disagreement over possible environmental effects?"

If the park service was impartial, all four of the questions deserved a "Yes" answer. To approve the incidental business permit, then Arches Superintendent Rock Smith needed all "No" answers. That's what Desert Highlights received.

The decision was a Pandora's box if there ever was one. The exploitation of the backcountry of a national park for profit is something new, and no one can be sure how successful operations like this will become. But there is a precedent, a reminder of another ill-fated National Park Service choice that environmentalists have regretted ever since.

Forty years ago, the commercial river running industry was in its infancy. No one dreamed that in the span of a decade or two commercial river use would grow exponentially and create a new industry. Motorized trips allowed the companies to significantly increase their business and profits; of course, with increased traffic came comparable impacts. By the time the National Park Service tried to get a handle on the motorized river industry, it was too late. The industry was too entrenched to be eliminated. Even Matt Moore wishes the motors could be banned, but he fails to see the parallel to his own business. Today commercial boaters are heavily regulated, but the river is overused. The same fate may await national park backcountry.

Yet, Desert Highlights continues to operate on a temporary permit, and park service officials continue to insist that the tours are not damaging Arches' once untouched backcountry. Nor are they sure how to address the future impacts as these tours expand and grow more popular. When the National Park Service did its very brief analysis, it concluded that "no affected publics" objected to the business. And that was true, not *one* environmental organization in Utah officially objected to this canyoneering company or *any* similar operation. There are now dozens of them. Why are they unwilling to cast a critical eye at the Arches commercial activity?

While impacts from nonmotorized recreation have never been a priority, groups like SUWA did actively oppose such activities in the past. A decade ago, SUWA fought EcoChallenge, a cross-country extreme sports marathon of sorts, created by television impresario Mark Burnett and shown on MTV. The event crossed or came near many wilderness study areas, and SUWA was, as one runner complained, "all over us like a cheap suit." Although the race was eventually allowed to proceed, SUWA's close monitoring of the event and the pressure it maintained on federal land agencies like the National Park Service and the BLM kept impacts to a minimum. Burnett, frustrated by all the restrictions, swore he "would never come back to Utah in a million years." Instead, he moved on to create the reality television series "Survivor," thus lowering the mentality of the medium to depths never dreamed possible. It still hasn't found the bottom.

But since then, opposition to these kinds of high-adrenalin, low-serenity activities by Utah environmental groups has all but disappeared, in part because many of these commercial outdoor enterprises have found a way to effectively co-opt environmental groups. "If you can't beat 'em, join 'em" has never rung truer. The fact that Desert Highlights prominently proclaims itself a "proud business supporter of the Southern Utah Wilderness Alliance" may have something to do with SUWA's reluctance to criticize commercial canyoneering, whether SUWA will admit it or not. This is the quandary environmental groups face: they want to build a constituency of businesses who support wilderness, but this is the kind of compromise they must make in order to achieve the support they want.

It gets worse. One of the most offensive canyoneering Web sites I've ever encountered was originally called "Select Circle of Few," now "Circle of Friends," operated by Shane Burrows of Draper, Utah. On his home page he writes, "Want to learn about a secret canyon before everyone else? Here is your big chance to join the 'Select Circle of Few' canyoneering program and be the first into newly identified canyons. . . . For the unbelievably low price of fifteen dollars, I will email you canyon information before it's published to the Climb Utah Web site." Yes, that is pretty unbelievable.

On the Web site, which Burrows maintains is a nonprofit organization, is a link to Desert Highlights, which in turn offers a link to SUWA. I don't believe *anyone* at SUWA would care to be a part of the Select Circle of Few. Yet, only two degrees of separation stand between them and an "unbelievably low price."

Perhaps SUWA and other environmental groups see no alternative but to embrace what Bill Brewster of ABC News called "one of the biggest, baddest, boomingest slices of the ever-swelling travel pie—adventure travel." In a 1999 story following a canyoneering tragedy in Switzerland that claimed fourteen lives, Brewster wrote that the adventure sport would grow, despite accidents and the loss of human life. He interviewed Matt Moore for the report. Under the subheading "Tragedy May Boost Popularity," Moore "had a slightly different take, saying that accidents like this week's and a similar one that killed eleven in Arizona in August 1997 give a sport like canyoneering a 'high profile' cachet."

In 2002 SUWA even got into the act itself when it sponsored and promoted slide shows by "legendary backcountry explorer and author Steve Allen." Allen called his show "Canyoneering Chronicles," and he took it to nine cities in Utah and Idaho, as well as New York City. In a related *Salt Lake Tribune* story, titled "Canyoneering Allen Says More People Should See Wilderness to Save It," Allen insisted that a mass influx of nonmotorized tourists to wilderness areas was the only way to preserve our threatened wildlands, "We need more people out there, not less. Right now, the wilderness lands are in flux. They're embattled. We need as many supporters as we can get. . . . If places get too crowded, we can take appropriate steps [to limit access]." Again, no one in the environmental community stepped forward to challenge Allen's strategy.

Numbers appeared to be the game that many organizations were and are playing, supposedly for the moral and philosophical support these groups *think* the nonmotorized recreationists could offer. There is no bigger numbers game to be played than the "24 Hours of Moab" bicycle race, held near Moab each fall. The first one was staged over a decade ago. Since then their numbers have swelled in excess of 5000, and in some locations the race route comes within feet of proposed Utah Wilderness Coalition wilderness areas. In fact, part of the course was once raced *inside* proposed wilderness. Environmental groups have steered clear of the event, despite obvious environmental impacts, because the event is such a shot in the arm to Moab's economy, if only for a couple days.

For more than a decade, environmentalists have wanted to believe that mountain bikers are true believers when it comes to wilderness. At first glance, that assumption sounds logical. Mountain bikers are nonmotorized, they enjoy the outdoors, they are generally affluent, and they express at least some understanding of environmental issues. In a 1995 *Zephyr* article, SUWA reported on one of the early "24" races with a very positive outlook. In the "Canyon Country Watchdog" section, SUWA described the event and added, "The mountain bike community in Moab is a large advocacy group aggressively promoting low impact recreation. We believe that both wilderness advocates and biking enthusiasts have a lot to gain by working together to keep potential wilderness areas as un-impacted as possible while Congress decides the fate of these outstanding lands."

Among mountain bikers, there certainly are many dedicated supporters of wilderness who treat public lands with reverence and respect. But as a recreational subculture, there is little reason to think the sport stands four-square behind wilderness. In fact, a recent press release by the International Mountain Bike Association confirms some of my worst fears about their understanding and appreciation of wilderness as a place for solitude and reflection. In part, the release said,

> The blanket ban on bicycling in Wilderness Areas and its effect on future trail access continues to be a focus for the International Mountain Bicycling Association (IMBA) in 2005. . . . IMBA believes mountain biking, a low-impact, muscle-powered recreation, is an appropriate use of trails on public lands and is consistent with the values of Wilderness land protection, which includes recreation in natural landscapes.
>
> When proposed Wilderness Areas include significant mountain biking opportunities, IMBA pursues boundary adjustments and alternative land designations that protect natural areas while preserving bicycle access. IMBA supports new Wilderness designations where they don't close single-track bicycling opportunities. IMBA members highly value land conservation, clean water and clean air. The first part of IMBA's strategy is to continue to build clout in the U.S. capital, where IMBA staff, volunteer advocates and a prominent D.C. law firm are lobbying to influence proposed Wilderness legislation and protect bicycle access.

When I passed the press release along to a SUWA staff attorney, he was unaware of IMBA's position. Later, he told me he'd looked at the IMBA Web site and "there appears to be significant dissent within the organization" in their forum section. I would hope so, but IMBA continues to press for wilderness loopholes for their beloved bikes, and environmental groups continue to pretend that all nonmotorized recreationists support their wilderness agenda. If ever there was a "hoist by my own petard" scenario, it's here.

The economy generated by extreme-adventure enterprises dominates Moab's business district. The word *adventure* is so commercially pervasive in Moab, it's hard to escape it or even remember what the word is supposed to mean. A quick Google search for "Moab" and "Adventure" provided almost 480,000 hits, including the Moab Adventure Center, Moab Adventure Xstream, Moab Adventure Headquarters, Moab Adventure Inn, Moab Adventure Package, Moab Adventure Guide, Moab Desert Adventures, Adventure Xscapes, Adventure Racing Retreats, and Moab Resort Adventure Package. A link to the Moab Adventure Park, from WWTI NewsWatch 50 in Watertown, New York, reported the following:

> MOAB, Utah—Riding down the ski lift from the highest point on the redrock rim overlooking the Moab Valley in Utah, our feet dangled some 800 feet in the air as Scott McFarland talked about the latest project for his Moab Adventure Park.
>
> "We're applying for permits for a zip-line, a 2500-foot-long cable that goes from the top of the hill to the bottom," McFarland said. "You get into a harness on the top and cruise to the bottom, kind of like you're flying. Without a braking system, you'd hit about 145 miles per hour. With the system, you'll go 50 or 60. That's on the computer, anyway. We'll see."
>
> One of the city's concerns in considering the permits was its noise ordinance. Nearby residents worried about screams coming from riders zipping down the cliff.

The report said it all. What one rarely hears mentioned when talking about any form of recreation these days is silence, or tranquility or spirituality, for that matter. When was the last time anyone used the reverential aspect of wilderness as an argument for preservation? It may be that environmentalists seek to avoid conflict with businesses like these for the very same reason these businesses exist. Ultimately, it's about the money, whether the motive is honest and well intentioned or not. That's how far we've descended.

They say that a fool and his money are soon parted. But what is it about twenty-first-century recreationists that makes them so eager to empty their wallets in the first place? What created the demand for such a cornucopia of sporting gear and planned "adventure activities"? There was a time when all a guy needed to go for a hike was a reasonably comfortable pair of shoes and an army surplus canteen. Now he requires a wardrobe and a gear checklist just to walk to the corner. I recently stopped at a sporting goods store looking for a canteen. The young sales clerk looked at me blankly.

"You know," I said. "A canteen. A water bottle."

"Oh," he replied. "You mean a portable hydration system."

A portable hydration system?

How did this happen? Why did Americans suddenly seem to need organized adventure? Going back ten or fifteen years to the Kelsey guidebook premonitions and the spiritual "get in touch with your green side" nature tour warnings, I had been puzzled by the need of so many adults to be told how to have fun, how to have a meaningful experience. When I first looked at the Desert Highlights Web site, I noticed that Moore posted photographs of every tour and its paid participants. I was shocked to discover that most of his customers were healthy young men and women who should have been able to walk the mile and a half required without adult supervision. Then it occurred to me—these people had never done *anything* without adult supervision. They had no idea how to entertain themselves.

I thought about my niece and nephews, who even fifteen years ago weren't allowed to go out and play in the yard because their mother thought they might be kidnapped or fall off a cliff. We were all at my parents' farm one winter, just after Christmas. It was a glorious 160-acre spread in northern Kentucky, with hay barns, spring-fed lakes, forests full of poison ivy and grape vines to swing from, and limestone ledges loaded with fossils. It was a kids' paradise.

My niece and nephews came to me and said, "We're *bored*, Unca Jim," so I proposed that we go outside and explore. They thought that was a pretty dumb idea, but I made them go. I took them to the barn and taught them how to build forts out of hay bales and how to knock the bales over once they were piled six or seven high. We walked to the pond, and I showed them how to punch holes in the ice with big rocks. They thought all this was great fun, but it had never occurred to them to do such things. Sad to say, it occurred to *me* that this little exercise was not going to change them at all. It was too late for them to create their own childhoods. The poor little kids, I thought. They have no idea what they missed.

Not being a parent myself, I hadn't noticed that almost all kids were like my little relatives. Now all of those children are young adults and about to have families of their own, and they have no hope of passing along any of those wonderful free-spirited adventures that I was so blessed with as a child. Such stories are merely hearsay to them, stories passed down from their elders, "Yep, kids. I kin remember when we wandered down to The Woods and almost drowned in the swamp. And that's when we were only five years old."

True to the twenty-first-century version of the American Way, someone has been able to attach an affliction to this condition. A new book by author Richard Louv, *Last Child in the Woods: Saving Our Children from Nature-Deficit Disorder*, gives credibility to the notion that kids no longer have any connection to nature, or to independent thought, for that matter. According to a *New York Times* article by Bradford McKee,

The days of free-range childhood seem to be over. And parents can now add a new worry to the list of things that make them feel inept: increasingly their children, as Woody Allen might say, are at two with nature.

The author Richard Louv calls the problem "nature-deficit disorder." He came up with the term, he said, to describe an environmental ennui flowing from children's fixation on artificial entertainment rather than natural wonders. Those who are obsessed with computer games or are driven from sport to sport, he maintains, miss the restorative effects that come with the nimbler bodies, broader minds and sharper senses that are developed during random running around at the relative edges of civilization.

"*Random* running around" is the key word there. Modern science will no doubt spend millions on research and development to produce a medication to cure this ailment, when all the afflicted really need is a long walk in the woods, by themselves. But the farther these denatured children stray from a spontaneous natural experience, the less likely they are to ever rediscover a world that seems to me impossible to live without. With a new and ever-expanding billion-dollar industry built around these dependent souls, it is in every sense of the term a codependent relationship.

A fool parting with his money is a necessary component of the amenities economy. Americans are likely to grow more foolish and adventure more expensive with every passing sunset, an experience that will eventually be arranged and conducted by the Sunset Adventure Tour Company. Sure, they may be a figment of my cynical imagination today, but give it some time. In the not too distant future of the Brave New West, we will make reservations and pay good money to be part of a tour that simply watches a nice sunset. It will not occur to us that we could have done it alone and for free.

The Amenities Boom and Meltdown

Patrick Diehl is an outspoken environmentalist and a strong advocate for change in the rural West. In fact, he'd like to dismantle it completely and start over again. Diehl ran for the U.S. Congress a few years ago on the Green Party ticket and received 2 percent of the vote, not bad for a guy who until recently lived in one of the most remote communities on the Colorado Plateau. Escalante, Utah, is still safe from becoming the next New West town. It is rural to its roots and proud of it. Escalante has earned a reputation with some for being one of the most intolerant towns in Utah, but even some environmentalists believe that the town simply wants to hold onto its lifestyle and its history. The clear message is "Don't try to change us." Diehl was ready for a change, or, more precisely, a revolution.

In 2002 the *Zephyr* published an interview with Diehl and his wife, Tori Woodard, at their home in Escalante. Their neighbor and *Zephyr* contributor Erica Walz interviewed Diehl at length about his views on what he called "the new economy":

> The amenities-economy idea that the Wilderness Society was putting out is what I think lies [ahead]. There's still a fair amount of merit to this concept. Between the extractive economy and the purely touristic economy is a third way in which you have people moving to an area to live there and be part of the local society and perhaps the local economy—in many cases bringing their jobs with them and telecommuting—and the reason people come there is because it's a beautiful place to live. It's not going to be healthy and beautiful if you degrade it through logging and mining and grazing. It involves replacing some of the extractive economies. But I'm much less confident in the future of this economy [in Escalante] than I was four years ago when we moved here, and I also see that the savagery of the local resistance exceeded even my expectations. People will go very far to make their area be extremely unattractive to outsiders. It has to do with political power. If you let outsiders in, if you allow them to organize and voice their point of view, you can easily lose control. These small towns have a lot to lose from a political standpoint if there's much influx from outside. So the chances of actually getting an amenities economy going in southern Utah is very bad in the short run because of the political situation.

Diehl wasn't willing to completely abandon the rural population, and he believed work could be found for them if this new economy took root. For instance, he believed a massive effort to remove the exotic plant tamarisk would attract a great number of the old locals, "if they were paid for it." But for the most part, Diehl wanted to see a dramatic turnover in small rural communities like Escalante, even its population, "I think this town needs to double in size. If we're going to have more towns in this part of the world, they should be more self-sustaining. They're really untenable. Not just in economic terms but as cultural units. Maybe 50 or 100 years ago when they were cut off from the outside world they had to create their own culture, but right now it feels like the further reaches of Provo to me—it's nothing, in itself."

Walz asked, "What about people who enjoy it the way it is?"

"I can't imagine enjoying it. I really loathe this town, and you can quote me. Socially it's a really loathsome place. You can put that in the paper. Absolutely. It's the worst place I've ever lived, and I've lived quite a few places. So some people like it—it's like there's no accounting for taste."

Ultimately, Diehl's failed vision of a New Escalante only frustrated and embittered him. When Diehl and Woodard left town for good, they left few friends behind. Escalante still holds onto its rural culture, backward as some people may see it, and intends to stay that way. Moab, on the other hand, could not have been riper for change.

Moab's "funky little town" reputation and its odd cultural diversity made us a prime target for the New West. Although we bickered and fought, the various factions in Moab at least coexisted. Albeit shaky at times, a level of tolerance existed in Moab that wouldn't have been found even fifty miles down the road in Monticello, Utah. Ultimately, it was people like me who in a perverse way made the Brave New West invasion possible.

Fifteen years ago, Lance Christie summed up the future in his *Zephyr* "Boom and Bust Baloney" essay when he wrote, "If a community uses wilderness amenities as a drawing card, then offers goods and services people want when they come to enjoy the local amenities, wilderness can make the people selling those goods a lot of money. If the community resents visitors and opposes wilderness for taking away the freedom to dig holes searching for treasure, then wilderness (or any tourism) won't make them money." Christie was prophetic in more ways than one when he added, "The whole economic debate over wilderness tends to distract us from the fact that the major reasons for designating wilderness arise from noneconomic values."

Indeed, yet that is exactly what happened. Moab's amenities economy really gathered steam in 1993, when seven motels were constructed in a matter of months and nationally franchised fast food eateries began to sprout along Main Street. Recreational visitation increased exponentially on surrounding public lands, but none of the major environmental organizations expressed concern—not SUWA, not the Sierra Club, not the Grand Canyon Trust, not the Wilderness Society. It was as if they didn't even notice.

Some environmentalists were loathe to praise the specific consequences of the amenities boom and privately expressed horror at the explosive and uncontrolled growth, but no one wanted to be on the record opposing it. After all, it was their idea. In fact, some organizations went to great lengths to praise the stunning changes occurring in Moab and elsewhere, but always in broad vague strokes.

In 2002 SUWA printed a feature story in its winter issue of *Red Rock Wilderness*, their quarterly newsletter. The article was called "The Local Economic Impacts of Protected Wildlands: Enhanced Economic Vitality" and was written by Thomas Michael Power, a professor of economics at the University of Montana. Power and his data asserted that protecting the rural West's wildlands did not damage local economies. On the contrary, he believed that "protected landscapes are often associated with enhanced economic vitality." But, considering the intent of the article, he followed that declaration with a curious caveat that was all but ignored by environmentalists:

> This does not mean that those seeking to preserve natural areas should base their case for preservation on the economic expansion it will stimulate. That could be a dangerous strategy in the long run and one that may not be very convincing besides. In fact, in the long run, ongoing economic growth may well threaten the ecological integrity of wildlands as growing population, human settlement, and commercial activities and their accompanying pollutants isolate and disrupt natural areas. *Even though wildlands may be good for local economic vitality, local economic vitality may not be good for the ecological integrity of those wildlands* [emphasis added].

In the remainder of the essay, Power moved away from that warning. Using the data he had gathered, Power struck several blows in support of the amenities economy. He noted, "higher percentages of county land protected by national park, national monument, and federal wilderness status were associated with higher rates of employment." Power discovered that population growth in areas near wilderness areas was higher than state averages, and he observed that wilderness "protection was associated with growth rates two to six times those for other nonmetropolitan areas."

Despite his warning, Power concluded, "It is not clear why wildlands advocates would not want to meet the economic critics of wildland protection on their own ground, while also continuing to make the ethical, cultural, and environmental arguments. After all, if you can take away the only powerful argument the anti-environmentalists have, why would you not do so?"

It was as if he was saying, "We can let the anti-wilderness people destroy the West on *their* terms or we can fight to destroy it on *our* terms. And aren't our terms of destruction better than theirs? After all, before we destroy the wilderness, we're going to protect it."

Environmentalists either failed to see or would not acknowledge the double-edged sword Power offered. In a subsequent issue of *Red Rock Wilderness*, SUWA attempted to put its own spin on Power's report with some additional numbers of its own. SUWA noted, "Total employment in Utah has increased by 45% in the last decade. . . . What is fueling Utah's pacesetting growth? Tourism and related services have been especially robust, and now provides more than a third of all jobs. . . . Growth is not limited to urban Utah. In Grand County, a tourism explosion helped to make it the third fastest growing county in Utah."

All of this was reported with almost evangelical enthusiasm. None of Power's warnings came to light in this particular spin. Finally, SUWA noted the ballooning Western population, which grew by 30 percent in the 1990s, "This tremendous regional growth, with Utah at its epicenter, is driven by Western quality of life factors like outdoor recreation, open space, and wilderness. . . . There is a very real place for wilderness in Utah's economic future. Protected by the BLM, wilderness can serve as a modest sustainable source for economic well-being and community development."

From today's perspective, there's nothing modest about Moab's transformation. Some environmentalists might argue that much of the explosive change in Moab has nothing to do with their efforts to support a clean, upscale amenities economy. They see the rowdy raunchy jeepers, the noisy noxious ATVers, and the rabid rock crawlers as having nothing much in common with the leg-powered bicyclists. It might be fairer to suggest that the amenities economy backfired in the environmentalists' very own faces.

Except for the annual Jeep Safari itself, Moab was never much of a tourist center. Travelers passed through Moab as quickly as a ride to the Arches and a daily raft trip required. It wasn't until the late 1980s, when bringing your bike to Moab was like making a trip to the Wailing Wall, that enterprising men and women everywhere began to seriously take note of our town. Clearly, Moab had achieved that special status reserved previously for places like Telluride, Aspen, Jackson, Santa Fe, and Sedona, just a handful of the small towns around the West that suddenly, one day, discovered they had cachet, that mystical indefinable quality that makes everyone want to be able to say, "I've been there."

What motivated entrepreneur could miss something like that? You could hear the wheels turning inside their minds, "Everyone knows about Moab now, and everyone thinks Moab is a cool place to be. If bicyclists will come here in huge numbers and spend massive amounts of money in this economy, why can't we do the same thing with other forms of recreation? Why not a hill climb for dune buggies? Why not a rock crawling event? Why not BASE jumping? Or rock climbing? Or canyoneering? Or skydiving? Or ATV jamborees and races? Why not anything that can make us a buck and pull more visitors to Moab? Who's going to complain?"

Truthfully, hardly anyone complained. Some environmentalists do bitterly oppose the dramatic growth in the use of ATVs in southeastern Utah and the subsequent resource damage, but how did the environmental community ever think it could limit the amenities economy to the kinds of activities only *they* approved of? There's little comfort in knowing that imitation is the highest form of flattery. But, the truth is, after Moab cut its teeth on bikes, the sky was the limit, no matter how dissimilar the activity might seem to some.

When Thomas Michael Power set out to analyze the effects of wilderness on the rural economy, he noted an anomaly that he could not initially explain, "Researchers, puzzled by the growth of population in western Montana, despite low wages and incomes, studied the location of new residential housing to determine what locational characteristics explained the decisions homebuilders were making. They found that the closer a location was to a designated wilderness area, the higher the likelihood of new construction. The same was true of national parks."

Power's bewilderment is old news to most of us who live in small communities near parks and wilderness. New home construction, which took off in Moab during the early 1990s, is often intended for part-time residents, people who have no intention or need to seek employment in the area. In fact, these homes and condominiums are very disconnected from the socioeconomic needs of the community to which they have, at least physically, joined. They exist in something of a vacuum, because so many of these part-timers are oblivious to the issues and problems that affect the town. They don't know much of the town's history and know few of its citizens. They don't get involved in local politics and don't vote. Although they do pay taxes, they don't impact the educational system because most part-time residents don't have school-aged children. But they still demand the services that they believe their tax dollars entitle them to. In almost every case, this kind of second-home community negatively impacts the tax base. In other words, when towns grow in this fashion, everyone pays more.

But rarely will the environmental community acknowledge such facts. Candor and the truth are the most effective weapons we can use to support our point of view. To me, candor and honesty have gone missing from our side of the debate for a very long time. Or perhaps it runs deeper than that, perhaps candor is a matter of interpretation. Within the conservation movement, there is a growing dichotomy between the more idealistic

Thoreau types and the New Environmentalists, who have embraced the kinds of land preservation strategies that concern me so deeply. The two groups can look at the same tree and see different colors. Let me offer an example.

Lance Christie frequently posts information, including his own and others' analyses, in emails to friends and associates. When an email came across my monitor titled "Rich Weasels in Aspen Do Something Right," I paused to give it a read. "Rich weasels" is a name I've used frequently in the *Zephyr*, so I had personal interest. Here was Lance's observation:

> Under the Pitkin County [Colorado] building code, every new and remodeled home in Pitkin County must meet a strict "energy budget" of approximately 40,000 British Thermal Units (BTU) per square foot. Nationwide, the average home consumes 63,000 BTU per square foot per year.
>
> Homes that do not meet the energy budget must pay a fee to the Renewable Energy Mitigation Program. The $1.7 million collected in its first three years has been channeled into projects that offset greenhouse gas emissions, ranging from car-sharing commuting programs to an energy-efficient revamp of a local ice rink and providing solar hot water heaters in affordable housing.

At first glance, the rule sounds encouraging. In fact, I read the email to several of my friends, without commentary, and each one of them nodded vaguely and said, "Well, they're trying at least." Maybe, but if you dig you'll recognize the absurdity in all this. Pitkin County is the home of Aspen, one of the wealthiest communities in the United States. It has been called the town "where the billionaires are running the millionaires out of the valley." Do these people or its government truly deserve a pat on the back? Who can better afford to employ the latest energy-saving technologies than these guys?

But what's more important is noting the restrictions that were *not* imposed on the new homebuilders. Specifically, did anyone think to limit the number of square feet on new home or remodel constructions? I doubt if it even occurred to anyone on the Pitkin County Commission. But it didn't take me long to do the calculations. A wealthy Aspenite living in a 15,000-square-foot home and using the mandated limit of 40,000 BTUs of energy per square foot will consume 600 million BTUs annually, while a redneck tool pusher living in a less-efficient 2000-square-foot doublewide can expect to use far less energy, about 126 million BTUs. It's a safe bet that this redneck lives in his drafty trailer twelve months a year, while many of the energy-efficient Aspenites spend a fraction of their time there.

How can we offer praise to some extravagantly consumptive part-time homeowner? Imagine how much energy it took to construct a mansion like that. Consider the natural materials, the cost to operate the heavy equipment, the energy to transport the workers to the job site (for it's doubtful that any of the contractors could afford to live anywhere near Aspen). The mind boggles.

Still, Lance Christie's praise for Pitkin County was sincere and well intentioned, and I respect him for that. Many, if not a majority, of environmentalists probably share his enthusiasm. But I'm not one of them. I can find no reason to celebrate or conclude, based on examples like this, that we're somehow becoming a more energy-aware, environmentally conscientious nation. In fact, I think this kind of misplaced optimism does us harm.

What about the land upon which these homes are built? In the small towns of the rural West, new residential developments are almost always built on what was agricultural or grazing land. Once again the "cows versus condos" debate raises its persistent head. No environmentalist worth his natural sea salt has much patience for the West's cattle industry and especially grazing on public lands, and the damage caused by some ranchers is well documented and disgraceful.

Although some environmentalists may believe that paving over alfalfa fields with something like Moab's Rim Village condo city is striking a blow for Mother Nature and the new economy of the West, we should remember Power's warning about the long-term view of this kind of development. Runaway tourism, growth, and expansion of towns like Moab should cause all of us to take notice and give pause, to *rethink* all of this. Exploding tourist numbers and a second-home culture transform a community, shifting the emphasis of the town away from the people who live there and toward those who don't. Moab doesn't exist for its citizens. It's there, in fact, for high-dollar transients. The amenities economy rarely benefits the small-town residents that were there during the tough times. It's the new arrivals with the capital to invest that flourish.

As much of Spanish Valley's laid-back potpourri of fields and pastures, junk cars, and funky homes yield to a sea of condo developments and faux adobe second homes, who can suggest that Rim Village is more aesthetically pleasing to the eye than the alfalfa field it replaced? Out of that shift comes a vital question for all environmentalists. When we talk about "highest and best use" of a piece of land, just what exactly do we mean, particularly when it comes to water and farmland? Often it comes down to a fight about cows.

I've always had a love-hate relationship with cows. I've cursed them loudly and with extreme prejudice when they turned my favorite mountain meadow, Nasty Flat, into a barren cow-pie-strewn wasteland, a devastating scene perhaps more worthy of the place name. But, then, cows *taste* so good.

On many occasions I've inched my way through a herd of these dull-witted beasts on some highway as their cowboy masters move them to summer range, winter range, or the feedlot, and I wonder if I could ever grow accustomed to a steady stream of green, smelly, fly-infested shit running down my flanks. But have you ever seen lovelier eyelashes than those adorning a Hereford cow? If any of my ex-girlfriends had been able or willing to bat eyelashes like *that* at me, who knows where those relationships might have gone.

When I see a herd of those heavy-set ungulates trampling yet another field or meadow,

I am appalled at the damage. But when I see yet another overgrazed field turned into a condo development, I ask myself, "Is a burned out meadow as bad as *this*?"

When I see a herd of Black Angus or Herefords, I'm struck with an instantaneous case of bovolexia, an affliction that actually brings me pleasure, satisfaction, and a sense of communication with these dumb animals. Bovolexia is an irresistible urge to moo when you see cows in a field. Without fail, as I drive along some rural highway, the sight of a cow forces me to roll down my window, hang my head into the wind, and moo as convincingly as I can. Sometimes I moo forcefully and lustily with a bullish spirit. Other times my moos are wistful and melancholy, as a poor steer might feel as he looks at all those heifers and wonders why he isn't interested. When the cows respond to my call and look up to acknowledge my moos, it pleases me immensely.

I can lose patience with ranchers who abuse and destroy the very land they make a living from, but I'm careful not to paint all ranchers with the same broad stroke. Ranchers run the spectrum like everyone else. For instance, if someone tried to tell me that rancher Heidi Redd didn't understand the heart and soul of the American West, I'd punch him in the nose. Heidi has lived most of a life at Dugout Ranch in San Juan County, Utah, and I'm glad she's there.

So, I face the issue of ranching with mixed feelings. I've been told repeatedly that cows are destroying the West, yet my heart doesn't seem to be totally committed to getting rid of them. I've been reminded that the cowboy myth is just that, but then I wonder, what's wrong with a myth? Isn't that what we need *more* of these days? What is it with today's cynical culture that makes us want to tear our myths and heroes apart? I'm not ready to abandon Gene Autry and Roy Rogers, not quite yet.

Beyond my irrational defense of the cowboy and his cow, I also find a more practical side to my emotions. It's the reality of a commodity-driven society and economy, where everything must have a dollar value, where everything must be marketed, sold, and show a comfortable profit.

Back in "the good old days" of twenty years ago, we didn't give much thought to the ranchers or the communities that were built upon ranching. We didn't consider what would happen to the ranches themselves, the old homes and barns tucked under century-old cottonwood trees, the alfalfa fields in the valleys that are as much a part of the Western landscape as the mountains that often rise above them. Environmentalists didn't consider then—and many don't care now—what the fate of the rural West might be if ranching on public lands was eliminated. In fact, for many urban environmentalists, eliminating the rural West is a key strategy, in their minds, to preserving it.

One morning a few summers ago, a friend and I were discussing the wildfires sweeping the West. When the conversation turned to water, my friend complained bitterly about the amount of water devoted to agriculture in Colorado.

"Did you know," he asked, "that eighty percent of the water in Colorado is used for agriculture, yet farming and ranching only constitute fourteen percent of the economy?" (My numbers are estimates of what he said.)

A decade ago, I might have nodded sympathetically and joined the chorus of dissent. But instead I said, "So what?"

"So what?" he growled in disbelief. "What are you talking about? You think it's *good* that farmers use so much water?"

"Well, what would you prefer?" I answered. "Consider the agricultural lands in many of the valleys in Colorado. Would you rather see them save the water for human consumption and encourage fifty thousand people to move into the area? If you shut down the farms, surely there will be plenty of water for massive urban expansion."

"No," he replied. "I don't want that either."

I shook my head. "Well, it's going to be one or the other. As B. Traven once said, 'This is the real world, muchacho, and we are all in it.' Do you think they'll just let the water flow slowly to the sea? This is America, pal. Somebody's going to make money off that water."

This is a question about land use that all environmentalists need to answer. Imagine there is a 100-acre alfalfa field that requires 100,000 gallons of water a week to produce a healthy crop. If a condominium complex of 300 units could be built on that same 100 acres, and the water use by all those new condo residents could be cut by as much as 75 percent compared to what the farmer uses. Would the new construction represent a higher and better use of the land because it used less water? It's a question we all need to consider.

I still understand the points made by cow-free advocates. I still recognize the damage caused by reckless grazing practices. I know changes need to be made. But at a time when the amenities economy is rapidly creating an entirely new threat to the beauty, solitude, and health of the American West, a cow-free West as an end-all solution to resource degradation is foolish and simplistic. Never underestimate the greed of American entrepreneurialism. The marketing of beauty is a brand new industry that may one day make us all long for a chance to demonstrate our bovolexia, and there won't be a cow in sight to satisfy us.

▬▬▬ ▬▬▬ ▬▬▬ Not long ago, in winter cows roamed Johnson's Up on Top, a mesa just south of Moab. But a grandiose amenities project called Cloudrock Resort Development may someday exile the cows yet again, and again we'll long for our bovine friends.

Cloudrock was first introduced to Moab citizens in 2000, after months of secret negotiations by the developer, the State Institutional Trust Lands Administration (SITLA), and local elected officials. SITLA lands are state-owned sections that were created to generate income for Utah schools. If you look at a map, you'll notice a checkerboard pattern of squares dispersed across the state. Those are SITLA lands, and they are often surrounded by federal BLM land and national parks. For years Utah legislators have sought ways to exploit their holdings, but until recently Utah was old school in its thinking. Development of SITLA land meant cattle grazing or, more often, mining and drilling. This is where they figured the money was.

But a decade ago, it occurred to the SITLA czars that state lands surrounding New West towns like Moab had a value they hadn't considered. Since then, Utah has negotiated with the federal government to swap many of its scattered and isolated state lands for clusters of state sections. Sometimes the clusters are based on their mining potential, but lately SITLA has sought lands near boomtowns like Moab. The implications for the future are staggering. In the rural parts of most Western states, private land is limited. Rural towns are often like small islands in a sea of public domain—the opportunity for sprawl faced physical limitations. The SITLA land swaps changed that in Utah.

As originally proposed, Cloudrock would have three luxury lodges with 198 rooms, 50 condos, and 75 home sites and lots would start at $600,000. According to the Cloudrock development proposal, assembled by the project coordinator Michael Liss and obtained by the *Zephyr* in 2000, the plan was stunning.

> Our intention is to create a world-class wilderness destination resort community in the American Southwest for people who enjoy the beauty and cultural legacy of the region. The centerpiece of this community is the Cloudrock Desert Lodge, an intimate luxury wilderness lodge that will set the tone and standard for the entire community. . . . We expect our guests to return time and time again, finally deciding that this is where they want to build a second or third home. . . . We plan to spend the time, money, and creative energy necessary to create a real estate development that will deliver top prices.

As to who might be a candidate for a Cloudrock future, the proposal could not be clearer, "We will use a highly targeted approach, planning intimate get-togethers at the homes of our friends and initial clients, as many second home real estate purchasers are often as interested in who their eventual neighbors might be as in the property itself." It really said that.

To add insult to injury to anyone with a net worth less than $10 million, the marketing plan promised that, "Johnson's Up on Top will be marketed as a vacation community for affluent families and individuals. The Moab real estate market does not currently serve this segment well, with most developments targeted to a somewhat lower economic bracket. . . . The lodge and condominium units that will comprise this mesa village will form a dense complex in the spirit of the Italian hill towns like Siena and San Gimignano. . . . The Phase III condominiums will be built in the spirit of the Anasazi Cliff Dwellings of Mesa Verde."

Clearly, Cloudrock was selling itself to the wealthy, but more specifically to high-end visitors and future homebuyers who also considered themselves environmentalists. Liss was quick to point out the easy access to national parks and wilderness areas, some adjacent to Cloudrock itself.

There was a time when the environmental community might have been appalled by such an extravagant scheme. After all, the conservation movement is rooted in the word *conserve*. How could such an opulent, consumptive, and arrogant plan even dream of winning the acceptance of environmentalists? Unfortunately, in the amenities economy, anything is possible.

As Cloudrock became better known and the developers were required to submit the plan to governmental and public scrutiny, the Glen Canyon Group of the Sierra Club weighed in on the issue. On behalf of the group, Vice Chair Jean Binyon addressed its concerns in a February 2001 letter to Michael Liss. Binyon made it clear that, "It is our consensus that the best thing for Johnson's is no development at all." Having said that, however, the Sierra Club had no intention of putting up a fight. "We realize you are making efforts to ensure that Cloudrock meets standards above and beyond Grand County's. . . . We realize you are well on your way to completing the preliminary plat, and incorporating changes becomes more difficult with the passage of time. Never the less, we hope you will be receptive to our concerns."

What kind of concerns did the Sierra Club have, and what were their requests? Besides setting structures farther back from the rim of the canyon, Binyon made the following demands: "coloring roads to match the surrounding soil . . . parking lots colored to match the surrounding soil . . . utilizing medium to darker earth tones and nonreflective materials on all structures . . . outdoor lighting should be kept to a minimum." They were all simply cosmetic. The Sierra Club also encouraged restrictions on off-highway vehicles, "Next to cows, [this is] the most damaging thing currently happening on the mesa. Please be explicit in not permitting their use on the mesa." Apparently, keeping out cows and off-highway vehicles was an acceptable trade-off for a massive multimillion-dollar "wilderness" resort lodge and scores of condos and homes built on $600,000 lots.

Liss's reply could not have been more accommodating, "I would be happy to discuss our project with you and members of your Chapter." He added enthusiastically, "I am a member of the Sierra Club and greatly respect the work being done around the country."

No other environmental group in Utah even chose to express an opinion. How could any environmental group be so passive or silent in the face of a project that was absolutely contrary to the basic principles of conservation? These homes, regardless of whether they were constructed with the most energy-efficient, recyclable materials available, would be massive consumers of natural resources. They would be clearly visible from Arches National Park and other scenic areas, would be constructed adjacent to proposed wilderness, and would wreak havoc on the social fabric of nearby Moab by driving property values and taxes even higher. To recall Thomas Michael Power's warning, "ongoing economic growth may well threaten the ecological integrity of wildlands as growing population, human settlement, and commercial activities and their accompanying pollutants isolate and disrupt natural areas."

Environmentalists must sit idly by because they can't oppose the very economic strategy for the rural West that they have embraced philosophically for years, and especially because they fear the risk of biting the hands and dollars that feed them. In the battle for wilderness in Utah, fundraising plays a greater role with each successive session of the U.S. Congress, as wilderness advocates push for permanent legislation. Money is everything. As Chris Peterson, the former executive director of a Utah environmental group, put it, "It is felt that without playing the game on their opponents' terms, they don't stand a chance. So is it better to win or lose the fight? Those with experience in the field of environmental advocacy deem it necessary to play 'dirty' and enlist any and all means necessary to accomplish their goals, and believe that walking the alternative 'high road' is an exercise in futility and ultimately leads to failure."

How much dirt are environmentalists willing to endure? Try this on for size. John Hendricks is the CEO of the Discovery Channel. He says he has passionately loved the West since he was a kid, when his father told him that the most beautiful place on Earth was a seldom-visited red-rock paradise called Gateway, Colorado. A few decades later, John Hendricks bought it—lock, stock, and barrel. Hendricks is rich, and his attorneys made offers to local landowners that were hard to resist. By 2002 he had accumulated more than 6000 acres of property, some of which he intends to put into conservation easements. Hendricks also decided to build himself a home where he could survey his holdings. At last report the Hendricks home has just enough space for John and his wife to feel cozy, about 27,000 square feet. A few years ago it was reported to be the largest residential construction project in the United States. Now he's added a massive lodge, a restaurant, and a vintage car museum. He's turned a once quiet backwater into what he hopes will be a booming business. All this so he can "save" Gateway, Colorado.

The John Hendricks project is perhaps the most grandiose acquisition and construction in a frenzy of Western land buying by America's wealthy and elite. In the last decade it has become a familiar sight, mansions perched on the brink of some mesa or canyon or on a mountain side, staring down at the little people. The leader of an environmental group in western Colorado and I were lamenting the mega-homes and mansions being built everywhere in Colorado, from the Front Range to Glade Park. Eventually, Gateway came to mind.

"What about this John Hendricks guy and his castle at Gateway?" I said. "He's got to be the most extravagant of them all."

There was a long silence.

"Uh, I think Hendricks is trying to do the right thing," he said softly.

I paused briefly, then asked, "So how much money does he give your organization?"

Another brief pause, "A lot."

People like John Hendricks have found an age-old way of gaining respectability and even adoration: they simply *buy* it. They buy everyone. His contributions to worthy causes are significant. He has kept a few artists eating well, and contractors love him. Maybe a new feudal society is our only option, where the peasants and serfs wait and hope for their wealthy and hopefully benevolent masters to sustain them.

Environmental organizations have certainly benefited from large contributions. Consider SUWA's financial status. For years, it was the scrappy underdog, one more struggling environmental group trying to survive against the powerful ranching, mining, and ATV lobbies in Washington, D.C. It was supposed to be like that. In a 1999 story for the *Zephyr*, current SUWA Executive Director Scott Groene wrote in praise of his former boss, the environmental legend Brant Calkin:

> Brant offered his staff low pay but lots of autonomy to "do good and fight evil. The benefit of lousy pay is you get to experiment." Calkin offered low wages because no environmentalist should be in it for the money, and "Pay doesn't affect the quality of the staff." He offered as rationale both that environmentalists have an obligation to spend their members' money wisely and that small salaries ensure that only the passionate keep their jobs. He added that while experience is useful, it doesn't automatically result in better or

smarter actions: "Smart young people with fresh ideas are just as important as those who have been around the track a couple of times."

Brant never asked his staff do anything he wasn't already doing. For example, he and Susan Tixier earned a total annual salary of $20,000 between the two of them as Director and Associate Director, about a third of what the current SUWA director makes now [1999]. Brant never stopped working, whether it was leading the Utah Wilderness Coalition out of shaky consensus efforts, hustling money, or fixing a fleet of beater SUWA cars (he was renowned for resurrecting aging office equipment and trucks). And when it seemed everything was done, he'd start cleaning the office.

But today SUWA is awash in money. Its 2004 Form 990 report, available to anyone who requests it because of the organization's nonprofit status, shows that SUWA had net assets or fund balances worth $4,777,352, up $1,128,211 from the previous year. Salaries and benefits exceeded $1 million. Its executive director earned an income of $70,775 in salary and benefits. The organization even had a mutual fund and stock investments worth $894,986. SUWA recently purchased a grand old home in downtown Salt Lake City for $800,000 as its new headquarters and spent another $500,000 renovating it. Clearly, the need for legends like Brant Calkin to "renovate aging office equipment" has passed. The idea almost seems quaint. Although many nonprofits invest their revenues in such ventures, it probably rarely occurs to most grassroots contributors that their membership dues might end up on Wall Street or in real estate. Much of SUWA's new wealth comes from one of its board members, Hansjorg Wyss, who was recently estimated to be worth $8 billion.

In the end, money ultimately doesn't seem to be swaying anyone in the decades-long fight for wilderness. Ten years ago, SUWA's staff was half the size it is now. The organization's starting salaries, in keeping with Brant Calkin's admonition, were about $16,000. Now, with more money than they can even hope to spend, SUWA and the Utah Wilderness Coalition are no closer to the passage of a statewide wilderness bill than they were then. In fact, while SUWA's assets have grown dramatically, its membership rolls have dropped significantly. According to a SUWA source, membership has fallen "from 21,000 in 1995 to less than 14,000 now."

There *are* voices of dissent as environmentalism falls further away from its ethical roots. A letter from David Jorgensen of Salt Lake City to "The Public Forum" in the *Salt Lake Tribune* caught my eye not long ago. "It is unfortunate," he wrote, "that wilderness advocates must resort to economic arguments as part of their advocacy. There are some areas that . . . should be left alone for their own *intrinsic worth* and not just for human economics or even human enjoyment."

But a front-page article in the same issue only confirmed Jorgensen's fears about the future of the environmental movement. The headline read, "Outdoor Group Threatens to Leave Utah over Land Deal." In response to a disastrous plan by Secretary of the Interior Gale Norton to cut millions of acres of BLM wilderness from Utah, a plan supported by Governor Mike Leavitt, enviropreneur Peter Metcalfe threatened to move the Outdoor Retailers Association trade show, worth $24 million to the state's economy, somewhere else. Suddenly Leavitt was in a panic, and he quickly scheduled a meeting with Metcalfe and other outdoor industry representatives, "in hopes of selling them on his environmental bona fides." It was clear who had become the most powerful environmental lobby in Utah. It wasn't the Sierra Club. It wasn't SUWA. It was the Outdoor Retailers Association.

Selling was the key word here. All the intrinsic reasons for wilderness are being trampled in the hard sell, not just by the people who oppose wilderness designation but by those who support it as well. All the eloquence of John Muir, David Brower, Wallace Stegner, and Ed Abbey, among many others, couldn't move hearts and minds to pass a decent wilderness bill. The fact that eloquence, values, and integrity have given way to trade-show boycotts, the commodification of nature, and the marketing of beauty as our most powerful tools for wilderness preservation somehow fouls the very meaning of wilderness itself. The outdoor industry needs pristine wilderness to make money, so what better reason to preserve it? For the environmental community to embrace or even cast a blind eye toward that philosophy is more than many can bear.

At the core of the environmental movement has always been the belief that its constituents must adhere to the ethics and values that make them environmentalists in the first place. It's much easier to be a consumer than a conservationist. From the beginning, we've embraced the idea of living a simpler life, leaving a much smaller footprint on this trampled old planet of ours, honoring and respecting the natural world, and even making a sacrifice to assure that some part of Earth is left unscathed by the works of man. Our purpose has always been to pay tribute to the land itself.

Can environmentalists escape the label of hypocrisy? How can we condemn oil exploration when our own consumption of oil is staggering? How can we condemn the impacts of motorized recreation while turning a blind eye to the damage caused by ever-growing numbers of nonmotorized recreationists? How can we heed Abbey's warning of industrial tourism when, at its heart, *that* kind of economy is the future many environmentalists have embraced for fifteen years? How can we condemn the timber industry when we continue to build homes at an alarming rate, homes that encroach on the habitat of the very wildlife we want to protect and are far larger than anything we'd ever need? When some of our biggest contributors consume massive amounts of natural resources to build monstrous part-time homes, how can we possibly accept their donations?

Like a civil rights organization in the 1960s accepting money from a man who belonged to an all-white country club, these are the contradictions that destroy our credibility. And like the civil rights movement of forty years ago, saving what's left of the wild American West is a moral issue, first and foremost. We didn't fight for the rights of African-Americans because there was a dollar to be made. Nor should that be our motivation as environmentalists to save wilderness. If we continue to follow this dangerous path, someday we may wonder if the road to victory was worth it.

Or what it is we actually won.

Optimistic Aspects of Outrage and Dissent

Not long ago, I was chatting with one of my favorite abstract performance artists, a hopelessly cheery woman whom I adore. But I was shocked almost to tears when she accused me of being too negative.

Here we go again. Negative? *Me?*

"You'll never believe this," I told her, "but I am one of the most optimistic people you will ever meet."

She thought that was pretty funny. After she'd caught her breath and I'd helped her off the floor, I attempted to explain myself.

"Look, do you know what I think one of the most striking and significant characteristics of an optimistic person is?"

She shook her head dubiously.

"Outrage," I told her. "Controlled and properly applied outrage."

My friend shifted uncomfortably from foot to foot. "What in the world are you talking about?" she asked, as she gazed at me with studied bewilderment.

"Okay, stay with me a minute. Do you mind if I sit down?"

Now she was really worried. "How long is this going to take?"

"Not long. You'll be out of here by noon."

"But it's only nine-thirty!"

"Okay, eleven. Please listen to me. In this crazed world of ours, when we see something happening around us that we think is wrong, we have two choices. We can either act to change it, or we can simply accept it and prepare for the consequences."

She seemed unmoved.

"Only by being outraged will any of us make the effort or take the time to do the right thing. Outrage led to the Declaration of Independence, the Emancipation Proclamation, women's suffrage, and the Civil Rights Act. Outrage created the Wilderness Act and the Clean Air Act. It was when people got mad enough, *outraged* enough to take action, that any of these changes occurred."

"Haven't you written about this before?"

"Probably, but it's a recurring theme that should be restated from time to time."

My friend sighed and sat down next to me. "I sort of see your point, but I just can't stand all the pessimism that comes from Gloomy Gus types like you. It just never stops."

"That's not true and you know it," I said defensively. "First of all, you know that I can be one of the silliest and dumbest individuals you've ever encountered. I offer all kinds of comic relief to soften the grim nature of my oft-repeated doomsday predictions."

"Dumb, for sure," she said.

"But second, and much more importantly, do you want me to tell you what a real pessimist sounds like?" I challenged.

"Uh, not really."

"Well, I'll tell you anyway. My idea of a pessimist is somebody who hears about a new tram in Moab, another condo development, or another bonehead move by a Utah congressman, hears the outrage from others, and puts his hands over his ears and says, 'Like, this is all so *negative*. I think this kind of negative energy is, like, really saaaad. I can find such happiness in my organic garden and taking hikes with my friends and just being, like, happy. I mean, I recycle. Why can't you people just be happy? There are still nice places to hike. You can't stop any of this anyway, so, like, why make yourselves miserable?' Now *that* is a pessimistic person, someone in such denial that she refuses to acknowledge the reality around her and the responsibility to defend the very things that she allegedly finds most precious in her life. It's stumbling through life with blinders on. It's ignoring the obvious. It's outrageous and hypocritical to boot! On the other hand, someone who is outraged enough to act believes that things can get better, that positive change is possible, that it's worth the screaming and elevated blood pressure to see something through to its conclusion, win or lose."

"I never say 'like' in a sentence," she glared.

"My dear friend, I'm not even talking about you. Your grasp of the English language is to be commended, and I know you have a great passion for right and wrong. I was creating a hyperbolic stereotype to make a point. Just don't assume that outrage is a bad thing. It has its place."

"So, the bottom line is that you're a positive upbeat optimist because you're constantly outraged and annoyed, and if the world were similarly infuriated, it would be a better place to live?"

"Something like that."

"Nobody will ever believe it."

"Probably not."

▬▬▬ ▬▬▬ ▬▬▬ Later I had to question my own argument. Did getting angry or passionately involved ultimately make any difference? Is the rural West doomed to the same plastic homogenous fate that keeps slurping up the rest of the country? Is there not a damn thing we can do about it? I always turn to Cactus Ed at a time like this, and I recall Abbey's admonition from the introduction to *Desert Solitaire*: "Throw a rock at something big and glassy. . . . What have you got to lose?"

About ten years ago, Ken Sleight saddled up his horse and attacked a D9 bulldozer that was tearing up pinyon-juniper woodlands on the mesa above his ranch. It was something of a mismatch. I have no idea how many horsepower a D9 bulldozer generates, but it's definitely more than Ken's horse, Knothead. Perhaps Sleight's charge was nothing but a symbol of his frustration, but I'd swear that in that critical moment when Ken and steed faced off with twenty tons of steel, Ken thought he just might win.

There was a lesson to be learned there. Ken's been tilting windmills for more than half a century. He was part of a handful of river runners in the 1950s who actively opposed the construction of Glen Canyon Dam, even when the Sierra Club had folded on the issue. Ken opposed road building in San Juan County, and he almost got himself flattened trying to block the forward momentum of a road grader when he was seventy-two years old. He annoys the San Juan County Commission to tears whenever he feels the need to appear before the commission to rail against . . . well, whatever it is he's currently railing against. Ken Sleight never gives up. He's probably lost a lot more battles than he's won, but I don't think Ken ever looks at it in those terms. For him, to do nothing would have been the ultimate defeat, something I doubt he could have lived with.

To me that's what "giving a damn" is all about—putting conscience and honor before complacency or the prevailing wisdom of the time, in the face of certain opposition, even defeat. At least in the beginning, most moral battles are waged against overwhelming odds and the cause worth fighting for may not yet be well defined. It can seem absurd to many, a folly to most. But there are some, just a relative handful, really, who can't accept the word *inevitable*. Nothing is a foregone conclusion to them. Here are a few of their stories.

Rich Ingebretsen: The Crazed Mormon Doctor/Restorer of Glen Canyon

Abbey died before he ever had a chance to meet Dr. Richard Ingebretsen, the president of the Glen Canyon Institute and a man as devoted to a lost cause as anyone I've ever met. I would have loved to see the two of them together, standing in the twilight along the Colorado River, discussing the issues of the day.

I can see Ed, bushy, bearded, and scraggly, his calloused and dirty feet hanging over the edge of a worn-out pair of flip-flops, sipping a beer and spewing hot rhetoric and occasional profanity. Then there's Rich, neatly trimmed, shirttail tucked inside his Dockers, cap placed squarely above his clean-shaven face, sipping lemonade and complaining about that gosh-darned lake. Ed's Rasputin looks concealed a gentle side, and Rich's Mormon manners belie an intense activist passion. These guys would have loved each other.

I met Rich Ingebretsen almost ten years ago at a Glen Canyon Institute gathering at Ken Sleight's Pack Creek Ranch. Rich had created the institute a year earlier, despite the warnings of friends who thought he just might be corseted up in a straitjacket and hauled away by Mormon elders if he publicly pursued such a crazy dream. Rich forged ahead anyway, driven by a dream and a memory.

Rich had seen Glen Canyon when he was a kid, just a few months before the dam was completed and the reservoir started to grow behind it. He was with his Boy Scout troop hiking up Forbidden Canyon to see Rainbow Bridge, when his scoutmaster mentioned the dam to them for the first time. He told the boys to look high up on the canyon walls, "Do you see that pinnacle up there? When the lake is full, that rock will be under water. All of this will be flooded, and you'll be riding in boats way up there."

Rich scanned the scenery around him. He saw the pools of water that they'd just emerged from, the pools that had offered such cool relief on a hot summer day. They would disappear under the lake. He saw violet green swallows darting overhead, coming and going from their mud nests in the alcove above. All that would be gone. He touched the inscriptions of ancient Anasazi Indians and more recent signatures, chiseled into the sandstone by pioneering river runners like John Wesley Powell, Fred Dellenbaugh, and the Kolb Brothers. Their images and names would be flooded forever. All that history would be gone.

He couldn't quite believe it. His mind simply could not compute the immensity of the project. After the trip was over and he'd returned home to Salt Lake City, Rich tried to put the image of the flooded canyon out of his mind, but it wouldn't leave. Two years later, he returned with his scout troop, and it was just as his scoutmaster had predicted. Glen Canyon was beneath him now. From a motorboat, he stared into the deep green water and could see nothing. He thought about the pools, the swallows, the inscriptions. All of it was in the dark green depths of Lake Powell now. But he vowed to remember what was there. He would not forget.

Thirty years on, Rich kept his promise. On behalf of the Glen Canyon Institute, he faced anyone who would talk about Glen Canyon. He walked into hostile water-board meetings and debated motorboat enthusiasts. He challenged other environmentalists to take a bold stand. Rich always approached his adversaries with gentle grace and a soft voice, which totally disarmed his most vitriolic opponents. His greatest tools were the facts, but he never threw them at anyone.

Then his ultimate lost cause got a helping hand from Mother Nature. In 1999 the Southwest saw the first of what would be six years of extreme drought. Its effect was stunning, and no one can say for sure that it's over. Cities and towns from northern Utah to southern Arizona saw their water supplies dwindle to a trickle. Mandatory rationing was instituted, and lawns and gardens became a memory. Ranchers suffered the most, as they watched their rangelands dry up and blow away. Great ponderosa pine forests withered and died. Here in southeastern Utah, millions of pinyon pines met the same fate. Wildfires consumed millions of acres. The landscape was changing before our very eyes.

One unexpected benefit of the drought was the effect it had on Lake Powell. By 2002 the lake level had fallen 80 feet from its maximum pool level of 3700 feet above sea level. After forty years, features began to emerge from the water. Rapids at the northern end of the lake reappeared. The Colorado River ran again at Hite Crossing, and the marina there closed because the boat ramp ended 300 feet from the lake's edge.

As we watched the reservoir recede, one thought dominated our hopes as we realized Glen Canyon was coming back to life. One day in early March 2002, Rich and I decided to search for the Cathedral in the Desert. We found it, looking more like Phil Hyde's 1964 photograph.

I first saw Hyde's classic image of Glen Canyon's Cathedral in the Desert more than twenty-five years ago. Even then, a full decade had come and gone since the rising waters of Lake Powell inundated this extraordinary work of nature in 150 feet of stagnant water. For most of us, it was as if the Cathedral simply didn't exist anymore. Only Ed Abbey was wise enough to remind all of us that the Cathedral and the rest of Glen Canyon weren't gone at all. They were, he insisted, simply in "liquid storage." Ed was more right than even he knew.

By the spring of 2005, Lake Powell had dropped another sixty feet. According to the institute's calculations, the Cathedral should be completely out of the water. Rich and I decided to take a look. We traveled to the Cathedral via motorboat, the very form of transportation that would become obsolete if the reservoir ever runs dry. Both Rich and I noted the irony, for the lake has made it almost impossible to explore much of Glen Canyon by any other means. So there we were, in a $20,000 rented motorboat, spewing a spray of lake water in our wake, trying to grow accustomed to the smell of two-cycle motor oil and the roar of the outboard engine. We did this to see one of the most stunning sights on Earth, one that no one had viewed in its entirety in almost forty years.

It took us an hour to go from Hall's Crossing to the mouth of the Escalante River and then up Clear Creek to a point where the canyon appeared to close in. It was just as Harlon Beamont and Burnett Hendrix, two writers for *National Geographic*, had noted a half-century before. They had given the Cathedral its name. Rich observed that for most of its named lifetime, the Cathedral had been buried in water. Now, maybe, it was finally free from its watery grave. We were still in the boat, passing over the skeletal remains of cottonwoods that once filled this magnificent canyon with colors and aromas unmatched anywhere. There was a slot at the back of the chamber, easier seen now than then, that allowed us to move a bit farther upstream. We made one final turn to the right. *There it was.*

The Cathedral in the Desert had been perfectly preserved in almost all respects. The waterfall now flowed freely, and the spring runoff cascaded over the sculptured lip of the drop-off and spattered in a pool fifty feet below. The ancient dark desert varnish around the waterfall had not faded in forty years. The concoidal striations that were so clearly visible in Hyde's images were just as sharply defined. We looked at each other, almost in disbelief. Rich and I found ourselves speaking in whispered tones. It had been a long time since I'd experienced silence like that.

We traveled back to the talus slope where Hyde had taken his 1964 photograph. (At the time the reservoir was already rising, and Hyde knew the scenes he was shooting would be lost within a year.) Incredibly, even the broken rocks had changed little; we found one large flat boulder near the top of the talus that must have served as the ultimate viewpoint. Rich kept saying softly, "This is where Hyde stood." It was all still there, just waiting for nature to expose the rock and for us to return.

From time to time, we came upon an old beer can, a piece of rope, or a lost thermos cup, the detritus of the last forty years of motorized recreation in this holy chamber. But what surprised us was how *little* garbage there was to be found.

We noted the seeps oozing from the canyon walls and a subtle hint of green around those wet places in the Navajo sandstone. Nature was already at work. Along the wash bottom, signs of new growth were everywhere. We could see how the runoff continued to scour the canyon of sediments and push it farther downstream, toward the Gulf of California, where it ultimately must someday be allowed to go. Without any help from us, the Cathedral in the Desert was, in the most tranquil way imaginable, one tiny step at a time, being restored. Nature was trying to put back what we had taken away. All it needs is time, that most precious of commodities.

It occurred to Rich and me that our greatest task was to run interference for nature. *We* weren't restoring Glen Canyon, *nature* was. We could pick up a few old beer cans, a chair or two thrown from the deck of a boat years ago, no doubt by a drunken tourist. But nature was doing the work.

The fact that the drought coincided with our pleas and laments was totally unexpected, it was a shock and a surprise to us all. But I'm too cynical to think that nature intended to be our partners in all this. Nature would be just as agreeable to drowning *us* in a sudden desert flash flood as it would members of the Bureau of Reclamation. I don't believe nature takes sides, even when one side wants to destroy it.

But how do we help Glen Canyon save itself? The easy answer is to leave it alone. Convincing supporters of the reservoir won't be easy at all; in fact, it might be impossible. But if the reservoir continues to shrink, the pro–Lake Powell arguments may become irrelevant.

As Rich and I motored out of the Cathedral, we already knew that this year's spring runoff would be massive and that the reservoir could rise at least thirty feet, perhaps fifty, maybe more. If the scientists are wrong, which has happened before, this may be Cathedral in the Desert's one brief moment to see the light of day. But I'll take comfort in knowing that it really is down there, in liquid storage, waiting for an enlightened future to let it shine again.

Meanwhile Rich Ingebretsen will not rest until he's told the world about the beauty that lies beneath Lake Powell. He proclaims to anyone who will listen, "I absolutely believe that I will see Glen Canyon again in my lifetime!" Sometimes, when I watch him very closely and listen to the conviction in his voice, I realize that this crazy Mormon really believes what he's saying. What a relief.

Waldo Wilcox: Keeping Secrets

The dilemma is knowing when to keep your mouth shut. When is staying silent more heroic than speaking up? Just *trying* to keep a secret is almost impossible in the Information Age, but rancher Waldo Wilcox kept a good one for half a century. In 2004, when his secret was finally revealed, it became the second largest global online news story of the day. Since 1951 Mr. Wilcox has protected one of the most remarkable archaeological treasures ever found in the American Southwest. Even the Wetherills would have been impressed. He protected them simply by not telling anyone. Like Wilcox said, "The less people who know about this, the better."

Strung along twelve miles of a mountain creek, deep in the rugged Book Cliffs of southern Utah, is a series of prehistoric Native American villages that have remained untouched and virtually unseen by anyone but Wilcox and his close friends and family for a thousand years. The ancient villages were occupied for more than 3000 years by the Fremont Indians until they were suddenly abandoned almost a millennium ago. Since then, only the wind and the rain have touched the thousands of artifacts left behind—until now.

Wilcox, who worried that after his passing the villages might be vandalized and destroyed, decided to sell his secret treasures. He was paid $2.5 million and retired to Green River, Utah. Ownership of the 4200 acres was transferred to the state and federal government. Naturally, the first thing state archaeologists did was to shuttle news organizations to the remote site. It was a media circus.

As I watched the coverage that evening on the Salt Lake news channels, Waldo Wilcox looked utterly bewildered. You could almost see him thinking, "What have I done?" I don't blame him for worrying, although I don't know what other options he had. Later, updated news reports indicated that the sites had already been vandalized by the very members of the media who traveled there.

So what happens now that the world has been informed? In an age where everyone feels they have a right to experience first-hand every secret treasure our shrinking planet conceals, what can we expect? Guided tours? A canyoneering-archaeological adventure trip? A state lottery for an opportunity to visit the villages? Will local chambers of commerce demand easier and faster access so that their tourism economies can grow? Will the government need to construct a thirty-mile cyclone fence around the site to keep the human scavengers out? I don't limit my scavenger label to just gravediggers and moki poachers. Every eco-tourist who wants to say he or she "did Waldo's artifacts" will bear part of the responsibility for its eventual degradation.

In fact, the idea of protecting special places by keeping them a secret has stirred debate even among environmentalists. I keep remembering what Steve Allen, the guidebook writer, canyoneering tour operator, and sometime SUWA spokesman, said about protecting wilderness areas, "We need more people out there, not less. Right now, the wilderness lands of southern Utah are in flux. . . . We need as many wilderness supporters as we can get."

There may be logic to his argument, but it still scares me. What of growing concerns that too many people, no matter how well intentioned, run the risk of loving such natural treasures to death? I'd imagine Wilcox shares my worries. For very unselfish reasons, this rancher protected a priceless treasure for half a century. Critics have already begun to question Wilcox's motives and look for reasons to dispute his good intentions. For those who will argue that he did it for the money, remember that he sold his land for less than $600 an acre—not exactly ranchette prices. Also consider how many government bureaucrats, at how great an expense, and with what degree of success will be required to perform the job he did alone.

We should leave the village alone. Take comfort that the Book Cliff sites are there and forget about them. Do it for the Fremont, and do it for Waldo Wilcox. The last I heard, he's still wondering if he made the right decision and worrying about those treasures that he guarded with his silence for fifty years.

Jennifer Speers: Thinking Outside the Deconstructed Box

Over the years, as I made one disparaging comment after another about wealthy people in the *Zephyr*, I knew that someday my rhetoric would come back to bite me on the ass. I often exacerbated the situation by calling some of them "rich weasels." I also didn't spare the "benevolent rich weasels," those who try to assuage their consciences by making large donations to their favorite environmental group, while building obscenely extravagant, absurdly consumptive dwellings for themselves, hoping for recognition in both *Architectural Digest* and *Sierra* magazine. Of course, considering the compromised, money-hungry attitude of most environmental groups these days, such dual recognition is not only within the realm of possibility, but a fact. Just ask Gateway's John Hendricks.

Then along came Jennifer Speers. Every time I even think about this woman, I feel the need, the responsibility, right here, right now, to get down on my knees and grovel for forgiveness. I feel obligated to lash myself with wet leather straps. I would allow her to bury me in sand, pour maple syrup on my head, and cover me with fire ants. I want to tell her in a striking way, "I'm *sorry.*"

Jennifer Speers came to northern Utah from New York several decades ago to attend college. She picked the University of Utah because it was a thirty-minute drive from the campus to the ski slopes. She came to Utah for the powder; college was her excuse.

Speers first traveled south to Moab in 1975 on the back of a Harley with her future husband. It was the beginning of her love affair with the canyon country. Back then, she had no idea what role she might play in its future. Although Speers was born to wealth, she doesn't wear it very conspicuously. In fact, she hardly wears it at all.

A few years ago while looking for property to buy in Grand County, she approached a few realtors. Several pieces of property caught her eye. First she bought Proudfoot Bend Ranch, north of Dewey Bridge and Moab on State Route 128, to assure its cow pastures and open space would never be covered in condos. That was good enough, but she didn't stop there—and this is where we enter the realm of *the unheard of.*

Adjacent to Dewey Bridge was the Rio Colorado Estates subdivision. An out-of-state developer bought the river frontage land several years ago. He bulldozed and graded the hills and gullies, bladed every plant and piece of grass on the ground into pulp, until the river bottom looked like an unpaved parking lot. He installed a paved road and curbs, established power and water services, and carved up the acreage into expensive lots. He built a big faux adobe gateway to his high-end, rich-weasel project and planted many nonnative trees around it to give it a warm and natural feel. Then he built a $600,000 home on the banks of the Colorado River to, I would guess, prime the real estate pump. But nobody was interested. The subdivision languished for a few years, until Jennifer Speers came along.

The developer was eager to unload the subdivision. He never dreamed one buyer might want the whole enchilada, but there she was with an offer he couldn't refuse. He assumed Speers wanted to market the lots herself, and maybe she'd have better luck. He was probably grateful to recover part of his losses and get out. So she bought all the lots, the whole damn subdivision. And then she *tore down* the house.

Speers and her ranch foreman attacked the house with crowbars, hammers, and mauls. They removed all the windows and doors, counter tops, wood trim, anything salvageable that they could pull out of the mansion. Then she contracted a bulldozer to knock the adobe walls down, and she cleared the premises of any debris. Not a trace of the monstrous, out-of-place mansion, just across the river from a public campground, survived her restoration efforts.

But that still wasn't enough. Speers had workers remove the street, the curbs, the underground utilities, and the pump house that was to provide water for the entire subdivision. She had them bulldoze the gaudy entrance sign, and they pulled up the nonnative trees. The ground was recontoured and seeded with native grasses and plants. When she was finished, not a hint of the Rio Colorado Estates was evident.

People were bewildered when they drove by and saw the other side of the river looking much as it had ten years earlier. What Speers did had been unthinkable before she did it. For all of us in Grand County, the subdivision was a foregone conclusion. Speers thought otherwise.

Now, whenever I drive past Dewey Bridge, I cannot stifle a smile. I don't know anyone else who doesn't react in the same fashion. I hope that Jennifer Speers becomes a role model for other wealthy people, that this is precedent setting. If all rich people would tear down just *one* of their mansions, I would sing their praises as well.

▬▬▬ ▬▬▬ ▬▬▬ What is so striking about Rich Ingebretsen, Waldo Wilcox, and Jennifer Speers is their basic decency and their conspicuous lack of self-promotion. All three chose to do something quite remarkable and set out to do it in a most unremarkable way. None of them sought the limelight, even if it finally found them. They are without guile, and I love that about them.

Rich Ingebretsen took on a cause that was laughable before he stepped to the microphone. Nobody took the idea of restoring Glen Canyon seriously. Even we who protested and demonstrated didn't expect results. Now the idea of decommissioning dams across America is on the table. That's why politicians are so vehemently defending Glen Canyon Dam now, and it's why we protesters are so optimistic. When politicians get blustery and bellicose, they're scared. They think we just might pull it off.

In these indiscreet times, who can keep a secret for more than a minute? And who won't sell a secret when tempted with a lot of cash? Waldo Wilcox kept his secret for half a century and honored the people who lived in those rocky canyons more sincerely and more poignantly than any museum could ever hope to do.

Jennifer Speers, in her own kind and gentle way, created another new set of possibilities. No one ever dreamed that an ugly, expensive home, no matter how out of place, unnecessary, or inappropriate it might be, could ever be torn down and cleansed from the face of the Earth. But that's what she did. Now the idea of deconstructing an eyesore seems plausible, even possible.

A decade ago, a well-meaning but misguided group of Moabites proposed to build a 2200-foot tram up the side of the red cliffs near the Portal. I was convinced that if our fight to stop it in the planning stages failed, the tram's construction would be a permanent scar on the land. We lost, and the tram was built. But it was an economic failure, and after the property traded hands a few times, the Nature Conservancy (the only environmental group I can unflinchingly honor) bought the tram. One Saturday morning a reclamation crew went to work, and by noon the tram was gone. It was that easy. I've started to call this "The Speers Effect." It just might catch on.

And always, my dearest friend of all, Ken Sleight, the last Don Quixote, the grinning idealist, is still attacking bulldozers on a horse, still implacably determined to go forward. May Ken live forever.

Over the years, I've always been impressed by the power that individuals can wield when they have the courage to challenge conventional wisdom, especially when they know such wisdom is dead wrong. In these cynical times, it's easy to assume our impotence is eternal and that values we once cherished are gone forever. But I have to believe that voices of people like Rich, Waldo, Jennifer, and Ken make a difference, and that all of us, deep down in our souls, have the power to be just like them.

Finally, the Naked West Comes to Moab

One fine morning, I awoke to find the world exactly the way I had anticipated it would someday be. The planet, as John Steinbeck once said, was spinning in greased grooves after all. "Perfect," I thought to myself, "I'm a goddamn visionary." I thought of Hunter S. Thompson, who should have been here for this final transformation and who would have been delighted. He may well have even participated. Although nothing was ever quite strange enough for Dr. Gonzo, it finally got weird enough for me.

The future had finally arrived, just a little ahead of schedule, at Sorrel River Ranch, the luxury lodge north of Moab that spreads sanguinely like a centerfold on the edge of the Colorado River. True, the full frontal exposure took me by surprise, but there could remain no doubt in anyone's mind about the rapidly changing physical and cultural landscape in the once remote and lonesome rural West.

On a late summer day in 2004, multimillionaire Robbie Levin, the owner of Sorrel River Ranch, applied for a state cabaret license. In Utah, that's what we call a liquor license. As part of the process, Levin requested a letter of support from the Grand County Council. This was supposed to show the state liquor authorities that Levin was a man of high moral character and unquestioned principles who was honored and respected by his peers and by the governing body of his home county. But things went badly for Levin. The council refused its support when one of its members, Councilman Al McLeod, accused Levin of operating a sexually oriented business. With just a couple months left in office, Al must have been feeling frisky that day, but he finally put an end to the rumors and laid out the naked truth for everyone to see. Here's what happened.

In 2003 thirteen episodes of the HBO series "Hotel Erotica" were shot on Levin's property. The television crew shot scenes in the rooms, in the spas, in the parking lot, along the river, and a lot of scenes were filmed in the bushes. The show features a great deal of simulated sex and humping, a plethora of shrieks and moans, and more than a fair share of "Oh God!" and "Oh baby!" HBO's Web site says the series contains "adult content, nudity, strong sexual content, and adult language."

Councilman McLeod said it amounted to soft-core pornography, and "that skates pretty close to state liquor laws," which ban cabaret licenses to sexually oriented businesses. The council voted on Levin's request and, based on a 3-3 tie vote, denied Levin its support.

In a telephone interview with reporter Lisa Church of the Moab *Times-Independent*, Levin conceded that rooms had been rented to the production company for the filming of "Hotel Erotica," but that it was a one-time occurrence. Then Levin went ballistic. He told Church, "How do you respond to something so stupid and ignorant? We are completely family oriented here. . . . Our property has nothing to do with sex or a sexually oriented business. It's silly to be labeled that. Al [McLeod] should get his facts straight."

Rumors that Levin planned to sue the council and its members spread like a sexually transmitted rash. His friends and employees fired off angry letters to the *Times-Independent*. Sorrel River Ranch Assistant Manager Sara Snider criticized Councilpersons McLeod and Joette Langianese, writing, "The recklessly unfounded remarks made by this uninformed duo are personally offensive and morally appalling. . . . Whether compelled by malice, ignorance, or other motives, you have intentionally caused harm with your unsubstantiated and viciously inaccurate statements."

Local developer Tom Shellenberger observed, "Never have we seen any hint of impropriety at the ranch. The filming that took place at the ranch was conducted in private. . . . Robbie and Hope Levin have created a four diamond resort in our community, the level of which has never been seen before in Grand County."

Levin certainly had taken us to levels never dreamed possible. Meanwhile, stories of these alleged soft-porn shenanigans fueled Moab's propensity for gossip and innuendo. Already, for some citizens Levin's plush Sorrel River Ranch had become "Oral River Ranch" or "Oral River Rash." The play on words was endless.

Personally, I wasn't offended at all. I'm as lusty as the next guy, maybe more so. I don't really care what goes on between consenting adults behind closed doors, whether it's across the street or twenty miles up the Colorado River. It didn't matter to me a whit if those activities were for fun, for profit, or both. Everybody's got to make a living. Besides, all that poor Robbie Levin wanted was a liquor license, a simple procedure practically anywhere else in America, but one that can become an ordeal in Utah. I could understand Levin's frustration at times.

For Levin, the problem was his venue. Utah is perhaps the most conservative state in America, a state where even buying a mixed drink is a challenge. Utah is heavily influenced by the dominance of the Church of Latter Day Saints, whose doctrines also frown upon the consumption of coffee and Coca-Cola. Utahns elect Republican presidents with 75 percent of the vote. When we swear, we say, "my heck" and "flip." Lime Jell-o is our favorite food.

Still most of us chose to live here. Nobody held a gun to my head and forced me to move to Utah. I came because I loved the red rocks, and I have no one to blame but myself.

My values may be a bit different from the Utah mainstream, but I have no desire to impose them on 75 percent of Utah's population. So no one could fault Al McLeod, as an elected official representing the best interests of *all* Grand County residents, for raising these issues. In fact, it was puzzling that the most conservative-leaning members of the council voted in favor of Levin's cabaret license. Utah is steeped in irony and contradiction, and this was just another example of it.

When it comes to Old West versus New West values, money and the greed it stimulates always have a way of complicating matters. Old Westerners have traditionally been torn by two very conflicting belief systems. On the one hand, they cannot stand to be dictated to by outsiders and resent, even despise, any intrusion into their rural way of life. On the other hand, they embrace individual property rights and the free enterprise system with almost religious fervor.

Old Westerners simply wanted to be left alone to pursue the kind of life they preferred. In the rural West it was possible to accomplish that, but only because very few people wanted to live such a solitary and acetic existence. Mormons consistently opposed any intervention by misguided heathens not of the true faith who attempted to impose different values or laws upon them. In 1857, when a federal judge was sent by President Buchanan to enforce federal law in Utah, he was summarily run out of the Salt Lake Valley on a rail. The unappreciated judge's name was George Stiles. Whether he's a relative of mine or not, it's an interesting point of trivia that I do not share with historically knowledgeable Mormons.

Rural Westerners' full embrace of individual property rights and free enterprise has been their undoing. They love their remote lifestyle but sometimes fail to see the connection between their lives and the land they've built those lives upon. Selling to the highest bidder is a capitalistic concept that any good American can understand. But sometimes the highest bidder isn't the fellow you'd choose for a neighbor. These conflicting values tend to blur ideological lines to the point where it's difficult to grasp just what the disagreement is.

Consider the downright baffling contradictions that stemmed from a recent local election campaign. Follow me closely. The incumbent county councilman, Jim Lewis, is considered the more liberal of the two candidates, but keep in mind that this is Utah. His challenger, longtime Moabite and contractor Dave Cozzins, is very conservative, listens to Rush Limbaugh, promotes the social values agenda promulgated by Bush and friends, and vehemently opposes environmentalists. Cozzins almost froths at the mere mention of SUWA.

As the campaign turned ugly, the rumors flew like biting gnats on a summer evening. Allegations flashed across my computer in a variety of e-mails. Supporters of Lewis (though I never heard this from Jim himself) believed that Robbie Levin, the host to soft-porn filmmakers, was funding Cozzins's campaign to the tune of $6000. This claim was denied by Cozzins. On the other hand, Cozzins believed that SUWA was contributing to Lewis's campaign and was also responsible for spreading the Robbie Levin funding rumor and other scurrilous lies. All of this was denied by SUWA. When Cozzins's construction equipment was vandalized, he held SUWA responsible. I informed Cozzins that since most of the SUWA staff are attorneys from urban areas, even if they had the inclination, none of them would know *how* to disable a bulldozer. I later realized that, when it came to SUWA, attempts at levity with Dave Cozzins were futile.

If I believed the rumors and the rhetoric, I might draw two conclusions here. Cozzins has no use for SUWA or its environmental policies and political agenda, and SUWA opposes pro-development types like Cozzins and Levin's ever-expanding, sometimes naked empire at Sorrel River Ranch.

Here's the reality and where it gets so complicated. Cozzins is Old West. He's been in Moab for decades, is a heavy equipment operator and independent contractor, and opposes federal wilderness designation. SUWA is New West. It supports wilderness and opposes the traditional extractive industry that was the economic backbone of the rural West for a century. Levin's high-end luxury lodge, with an occasional soft-porn production company from Hollywood, pumps thousands of dollars into the Grand County and

Moab economies and is *precisely* the kind of nonpolluting, tourist-oriented business that the environmental community has promoted as the future of the rural West for fifteen years. Sorrel River Ranch, bare nipples and all, *is* their kind of industry.

While Cozzins maintains he's Old West and upholds strong Christian values, he openly supports businesses like Sorrel River Ranch. (Putting the soft-core porn aside for just a minute, wasn't it Jesus Christ himself who once said, "It is easier for a camel to pass through the eye of a needle than for a rich man to enter the Kingdom of Heaven"?) I doubt if Cozzins ever sheds a tear for the good old days when Bill Boulden ran a few cows on that property.

The irony-driven truth must be acknowledged. Dave Cozzins, legendary right-wing, anti-environmentalist, free market capitalist, and SUWA, legendary left-wing, tree hugging, commie pinkos are on the same team—and they have been for years. The Old Westerners who bitterly complain about the changes to their beloved lands are, more often than not, willing accomplices who have profited handsomely from the New West invasion. Environmentalists privately decry the likes of Sorrel River Ranch but refuse to admit their own culpability. Old West versus New West? Sometimes it's difficult to tell that anything has changed at all. The extractive industries are alive and well. The glitter has a different glint, that's all.

■■■■ ■■■■ ■■■■ But politics is never as interesting as sex or a woman's naked body, and the "Hotel Erotica" story still had another chapter or two to titillate us with. Although Levin continued to assert that he merely rented rooms to the "Hotel Erotica" production company and that he runs his lodge as a "completely family-oriented" business, it just didn't ring true with a lot of people. A dash of candor would have been appreciated, even admired. I would have respected Levin if he'd said, "Yeah, they shot a soft-core porn series here. It made us a lot of money and brought a lot of revenue to Grand

County. This is the future of Grand County, and if you don't like it, you better step aside, because the future is here and it's not wearing clothes."

But that didn't happen. Levin kept ranting against his enemies, real or perceived, that he'd been slandered. Worst of all, he kept threatening retribution in the form of lawsuits. Finally, I'd had a gut full. We've all grown sick and weary of that kind of attempted intimidation from rich weasels who can act threateningly simply because they have more money than the rest of us.

So, I did a Google search on Sorrel River Ranch. Levin's claim that he served only as an innkeeper for the "Hotel Erotica" crew and that the relationship was purely business got a bit shaky when I discovered that his beautiful wife, former Playboy Playmate of the Month Hope Levin, appeared in the series. In fact, I found an entire page called "Hotel Erotica: Cast Guide" that listed the stars, including "Hope Levin, Lauren Hays, and Tina Leiu." I learned from an accompanying episode guide that Hope Levin starred as maid supervisor Agnes in an episode called "Maid Service" and in the role of Queen Theodosius in an episode entitled "Bewitched and Bewildered." Bewitched and bewildered, indeed.

Finally, I found some images from the "Hotel Erotica" series on another Web site. For a few bucks, I could have downloaded the steamy streaming video of some lesbian love scenes filmed on the banks of the Colorado River in broad daylight and in clear view of anyone who happened to be paddling downstream from the Hittle Bottom put-in. Had Dave Cozzins been floating downstream that day, his "family values" may have taken a beating, but the view would have been spectacular. One thing is for sure, referring to the "bottomland" along the Colorado River has an entirely new meaning in the early years of the twenty-first century.

I can still recall my first journey down the old river road, decades ago, when it was dirt and gravel and the most exciting part of the forty-mile drive was the hazardous crossing of the old one-lane Dewey Bridge. Back then, most of the bottomland was owned by real ranchers. They grew alfalfa and raised cattle. Later the ranchers came to be targets of the environmental community. As the amenities economy continues to generate a demand for rural property, most Old Westerners are unable to resist the staggering sums offered for that land. The wide-open lonesome West isn't nearly as lonesome as it used to be. The New West is here in all its naked glory.

Hollywood had discovered this land long before Hope Levin's stunning performance in "Bewitched and Bewildered." Going as far back as the 1940s, directors such as John Ford were producing classic films like "She Wore a Yellow Ribbon," all shot on location right here in God's country, in the heart of Utah's red-rock canyons. Perhaps some day we'll see something of a remake. I can almost see the title on the DVD, "She Wore Only a Yellow Ribbon."

The Brave New Naked West.

"Something Entirely Different"

The Naked West, the Nouveau West, the Brave New West, the extractive economy, the amenities economy, motorized recreation, nonmotorized recreation, wilderness as a concept, wilderness as a regulation. When did it become so complicated? Who are my allies and who are my adversaries? Is the Brave New West an improvement on the Old West? Are bare-breasted women at Sorrel River Ranch an economic and spiritual step up from swaying udders on Black Angus cows? Are 7000 bicyclists preferable to 500 jeeps? Why do I miss old miners and old cowboys, even when they exhibit narrow-minded behavior that infuriates me? Why do I find New Westerners infuriating even when they *do* agree with me? Do they exhibit a narrow-minded behavior all their own? Do I? Life was much easier when I viewed the world through a black-and-white lens.

Maybe I'm a hopeless sentimentalist, but I don't think I stand alone. Surely, there is something of this Old West worth saving. Does it all need to be thrown out and forgot-

ten? Does honest, genuine behavior, for example, count for something even when it's wrongheaded? I'd love to have an honest conversation with someone who totally disagrees with me but is willing to talk. I've come to recognize intolerance from both ends of the entrenched ideological spectrum. A real redneck right-winger will hear something that doesn't suit him, get angry, turn red in the face, and the vein in his temple might start to throb. He'll look you in the face and spit, "You say something stupid like that again, and I'll shove your teeth down your throat!"

But a liberal? His expression won't change, save a raised eyebrow perhaps. He'll lift his nose, fold his arms, turn slowly away and sniff, "I won't even dignify that with a response."

I've been attempting, *begging* for an honest, no-holds-barred conversation with my old pals at SUWA for years now. They give me nothing, nothing at all, other than an occasional "Why are you trying to trash us?" plea of exasperation. Recently, SUWA publicly proclaimed me to be "irrelevant." It's the old bunker mentality. If you dare to disagree with us, you must be against us. Therefore, you must be our enemy, and we will not acknowledge you. Nixon never stonewalled this well. At this point, I'd prefer throbbing temples and a face full of spittle. I yearn for a conversation, even if it's hotly shouted.

If *you* are wrong-headed or *I* am, then let's be truthful about it. That's the beauty of honesty. Boneheads talking to boneheads. Occasionally my Honest Bonehead Theory strikes a chord with someone, and when that happens, I know I've found a kindred spirit. Maybe that's all we can even hope for, finding the odd honest soul with whom we can commiserate. I'd like to hope for more, but maybe that's stretching it a bit.

How do we gather the kindred spirits? How do we pursue the common ground, now that we've found its contradictory vortex? The *Zephyr* has always been a gathering place of sorts. I was always proud when a *Zephyr* reviewer, Dave Swift of Jackson, Wyoming, insisted my paper was "full of boneheaded radicals and radical boneheads." He was exactly correct.

For a while I contemplated creating yet another activist organization. I wanted to call it Mormons and Heathens for a Better Utah or MAHBU. Of course, I recognized that not everyone on one side of the ideological fence is a member of the Church of Latter Day Saints, and not all people on the opposite side are heathens. To begin with, I searched for an acronym, one that might best suit Utahns, since that is, after all, my home base. Then I stumbled upon MAHBU. It sounded as if I'd morphed Nauvoo, the site of the original Mormon temple in Illinois, with SUWA, a frightening prospect for everyone involved regardless of their affiliation. But the point was to force everyone to be uncomfortable with their proximity to each other, instead of exchanging pot shots from the relative safety across the fence.

I knew that to address the issues, we had to clearly and more concisely identify them. At the heart of *this* war in the American West—and that's what we should call it—is a fundamental conflict of cultures over the future of its landscape. The vast majority of Americans who call themselves environmentalists, 78 percent in one survey, live in urban areas. Their connection to the land has usually been as observers, recreationists, and infrequent visitors. When they decide to become a part of a small rural community, these New Westerners bring their urban mind set with them. Most of those who oppose the environmental movement have actually lived and worked in the small rural communities of the West, and many of them have made their living from the land itself. They still represent the Old West. For the urban enviros, there's the rub.

In the last three decades, each side of the conflict has so savagely misrepresented the other, so excessively caricatured their opponents, that they've turned themselves into laughable cartoon characters as well. There is nothing like bloated self-righteousness to make someone seem ridiculous. To me everybody looks goofy these days. So, let's review once more the contentious issues driving this debate.

Rural Americans live in small towns, and the core of their economies has always been extractive—ranching, mining, and timber. To deny that the extractive industries have wreaked stunning and long-term destruction upon the Western landscape and its ecology is absurd.

Urban Americans want to eliminate these industries or at least curtail them to a large extent. They believe that the amenities economy is a clean and viable alternative to ranching, mining, and timber. Urban environmentalists are convinced it can allow the rural West to prosper and prevail, without further degradation to the resource. To deny that this kind of transformation of the rural West has bleak and destructive consequences of its own is equally absurd. The amenities economy is just another extractive industry, and it should be regarded by environmentalists with the same concern.

What is the unvarnished truth about *both* sides of this debate? From where I'm standing, it's this. Think of this list as a primer, the barely scratched contentious surface.

Most Old Westerners oppose wilderness because they believe it will limit their access to public lands. Sometimes their physical abuse of the land itself is dramatic and the damage is long term. But Old Westerners understand one key component of wilderness far better than their adversaries. They understand solitude, quiet, serenity, the emptiness of the rural West. They *like* the emptiness.

New Westerners are individually more sensitive to the resource but are terrified of solitude. They'll walk around cryptobiotic crust, but leave them alone in the canyons without a cell phone and a group of companions and they'd be lost, both physically and metaphysically. Because New Westerners need to travel in packs, the collective resource damage is far more than they might realize.

Old Westerners like their jeeps and their ATVs. Among these thousands of motorized recreationists are a minority of reckless and thoughtless idiots who cause a disproportionate share of the resource damage. Many of their peers know this and don't like it, but they don't apply peer pressure because the one thing they'd rather *not* do is be seen agreeing with an environmentalist.

New Westerners drive hundreds or thousands of miles in gas-consuming vehicles so they can pedal their bicycles for ten, and then they claim they're nonmotorized recreationists. Bicyclists gather for rallies and races just like their motorized cousins and cause extraordinary damage when their numbers are high enough. Yet, environmentalists refuse to acknowledge that many, many bicycles can sometimes cause as much damage as ATVs.

Old Westerners like cows. Millions of cattle still graze on public lands, and some ranchers who hold federal grazing allotments are terrible stewards of that land. They allow overgrazing, destroy valuable and rare riparian habitat, and turn some public lands into barren wastelands.

New Westerners hate cows. They think *all* ranchers are bad stewards. They want to eliminate all grazing on public lands. But when they buy a condo in a New West town, they love the view of the adjacent alfalfa field from their picture window and complain bitterly when yet another development wipes out the pastoral scene. Cows eat alfalfa.

Some Old Westerners like to hunt, mostly deer and elk. Each year a few hundred hunters in Utah get a permit to kill a cougar. They chase the big cat with their dogs, run it up a tree, and shoot it. Sounds pretty barbaric to me.

Most New Westerners don't hunt, and they would never kill a cougar. But when thousands of cougar-loving recreationists invade once empty public lands that are habitat for wild animals, it's a hunt of sorts already, a hunt to eliminate the habitat that wild and reclusive animals like cougars need. Conflict is inevitable. New Westerners build their homes farther into wildlands, so they can "live amid nature," but when a cougar has a favorite shih tzu for lunch, retribution suddenly becomes acceptable.

Most Old Westerners actually live the more modest and simple lifestyle that their New West adversaries claim to admire. Their homes are smaller, and their cars are older. They recycle their junk—or at least don't throw it away—and generally do without a lot of luxuries that a New Westerner could never endure. They despise the smug arrogance and urban ways of their New West neighbors. But if Old Westerners had more money, they would probably live just as extravagantly.

Most New Westerners long for the simple life and want to move to a small town. But they hold the Old Westerners in low esteem and abhor their politics. When they move to a small town, New Westerners build oversized homes, complain about the lack of amenities, and try to change everything.

Old Westerners long for the "good old days" of ranching and mining and detest the tourists and the New West image of their towns. But they never hesitate to make a buck from the amenities economy themselves when the opportunity presents itself. Many Old Westerners are millionaires today because land they bought for next to nothing in the 1960s or 1970s is now worth a fortune.

New Westerners claim that the uncontrolled growth of the amenities economy is out of their hands, that market forces and the whims of American culture are driving the New West, not them. As one Utah environmentalist said defensively, "It would have happened anyway." In effect New Westerners now refuse to take credit for the extraordinary success of the very economy they claimed would save the West. They actually distance themselves from the solution they continue to promote. Every ATV rally, every new convenience store, every condo development, every golf course, every four-star restaurant in a town with a population of 5000 is an extension of the amenities economy.

Old Westerners love seismic exploration work because it brings money to the rural economy. But it also leaves a swath of destruction in its path. While restrictions have reduced the amount of damage that seismic work once caused, its effects can still be seen years later. Once the work is done, though, the land returns to normal as far as the habitat goes. Wildlife is most adversely affected by constant human intrusions. The one good aspect of a seismic crew is that when they complete their work, they leave.

New Westerners hate seismic exploration so much that they often hold on-site protests. But to some animals, *their* long-term presence is more offensive than the thumper trucks. The fact that desert bighorns have vanished from the Gemini Bridges area near Moab is not because of the seismic work that environmentalists fought in the early 1990s. It's recreationists, both motorized and nonmotorized, that have driven them into hiding. Also, many seismic trail habitats never get a chance to recover because bicyclists and ATVers keep using them.

Old Westerners are unlikely to go backpacking or exploring for the sheer pleasure of it. Many of them would think such an effort to be pure folly. Sometimes they seem oblivious to the beauty that surrounds them. But if they broke down or got stranded in the backcountry, they would probably be able to take care of themselves because most of them have lived close to the land all their lives.

New Westerners love to go backpacking and exploring, but many of them simply don't have the skills necessary to survive if something goes wrong. As a result, the search-and-rescue budgets of many rural Western communities have increased astronomically in recent years. Most members of search-and-rescue teams are Old Westerners.

Old Westerners advocate support the federal government's unprecedented efforts to increase oil and gas development on public lands, and they insist increased production is absolutely necessary to reduce our dependence on foreign oil. Many of those same people mock efforts to reduce U.S. dependence through conservation efforts, which is really stupid. Why would conservatives oppose conservation? Because they're afraid to be linked with anything remotely supporting an environmentalist perspective.

New Westerners oppose increased oil and gas exploration and advocate conservation efforts. Yet, most of them are bigger consumers of natural resources than the people who defend drilling in the public domain. While New Westerners decry the loss of wildlife habitat, the fact is, most wildlife adapts quite well to inanimate objects, including oil wells. It's constant human intrusions that can critically disrupt wildlife habitat.

Most Old Westerners love the owners, major stockholders, and corporate heads of oil and gas companies, who are mostly rich, arrogant bastards with friends like Vice President Dick Cheney. Most field employees of oil and gas companies are hard-working middle-class Old Westerners, trying to keep food on the table.

Most New Westerners despise the owners, stockholders, and corporate heads, not to mention the vice president. But they also detest the field employees, which is about as wrong-headed as the Old Westerners' admiration of Dick Cheney.

Most Old Westerners hate Ed Abbey, who once said, "If America could be, once again, a nation of self-reliant farmers, craftsmen, hunters, ranchers and artists, then the rich would have little power to dominate others. Neither to serve nor to rule. That was the American Dream." Despite such sentiments, Old Westerners still despise him, and they stubbornly refuse to read his books.

Most New Westerners love Ed Abbey, even though they despise half of the people Ed honored in the preceding quote. They've read all his books and own cherished signed copies, but New Westerners understand far less about Abbey's ideas than they realize.

As long as Westerners, both Old and New, refuse to acknowledge the fruitlessness of their own entrenched and inflexible positions, the West will suffer for our stubbornness. This is not about compromise, it's about dialogue, discussion, and just maybe enlightenment. There have been times when the battle lines weren't nearly as clear as I thought.

▬▬▬ ▬▬▬ ▬▬▬ About fifteen years ago, for example, I participated in a protest against a chaining project by the BLM on a high wooded mesa called Amasas Back south of Moab. Chaining is a process developed by the U.S. Forest Service to easily although brutally remove thousands of pinyon and juniper trees from public lands, usually for the purpose of converting that land to an agricultural use. They call it "range improvement," an odorous euphemism if I ever heard one. Two D9 bulldozers, connected by 100 yards of heavy anchor chain, drive along parallel lines into the pinyon-juniper forest, ripping up everything in their path.

As I walked through the trees targeted for destruction, as I examined for the last time gnarled and venerable old junipers that must have taken root about the time the Pilgrims landed at Plymouth Rock, the whole project seemed impossible. For a moment I deluded myself with the silly notion that the trees simply would not stand for it—that they would reach down deep into the rocky earth and deny the destructors their bitter victory. The trees would win in the end, I thought. No bulldozer, no chain is strong enough to uproot a life so long and well deserved. When I saw the dozers and their chain up close, reality came back quickly and stayed there like a tumor.

Some of the government officials overseeing the project agonized personally over the decision to proceed. But reporters from Salt Lake City had come to film the chaining and, hopefully, a good confrontation between the protestors, who had arrived from both sides to either decry or defend the massive tree removal project. When a television camera blinked on or a microphone was shoved under a government nose, the company line flowed mellifluously through the whispering pines—the language of bureaucratese, the ambiguity dialect, "In so much as we have considered all the options and examined the concerns, and we certainly and always appreciate the concerns and input of the public, because without your participation, these kinds of projects cannot succeed. And so we will begin this project and look forward to the successful completion of the project."

A cloud of dust and the whine of diesel engines under stress shattered the morning silence. All around us the two D9s and the anchor chain did their work. Every tree on one side of the road was down. But not *just* down, the pinyons and junipers were ripped and torn completely from the earth, shattered to splinters the way a tornado shreds everything in its path. I'd never seen such utter devastation performed so quickly or so clinically. The whole thing took about an hour.

The television crews captured a few minutes of "good video" when a heated argument broke out between the environmentalists and some miners from Moab who had arrived to defend the project. Early on, I was puzzled by the miners' presence. After a few minutes, the press had all the video it needed and began packing up its gear, heading back to Moab and a beer at the brewpub, no doubt. But I lingered for a while with the miners, curious about their motivation for coming. After all, range improvement offered no benefit to a hard rock miner.

It was a blistering hot day, even at 7000 feet up on Amasas Back. Maybe out of exhaustion from the heat, we hunkered down in the shade of one of the few remaining junipers and talked, just talked. As the afternoon wore on, we began to look human to each other.

"Look," I said slowly. "None of us seems nearly as bad as we thought of each other an hour ago. I can even see your point of view in some of the ways things are changing around here. I might even say that sometimes I feel more comfortable on *your* side than mine. But on *that*," I said, pointing to the chaining, "on that I could never agree with you. You'll never get me to agree this is a good thing."

One of the miners, a tall skinny man named Johnny with a weathered but understanding face, glanced about, as if to assure himself there were no eavesdroppers hiding in the brush. "Shit," he said, "I don't much care for it either."

The other miners nodded solemnly.

"What?" I said. "What do you mean? We've been arguing all morning. I don't get it."

"Well," explained Johnny, "you environmentalists are coming in here and taking over land that we've been using, working on, hunting on, and even just plain enjoying for a hundred years. Now you all come in here and start telling us we can do this, but we can't do that. And we can stay here for so long but over there we can never go there again. But I got no use for this chaining business. I think it's bullshit, if you ask me. And it does a lot more damage than me out here with a pick and shovel, too. Hell, I used to like coming into these trees. I'm gonna miss them. *But*, I'll be goddamned if I'm going to be seen siding with you environmentalists! And that's final!"

It was final, and that was more than a decade ago. The polarization between the Old West and New West has never been more intense. The system is not working for any of us any more. I can't tell the difference between the "good guys" and the "bad guys." It's become a standoff between well-paid lobbyists, with each side trying to outspend the other in the quest for influence and power. Both sides have a phony commitment that's usually motivated more by issues of personal comfort and the right to play and display their toys than a genuine dedication to a cause. It's like that old saying, "Their commitment is like a big puddle—a mile wide and an inch deep."

Ed Abbey once said, "What our perishing republic needs is something different . . . something *entirely* different." He was absolutely right. What could be more unique than an honest conversation?

As for MAHBU, I'd hoped it might be the beginning of a new global force akin to woman's suffrage, civil rights, or maybe even the Alice's Restaurant Anti-Massacree Movement, but I knew that more likely it was a wad of spit in a scum-filled pond that never makes a ripple. The truth generally survives only as a last resort. Certainly, isn't that where we are now? But the truth doesn't make anybody feel good in these times, and feeling good seems to be what counts the most. Marketing and packaging have relegated a serious and substantive discussion to the back seat, to the rumble seat, out in the cold.

Instead, we even give honesty the soft sell. We hide it in a subliminal message. In the twenty-first century, even the truth is a bait-and-switch ploy. I have my frustrated moments when I wish I was king. Then I could just slap this cursed American culture until it's silly and do what's good for it, give it what it deserves. The United States is so severely damaged by rampant greed and materialism, so twisted beyond recognition by this shallow, vapid pop culture we're wallowing in that it's nearly impossible to imagine the democratic process incrementally turning our weird culture around and leading it back to a place where we might actually be proud of it and ourselves.

Is it too late? Maybe not. In my search for solutions, I've considered taking a nihilistic approach. One definition of nihilism is the idea that something can be so badly damaged that the only way to fix it is to first completely destroy it. It just might work.

I momentarily considered a run for the President of the United States myself. I wanted to be the Nihilist Candidate, albeit a fun-loving nihilist: a doomsday optimist, a mellow misanthrope, a clear alternative to the inevitable. If elected, I knew I would need loftier, broader goals, objectives to challenge not just my local community but this nation and the world beyond it. After all, the stories told here about Moab, Grand County, and Utah are just snippets of the larger drama unfolding around us. What's happening in my backyard is happening in yours as well. Indeed, if elected I would start with *my* new home. I would bring a sense of humor to Washington, D.C., because God knows they need one. I'd plant dandelions on the White House lawn, rent the White House to the homeless and live in a yurt, and sell the presidential limousine and buy a moped.

Beyond that, I would pledge my support for universal free birth control, require all Christians to actually read the four gospels of the New Testament (there *will* be a quiz), and declare "Lonesome Dove" the official American Western. I'd promise to never obfuscate. I would restrict the size of all homes in America to 2000 square feet and require owners of existing homes larger than that to rent the additional space as low-income housing. I'd tax the hell out of rich weasels. I'd give tax credits for vegetable gardens and for miles driven on bicycles (the government will subsidize the cost of odometers for all bikes). I would make it a felony to use *any* public lands for profit and ban the use of eminent domain. I'd require compulsory nonmilitary, public service for all high school graduates. Duties would range from helping the poor in our cities to disaster victims around the world. Mandatory compassion is our last hope. I'd ban all reality shows, because real life is grim enough. I'd drain what's left of Lake Powell, and I'd subsidize western ranchers' alfalfa fields to prevent further condo development and to provide a guaranteed income for all family farms.

For my global environmental agenda, I would immediately order the withdrawal of all U.S. military forces around the world and terminate oil contracts with all nations, including those in the Middle East. I would mandate that all vehicles sold in this country have a fuel efficiency rating of at least fifty miles per gallon. So long, Hummers. I would subsidize the cost of these improvements with the $500 billion we'd save by terminating those military obligations.

But these measures would still not be enough to stave off a worldwide economic depression of catastrophic proportions caused by my oil imports ban. The global economy as we know it, thanks to President James Ogden Stiles Jr., would grind to a halt. The teeming masses would no longer be able to afford the plethora of crap that we all think is essential to our lives. Factories would shut down. Jobs would disappear. Service industries would dwindle and die because no one would have money for personal trainers and nose-lifts. Tourism worldwide would be devastated. Around the globe, people would have to survive by helping each other. We'd take our altered noses out of the PlayStations, the CNBC market report, or the Jerry Springer show and start having conversations again. We would have potluck picnics and play horseshoes. We'd actually start listening to the stories that our parents and grandparents have wanted to tell us for years, but nobody had time to listen. We'd have more sex (albeit safe sex). We'd quit taking most of these damn medications, and we'd die when we're supposed to and not a minute later. We would cherish our real time together because we'd suddenly realize we have more of it, now that we're not worrying about buying a Lexus as a third car or fretting about our blood pressures. By not fretting, our blood pressures would most likely go down anyway. We'd quit being depressed because we'd all be blissfully poor. We'd eat lots of fat and carbs and become fat and happy. Finally, the world population would start to decline.

Much of the world, or at least its most conspicuous consumers, is locked in a death grip with this insane free market global economy. This system requires that we continue to produce more stuff and invent new services that the exploding population will want to buy in order to provide employment for the exploding population that needs the work to buy more stuff. The new global economy also requires the consumption of the Earth's natural resources and open space at a rate that most of us cannot even begin to grasp.

I can't help but believe, though, that most environmentalists and most liberals feel that the population issue is beyond our reach. When it comes to dealing with future environmental crises, an expanding population is a given, at least for the foreseeable future, and we must operate within that framework when shaping our future battles. Many in the environmental community seem to be saying, "Okay, we can't do a thing about population growth, so what can we do to make things better, given the fact that we're going to become a nation of 400 million people by the middle of this century?" If we can find a way to more efficiently produce and use electricity, so that a United States with double today's population used no more energy than now, would that be a great environmental victory?

I often hear liberals say that conservation technologies will actually stimulate economic growth, create more jobs, and expand the gross domestic product. Is that a good thing? Are environmentalists really prepared to embrace a simpler, less materialistic life? Or do they still want all the stuff but in a more efficient way? A respected environmentalist in Utah recently wrote,

> Yes, population increase is the problem that undoes all efforts to build a sustainable, ecologically compatible life-support system for homo sap. Given what I see . . . I think we are already past the point of no return for massive population reduction by "natural" forces. All you have to do is look at the declining per capita production of grains, fish, and all other forms of food to read the writing on Malthus's wall. We are very close to the point where there will be no "surplus" grain or food to send to third-world nations suffering famine from drought, pestilence, and/or war. We haven't taken care of the population and carrying capacity overshoot problem intelligently, so Momma Gaia will do so in her usual fashion.

If that's true, why do we waste our time praising the Pitkin County commissioners for requiring more energy-efficient 12,000-square-foot homes for the billionaires in Aspen? If a worldwide economic collapse is coming, does it really matter if we replace all gas-powered SUVs with more efficient hybrids? Isn't this just a Band-aid on an avulsed wound? Why aren't we demanding that we *all* pursue a simpler, less consumptive lifestyle? Why not encourage us to prepare for the inevitable? Those of us who are living that simple life when the hammer falls would be much better prepared to deal with Momma Gaia. So, why do we continue to promote (or at least remain conspicuously silent on) an environmental strategy like the amenities economy, which encourages unlimited growth and development and the ever-increasing consumption of natural resources instead of demanding sacrifice and true economic reform?

Liberal Democrats aren't much different from conservative Republicans in one regard: neither group wants to see Americans live with less. Republicans think we should continue to live extravagantly and are convinced our energy resources will last forever. Democrats want to be able to live as extravagantly, but think we can live extravagantly in a more energy-efficient manner. When critics asked 2004 Democratic presidential candidate John Kerry how he hoped to pay for his massive health care bill, his answer was simple, "We'll grow the economy to pay for it." That means more big homes, expensive cars, massive shopping malls, and extravagant lifestyles and a materialistic society that sees more value in things than anything else. No one is out there on the political landscape willing to ask U.S. citizens to live with less.

I recently came upon some population projections by the U.S. Census Bureau that were prepared in the early 1990s. In predicting future U.S. growth, they offered three models. The worst-case scenario envisioned that the U.S. population would reach 295,911,000 by 2005 and would exceed 1 billion by 2100. In 2005 we passed 298 million, more than 2 million ahead of the worst-case scenario.

If Armageddon is the only viable answer to the population problem, we at least have a responsibility to prepare for it. And that includes being painfully honest. Instead, most environmentalists seem to embrace feel-good causes that allow them to think they're contributing to the cause, while continuing to ignore the actual problem. The fact is that in this global economy an expanding population is absolutely necessary—it requires that we constantly think of new products and services for that burgeoning population to buy. *That's* where the cycle has to be broken. It would be painful in the short term but no more so than waiting for Momma Gaia. Environmentalists at least have the responsibility to say all this out loud. If that kind of plain speaking causes "hopeless despair," as one of my enviro pals suggested, then so be it. That is how we save our country and save the world.

But we must start at home. Other small rural communities in the West, who already tremble with fear at the notion of "becoming another Moab," need to reassess their future in a way that never occurred to their economic development directors. This should become their mantra, "Support a simple life. Embrace poverty."

They should recognize the intrinsic values that make their small communities so special. Elected leaders spend too much time trying to quantify the value of these towns. It's always tax bases, public infrastructure, and how many jobs this proposed development will bring to the public coffers. They never give enough consideration of other intangibles that are so critical to a life with value.

Less than three months before his death, Robert Kennedy noted that if we judged our country's worth by its gross national product, it would include the cost of the locks on our jails, the "television programs that glorify violence," our air pollution and health care costs, the price of nuclear warheads, and "the loss of our natural wonder in chaotic sprawl."

What it would *not* reflect, he said, is "the health of our children . . . or the joy of their play . . . or the beauty of our poetry. It measures neither our wit nor our courage, neither our wisdom nor our learning, neither our compassion nor our devotion to country; it measures everything, in short, except that which makes life worthwhile. It can tell us everything about America except why we are proud we are Americans."

My nihilistic approach as president could, in the end, cause the collapse I'd hoped for. By trying to destroy the American way of life, we might just save it after all.

Return to Moab

By the summer of 1940, Toots McDougald was a blissfully married young woman living at the end of the world. When Dick Wright asked her to the Junior Prom in 1932, she fell instantly and forever in love. They'd both grown up poor and remarkably happy in a remote and forgotten corner of the American Southwest, and that suited Toots just fine. In many ways she could not have asked for a more idyllic life.

She was born Marilee, but her Uncle Ab always called her his "little Tootsie" and the name stuck. Eighty years later she was still listed as "Toots" in the Moab phone directory. Whether time sweetened her memories or she just loved life that much, only she can say for sure. But at eighty, Toots could find little fault with her childhood.

It was wonderful. We went on hikes and picnics and chicken fries. We had great watermelon busts. In fact, a man named Ollie Reardon planted a field of watermelons just for us kids to steal. He said we could steal from that patch all we wanted, if we left his other patch alone. . . . Everything was so free and easy. No pressures. No traffic. We didn't know anything about drugs. We thought we were pretty wild if we got a sip of homemade beer. My father's friend was a bootlegger. I'd tell you who it is, but they've still got family here.

By 1940 the Big Tree on First South was already a local landmark. Toots could see it from the far side of the rodeo grounds, which in those days was in the heart of town. Years earlier a circus had pitched its big top there, and she and her friends had been amazed to see elephants and camels coming down Main Street. But a few weeks later, a strange and noxious weed began to sprout on the lawns of nearby homes. It looked like a green wagon wheel, she said, with yokes stretching for ten feet or more. Each vine produced hundreds of spiny seeds that stuck in the soles of Toots's bare feet and even punched holes in her bicycle tires. Moabites called them goatheads, and later it was decided that these nasty weeds were left behind by the circus.

"Well the damn things must have been mixed up with the hay, because pretty soon those nasty little goatheads were popping up everywhere. I've got no use for goatheads at all," Toots told me.

By 1940 goatheads were a plague on Moab's lawns and gardens. Its citizens would still be fighting them half a century later, with Toots their most ardent foe.

Toots's stepfather, Marv Turnbow, was a prominent rancher in the 1920s and 1930s and the first custodian of Arches when it became a monument in 1927. Turnbow filed homestead papers on a ranch around 1915, and Toots had fond memories of her summers at Turnbow Cabin, in what would become Arches National Park.

We used to leave Moab in the morning on our horses and ride up Courthouse Wash for five or six miles. There was a good horse trail that would lead up to Balanced Rock and down into Salt Valley and the cabin . . . and we'd bring most of our food. We'd bring canned milk, and to this day, I can drink canned milk right out of the can. And flour and salt and coffee. And things Mother canned. We couldn't keep chickens out there or the coyotes would get them.

And Dad used to make flour sack biscuits. He never used a pan. He'd roll up the sleeves of his long-handled underwear, which he wore year-round. He'd scrub his hands, and he'd get this sack full of flour and roll the edges back. Then he'd form a hole in the flour, just smooth it out like a big bowl. Then he'd put in some baking powder, some salt, and some shortening and mix it all around. Then he'd start adding water, a little at a time, and just keep working it with his hands until it was all blended. Then he could just pinch off a piece to bake . . . there never was a single lump in those biscuits.

Toots and the family stayed at the cabin for weeks at a time, just down the trail from what would someday become the most famous natural stone arch in the world. Although most locals called it the School Marm's Bloomers, Toots had her own name. "I called it the 'Old Man's Pants' because it looked like they cut the top off a man and just left his feet and legs." Later the National Park Service named it Delicate Arch.

Toots told me, "We used to horseback up to the arch. We never saw anyone except other cattlemen from time to time. Jim Westwood had some cattle out here, and a man named Frank Graham did too." When the National Park Service hired her stepfather as the monument's first custodian, the pay was not too lucrative, "In those days, they called them 'dollar-a-year men.' You sure couldn't make a living on that."

By 1940 Toots had set aside her riding jeans for a dress and domesticity, but the real world seemed very far away. Standing at the corner of Main and Center Streets, it was hard to imagine that much of the civilized world was embroiled in yet another world war. Radio had reached Moab in the 1930s, and Toots remembered hearing her first broadcasts on Bish Taylor's old Crosley radio. They heard the news that Hitler's Blitzkrieg had crushed most of Europe that spring, and in June the Nazis marched through Paris. Roosevelt was preparing the nation for war, but it all seemed so abstract in this remote red-rock outpost.

As the November 1940 elections approached, Roosevelt faced Republican Wendell Willkie. South of Moab, sculptor Albert Christiensen was so impressed with both candidates that he proposed to build a massive Rushmoresque bas relief tribute to the two candidates. He completed a working model near his Hole 'n the Rock home, and Toots and Dick drove out for a look. It was the last time anyone in Utah felt compelled to honor both a Republican and a Democrat in such a fashion. Later, when the government land agency obliterated his work because it was on public land, Albert reluctantly gave up his plans for a giant sculpture and hated the federal government thereafter.

President Roosevelt had won Utah's votes in 1932 and 1936, and in 1940 most Utahns felt safe and secure under his leadership. A few years earlier, though, Roosevelt had created some animosities with southern Utahns that would last for decades. His secretary of the interior, Harold Ickes, proposed a vast 4.5 million-acre national monument in the heart of the Colorado Plateau. It was to be called "Escalante National Monument," and it would have straddled the Colorado River for more than 200 miles, from Moab all the way to Lee's Ferry in Arizona. Its boundaries would have encompassed all of what is today Canyonlands National Park, Grand Staircase/Escalante National Monument, and Glen Canyon National Recreation Area—all that, but with one significant difference: the 1936 monument would probably have stopped any serious consideration of a dam at Glen Canyon.

The issue dragged on for years, with Utah officials like Governor Henry Blood fearing a behind-the-scenes maneuver by the federal government. Blood would sound a prophetic note when he warned the Utah congressional delegation in 1939, "Some morning we may wake up and find that the Escalante National Monument has been created . . . and then it will be too late to forestall what we in Utah think would be a calamity."

Elsewhere, few Americans thought the new monument would be a calamity. Very few Americans spent much time thinking of southeastern Utah at all. In fact, most had likely never heard of it. The 1940 census showed that Moab was home to 883 residents and was the seat of government in Grand County. Roosevelt's Works Progress Administration put unemployed writers and photographers to work, compiling travel guides to all forty-eight states. Among their observations in the Utah Writers' Guide:

> Moab is the commercial center of an extensive sheep and cattle country, and since 1930 has achieved importance as a point of departure for scenic attractions in southeastern Utah. Though isolated, it has a small business district, selling everything from hay to gasoline to malted milk and liquor—the only "legal" liquor in the county. Squat red adobe houses stand neighbor to more pretentious firebrick houses. In the evening, neon lights illuminate the business district, but after midnight, except on Saturdays, the town does a complete "blackout."

At Arches, Custodian Hank Schmidt filed his monthly reports to Southwest Monuments Superintendent Hugh Miller, whether anybody noticed or not. Southeastern Utah's "importance as a point of departure for scenic attractions" was sometimes lost on Schmidt, who noted, "The majority of our visitors are of the hardy variety and don't seem to mind desert roads. It is possible that with the help of the CCC maintenance crews, we will be able to keep the sand dunes from causing the visitors too much trouble. . . . The Salt Valley road, to Delicate Arch and the Devils Garden sections, is passable but very rough."

Still, to Schmidt it looked like business was picking up. In late May 1940, he announced, "Two of our previous visitor records were broken this month. The total number of visitors, 553, is greater than that for any month on record, and the number of people, totaling 224, who visited the Windows Section on May 11 set a new record for a single day's travel into the area." These days, 553 visitors might enter the park in thirty minutes, if they could pay their ten-dollar entrance fee fast enough.

The Depression had reduced mining to a trickle, but occasional stories in Bish Taylor's ever-optimistic *Times-Independent* suggested that a mining boom lay just ahead. Oil exploration picked up some as the threat of war seemed more likely. In 1940 Howard Balsley still managed to eek out a living selling uranium to the Vitro Manufacturing Company for ceramic pigments. Nobody else was interested in competing with Balsley for the uranium market. A decade later, all that would change.

In 1940 the road to Moab from Crescent Junction was still dirt and gravel. According to lifetime southeastern Utah resident Gene Schafer, it was "still slicker than snot on a glass door knob" when it rained. Plans to improve and pave the highway had been announced in 1939, but the coming war put everything on hold for the duration. Nobody went to Moab for the weekend, because it took a whole weekend just to get there, even if you only lived in Salt Lake City. Kids rode their bicycles, but the bikes only had one gear and coaster brakes and the frames were not made from titanium alloys. Bikes didn't cost $3000 in 1940.

As Toots cut through backyards and orchards to Ollie Reardon's melons, she would not have seen men and women on the streets wearing skin-tight biking outfits of Lycra or Spandex. Toots was grateful to have anything to wear at all.

Nobody did the Slickrock Trail, except for the cattle that roamed the Sand Flats and the occasional rancher who was rounding them up. Nobody "did the daily" but a few of Toots's friends who fell into the Colorado River when they got too close to the eddies that swirl near Moose Park. More fishing poles than can be counted lie in the deep holes near the old stone picnic tables in Moose Park. And nobody did Satan's Throne, except for the ravens that floated effortlessly by, built nests in its crevices, and watched the world below with casual scorn.

Backyard hot tubs with super-turbo-powered jets were nowhere to be seen. By late summer, though, the potholes in the slickrock above town that still held water could feel very warm. Toots was glad to share the potholes with the thousands of frogs that hatched each summer and sang her to sleep at night.

A fairly decent cup of coffee could be had at the Club 66, but skinny double-decaf mocha lattes were unheard of. Beer was available, and it might have been home-brewed but it wasn't microbrewed. Beer was usually served cold, but regular power failures drew occasional complaints from Moabites.

Hardly anyone in Moab owned a new car in 1940. The Depression made sure of that. Old cars and trucks limped along, held together with baling wire in the days before duct tape, and horses still provided conveyance for many. Toots depended on her feet to get her just about anywhere her heart desired. Hummers, SUVs, ATVs, off-road vehicles, and even jeeps were beyond the realm of her imagination.

Toots McDougald's summer nights were unfettered by credit card debt, staggering mortgage payments, or time-share condo schemes. She did not suffer from late night indigestion from a Big Mac, a Whopper, a Soft Taco Supreme, or a Lean Cuisine frozen dinner. She never needed a Zantac 75. Her evenings were spent with Dick, watching the twilight fall over their little town, listening to the croaking and humming of frogs in Mill Creek or the rustle of a summer breeze through the towering branches of a cottonwood tree. She and Dick believed that it would be this way forever. Her life was a quiet adventure in the best sense of the word, and the experience didn't cost her a penny extra. Toots was blissfully ignorant of a future she would live to see, dramatic changes that would all happen within the span of her remarkable life.

The Golden Light

On a brilliant afternoon in late autumn, just a few weeks before the dawn of the new millennium, the Big Tree on First South began to uproot itself. The sidewalk buckled and split in two as the cottonwood's massive root system slowly lost its grip on the good earth that had sustained the tree for more than a century. Within the space of a few hours, the tree was visibly tilting toward the street. The news rippled from one end of Moab to the other, and by sunset scores of Moabites had gathered to watch and to mourn. City work crews, fearing the tree might topple completely, blocked traffic in both directions and sought advice from tree specialists at the University of Utah. They drove down from Salt Lake City the next day, but it only took a short while to assess the Big Tree's future—it was going to die. The city decided to put the tree out of its misery.

The Big Tree might have lingered for weeks or even months, but its collapse was inevitable. Within a few days, the slow and arduous task of tearing the tree down, one sacred limb at a time, began. Moabites, from young ones to octogenarians, all who had remembered the Big Tree as children and played in her shadows, now came to pay their respects, honor a lifetime friend, and gather remembrances. They collected small cross-sections of branches left by the woodcutters to take home as cherished relics, to preserve the memory of a Moab landmark.

I brought my camera and photographed the old cottonwood from every conceivable angle. I had passed beneath these branches, appreciated its shade on a hot summer day, and marveled at the translucent light that filtered through its leaves in the late afternoon countless times. To think these images would be the last, a death mask of sorts, seemed more than tragic. It seemed impossible.

Finally, only its central trunk remained, one naked gnarled battered arm extended toward the sky. A bulldozer prodded it a bit and brought the cottonwood down completely. I saw the small explosions of dust and debris and heard the snapping, cracking, and tearing of roots giving way. I watched the roots reluctantly relinquish their steady hold at last, after serving the Big Tree so well for so long. The body parts were chopped up and hauled away, the hole left by the tree's uprooting was filled and leveled. A construction crew, no longer impeded by the Big Tree, extended the curb to the corner and laid new asphalt. A month later, not even a hint suggested that a magnificent century-old cottonwood had ever lived at the corner of First South and Third East in Moab, Utah. Visitors and new residents alike, from that day forward, would pass by the site and have no idea what was once there. They could not mourn what they'd never experienced, and so they felt nothing at all as they hurried up or down the street. It became that way with Moab itself.

In the years that followed the Big Tree's demise, Moab would move farther and farther from the town's past and from the qualities that made it such a special place when I first arrived. For me, the Big Tree's death was a watershed moment, a dividing point. There was the Moab I knew before it fell, and there is the Moab that I've observed since. Admittedly, in those waning years before the tree's death, my grasp on Moab as the vortex of my soul had become tenuous at best. I had seen the changes coming, but I hadn't expected to observe such a shocking symbol of Moab's transformation. The tree, both literally and figuratively, was the breaking point.

The landscape changed at an accelerated, almost dizzying rate. Fields, orchards, and pastures we'd taken for granted just a few short years before, now all came face to face with heavy equipment and a developer's dream.

Resistance could scarcely be found. When the Cloudrock Resort Development project first gained notoriety in 2000, public anger was aroused for a while. A group of young activists calling themselves the Moab Citizens Alliance briefly tried to gather public opposition. I hoped they were the next generation of troublemakers, and when I attended one of their first organizational meetings I was encouraged. Someone claimed to have actually seen me smiling throughout most of it.

But it didn't last. Few seemed willing to commit to the fight for the long haul. Its leaders worried about retribution from Moab's pro-development faction, a nasty bunch to be sure. The Moab Citizens Alliance was afraid of being cast as "too negative" by friends and foes alike. They were uncomfortable being "against" something. I argued that opposing Cloudrock meant they were *for* lower taxes, *for* an affordable housing market, *for* a diverse community, and *for* open space. But opposition sputtered and shrank. Ultimately, it appeared the Cloudrock developer had outlasted almost everyone. By 2005 he even bragged that the "environmental community" supported the project, and he was, with a few courageous exceptions, right.

With Cloudrock still on the drawing board, the housing market exploded in Grand County. Lower and middle-income residents faced a gloomy future. Starter homes *started* at $150,000. My little bungalow, the 900-square-foot house I'd purchased in 1985 for $18,000, doubled and then tripled and quadrupled in value. Though my home wasn't on the market, when an out-of-town investor offered me $200,000, I had to pause. When he explained that he planned to bulldoze my home and every tree on the lot and build something "better suited" to his needs, I knew I could still pass up a deal like that.

Over the next few years, hundreds of new residents, thousands if you counted the part-timers, flocked to Grand County. By 2005 most homes in Grand County were owned by nonresidents. They were drawn to Moab by the hype, the promos, the sales pitches, the Web sites, and the slick imagery. Some said they wanted to experience the small-town, pastoral lifestyle, not realizing that their new faux adobe dwellings were built atop what had made Moab pastoral in the first place. But they'd never seen the foals in the pasture in the spring, trotting on the very spot they now parked their SUVs or soaked in their hot tubs. How could they mourn, or even feel guilty? In fact, not realizing what they'd missed, many set out to redefine Moab on their terms. Their unintended goal was often to re-create the urban nightmare they had just fled from and claimed to loathe.

"I just *love* it here! I love doing the daily river trips! And I love doing the Slickrock Bike Trail! The music festival is wonderful! And I really love how much quieter it is here than in L.A. . . . But I do wish we had a Wal-Mart. Then it would be *perfect*."

Walt Whitman once said, "But where is what I started for, and why is it yet unfound?" Maybe that's the way it has to be, the way it always will be. The world has always rede-fined itself, one day at a time. I suppose what happened to Moab was inevitable, in the same way change is occurring everywhere at breathtaking speed. I just thought we had a little more time.

I recently paused to take a photo of another tree, though I doubt it will live long enough to achieve landmark status. Near what was once the Clark Orchards, on the building site of what is now the final phase of the Orchard Villa subdivision, something foreign caught my eye as I drove down the recently widened and improved Fifth West. It was a fruit tree, a stunted twisted apple tree standing all by itself in a vacant lot. I doubt that its trunk was more than four or five inches in diameter, and it looked out of place in this otherwise barren landscape. New construction was underway across the street, and the little tree was surrounded on all sides by bright yellow dozers, graders, and earth-movers. Though it had been abandoned and unattended and the ground around it was dry, cracked, and strewn with weeds and construction waste, despite all that, the little apple tree was teeming with fruit. Amid all this cold-blooded heartbreak, the tree was determined to live and be bountiful, as long as the heavy equipment and construction schedules allowed. Now each time I pass by, I pause to salute the tree and wonder if it will be my last chance to pay homage.

I pay homage to all the lost trees, the lost pastures, the lost alfalfa fields, the lost orchards. I pay homage to the vast landscape that extends beyond the town, which used to be the source of so much mystery and surprise. Now, to a great degree, this landscape has been gridded, dissected, and explained as thoroughly as any city street. What hasn't been gridded will be soon.

I pay homage to the lost faces of Moab and the legends that once grew around them. Their presence used to be palpable, but now they're ghosts without names and without even a hint of recognition. I remember what Augustus McRae said to his friend Woodrow Call in *Lonesome Dove*, "The people are buildin' towns ever'where and it's our fault. . . . Well, we killed off all the Indians didn't we? Hung all the good bandits? Did it ever occur to you that ever'thing we done was a mistake? You and me did our work too well, Woodrow. Hell, we killed off most of the people that made this country interestin' to begin with." Moab is Gus's lament with twenty-first-century tactics.

Time to go.

■■■ ■■■ ■■■ Sometime in mid-August, something happens to the light in southeastern Utah. The color becomes softer in the mornings. Although it may still feel like summer, the days begin to *look* different. The light is not so harsh, the color assumes a more golden hue and begins to lose its white crystalline brilliance. For me it is a portent of autumn, with its cooler days and longer nights. This golden light means imminent escape from the summer heat, but it also leaves me with that apprehensive sense of melancholy as we tumble toward winter.

At times like this, my sentimental side always pulls me back, back in time to the home

I discovered in the desert, my well-kept secret, Moab. More than thirty years have passed since my first frigid view of the place that would become an integral part of my heart and soul. I remember Jack West's assessment of the "son-of-a-bitchin' snow" in January and Nelle Holmes's admonition to walk downtown from her cottage to the co-op. I still recall seeing only one man, my future friend Dave Baker, busily tending to his garden all afternoon under the late summer sun. I saw no one else, impressed that on a Labor Day Weekend Moab's streets were almost empty. Later that day, I made my way in an old Volkswagen microbus to the Island in the Sky campground, over winding corrugated dirt roads, the kind of road you curse at the moment and yearn for years later. There was nobody up there that weekend. I had the island to myself.

On a mid-August day not long ago, I retrieved a bottle of Kulmbacher beer from the back of my refrigerator, left there by Ed Abbey in 1987, and took a drive to the Green River Overlook. That tiny part of Canyonlands National Park has changed very little since my first visit, one of the few areas not "improved" by the National Park Service paving people.

Climbing the high sandstone fins adjacent to the Island in the Sky campground gave me a clear view of the massive pinyon-juniper graveyard that lies at the end of a service road, just out of public view. These thousands of rotting skeletal trees are the price we all paid to widen, straighten, and pave the Island Road. Visitors come and go constantly now and never even know of the sacrifice those pinyons and junipers made. But the road was built twenty years ago, and so much has happened to alter the face of southeastern Utah since then, the graveyard felt more like a minor intrusion to me that day. I turned away from that sordid scene, climbed to the top of a remarkable sandstone spire that stabs the sky like a knife, opened Abbey's prized gift, and let myself remember.

The golden light. Everything looked golden to me during those lazy first days at the Island in the Sky. I had no idea what the future held, no inkling of the events that would not only shape my life but the destiny of the land that stretched around me for as far as my eyes could see. In that golden light, I gave no thought to what I might be doing in twenty years. I wasn't sure then what I'd be doing in a month, or a week. But I knew *where* I'd be. I was certain of that. It's not often that any of us finds home with such clarity, and I'll always be grateful for that experience. It was one of the most hopeful times of my life.

If you get far enough away from Moab, there's still raw land that has changed very little in thirty years and rarely sees so much as a Vibram-soled footprint—so far, at least. When the oil companies can finally get their drill rigs in there, when ATV trails stretch farther into wilderness, when commercial tour operators can find a way to get their customers in and out of such places in under eight hours, when a teeming population searching for some open space all descends upon it at once, those untouched remnants will fall as well. With strict environmental regulations and user controls, it may be possible to "mitigate impacts," as land use agencies like to say, but it will never *feel* the same. Does it matter? It does to me.

As I drank my beer, I wondered if Moab could have turned out differently. Could its citizens have fought back the promoters, developers, and money schemers? Could we have found a way to save Moab from the invasion? Could we have come to appreciate the life we had there, in terms that bankers, accountants, politicians, and chambers of commerce can't measure? Absolutely.

We humans are a tragic lot, not because of our malevolence and greed but our indifference. It's never the bad guys that diminish our species, our culture, and our lands—their numbers are insignificant. We good guys empower them with our apathy. Our willingness to submit to things we know are wrong is always our undoing. It doesn't have to be like that.

From my vantage point atop the sandstone massif, I could see the landmarks and features that I've come to know so intimately over the last quarter century. I could feel them as well. For me, such places are cherished time capsules. When I reflect on my memories and the warmth and comfort they give me, it offers me hope. Will today's children find that same comfort in these red rocks decades from now? That is my fondest dream.

I finished Abbey's beer, wrote a note to myself similar to one I'd left in the same place three decades earlier, sealed it in the bottle, and buried it nearby. Maybe in another thirty years, I'll return, dig it up, and amuse myself with the recollection of *that* moment. That is, if I live that long, if I'm still clinging hopelessly to my past, and if I can drag my creaky bones up the cliff face.

A wind started to blow out of the northwest and the sky began to hurl lightning, so I packed my canteen, my notebook, and my memories and headed back to the truck. Bound now for an undisclosed location. What else was there to do? The golden light. Thirty years ago, I didn't notice that the light had changed.

Now I do.

About the Author

Jim Stiles moved to Moab, Utah, shortly after graduating from the University of Louisville in Kentucky. In the late 1970s, he became a seasonal ranger at Arches National Park and met his hero, the author Edward Abbey. Stiles would stay at Arches for a decade and remain a friend of Abbey's until Ed's death in 1989. That year, Stiles first published the independent newspaper the *Canyon Country Zephyr*, which remains a consistently controversial and passionate voice in defense of the rural West. Stiles illustrated Abbey's collection of essays *The Journey Home* and was one of the original *Earth First! Journal* cartoonists. His stories and essays have also appeared in numerous magazines and periodicals around the West.